CONTEMPORARY
Black
Biography

ISSN-1058-1316

CONTEMPORARY

Black
Biography

Profiles from the International Black Community

Volume 50

THOMSON

GALE

Detroit • New York • San Francisco • San Diego • New Haven, Conn. • Waterville, Maine • London • Munich

Contemporary Black Biography, Volume 50

Sara and Tom Pendergast

Project Editor
Pamela M. Kalte

Image Research and Acquisitions
Robyn V. Young

Editorial Support Services
Nataliya Mikheyeva

Rights and Permissions
Emma Hull, Lisa M. Kincade,
Andrew G. Specht

Manufacturing
Dorothy Maki, Rhonda Williams

Composition and Prepress
Mary Beth Trimper, Gary Leach

Imaging
Lezlie Light, Randy Bassett

ISBN 0-7876-7922-4
ISSN 1058-1316

Printed in the United States of America
10 9 8 7 6 5 4 3 2 1

Advisory Board

Contents

Introduction

Contemporary Black Biography provides informative biographical profiles of the important and influential persons of African heritage who form the international black community: men and women who have changed today's world and are shaping tomorrow's. *Contemporary Black Biography* covers persons of various nationalities in a wide variety of fields, including architecture, art, business, dance, education, fashion, film, industry, journalism, law, literature, medicine, music, politics and government, publishing, religion, science and technology, social issues, sports, television, theater, and others. In addition to in-depth coverage of names found in today's headlines, *Contemporary Black Biography* provides coverage of selected individuals from earlier in this century whose influence continues to impact on contemporary life. *Contemporary Black Biography* also provides coverage of important and influential persons who are not yet household names and are therefore likely to be ignored by other biographical reference series. Each volume also includes listee updates on names previously appearing in *CBB*.

Designed for Quick Research and Interesting Reading

- **Attractive page design** incorporates textual subheads, making it easy to find the information you're looking for.
- **Easy-to-locate data sections** provide quick access to vital personal statistics, career information, major awards, and mailing addresses, when available.
- **Informative biographical essays** trace the subject's personal and professional life with the kind of in-depth analysis you need.
- **To further enhance your appreciation** of the subject, most entries include photographic portraits.
- **Sources for additional information** direct the user to selected books, magazines, and newspapers where more information on the individuals can be obtained.

Helpful Indexes Make It Easy to Find the Information You Need

Contemporary Black Biography includes cumulative Nationality, Occupation, Subject, and Name indexes that make it easy to locate entries in a variety of useful ways.

Available in Electronic Formats

Diskette/Magnetic Tape. Contemporary Black Biography is available for licensing on magnetic tape or diskette in a fielded format. Either the complete database or a custom selection of entries may be ordered. The database is available for internal data processing and nonpublishing purposes only. For more information, call (800) 877-GALE.

On-line. Contemporary Black Biography is available on-line through Mead Data Central's NEXIS Service in the NEXIS, PEOPLE and SPORTS Libraries in the GALBIO file and Gale's Biography Resource Center.

Disclaimer

Contemporary Black Biography uses and lists websites as sources and these websites may become obsolete.

We Welcome Your Suggestions

The editors welcome your comments and suggestions for enhancing and improving *Contemporary Black Biography*. If you would like to suggest persons for inclusion in the series, please submit these names to the editors. Mail comments or suggestions to:

The Editor

Contemporary Black Biography

Thomson Gale

27500 Drake Rd.

Farmington Hills, MI 48331-3535

Phone: (800) 347-4253

Paul Regan Adams

1977—

Cricket player

Adams, Paul, photograph. Touchline/Getty Images.

With an unusual bowling (pitching) style and skill beyond his years, Paul Adams gained a reputation as an up and coming cricket player in the mid-1990s. His success, however, was hard earned. In high school, opponents often laughed at Adams' method of bowling, and because he did not attend the better-known cricket schools, many refused to take the talented player seriously. But cricket player and coach Eddie Barlow was convinced of Adams' potential, and helped place him on the Western Province (South Africa) cricket team. In a short time, Adams progressed from Western Province B to Western Province A, and soon took his place among South Africa's best cricket players.

Adams was born on January 20, 1977, in Grassy Park in Cape Town, South Africa, the son of William and Anne Adams. As a young boy he played cricket at school and in the Blue Bells, a local lower division club. Although he started off as a batsman, his teacher at Plumstead High School asked him to bowl spinners (bowling is similar to being a pitcher in American baseball; a player can bowl the ball fast, or add some spin.) In a cricket match, the bowler can try to get the batsman out by hitting the wicket, so having a skillful bowling style is an asset. "When he first bowled the other team used to laugh at the way he bowled," his teacher, as quoted by Eugene Abrahams in *Paul Adams*, said. "But when he started taking their wickets, they were not laughing anymore." Adams later joined the SA Colts, the school's C-side team, but he was passed over when South Africa formed its under-19 team to tour England in 1995. He was also turned down for Clive Rice's Plascon Cricket Academy.

Adams' prospects improved when he met Eddie Barlow, a popular cricket player and coach. Barlow was impressed with the young player's ability, and asked the selectors to choose Adams for the Western Province team. "I have never come across a wrist spinner who has such amazing control of length," Barlow said, as quoted by Abrahams. Adams quickly proved himself on the Western Province B team in a game against Eastern Transvaal, leading to his inclusion on the A team for another match against Northern Transvaal. He played so well in the game, scoring nine wickets in two innings, that he was chosen to play on the South African A team against England in November of 1995. "Adams' parents drove all the way to Kimberley to watch the

At a Glance . . .

Born Paul Regan Adams on January 20, 1977, in Cape Town, South Africa; son of William and Anne Adams.

Career: Professional cricket player, 1995–.

Awards: Named Outstanding Cricket Player by United Cricket Board of South Africa, 2001/2002.

match," wrote Abrahams. "Adams dismissed two top England batsmen Hick and Thorpe, in one over." He also received the affectionate nickname Gogga—meaning insect—from Brian McMillan during this time.

Adams received a great deal of attention due to his highly unusual bowling method, referred to as the "chinaman" or "frog in the blender" style. With his head pointed at the sky, Adams released the ball with his left hand, a style that amused many of his English opponents, giving them the impression that he could not see the batsman "People think I can't see the batsman when I bowl, but I can," Adams said, as quoted by Abrahams. "When I drop my head, I can still see him in my mind's eye. It comes from practice. It is not just luck."

Despite his success, Adams frequently faced controversy. Critics often mentioned his youth and lack of experience when he joined the national team at the age of 18 (the youngest player chosen). "The youngest player to win a South African test cap has been subjected to a variety of comment about his bowling action," wrote Trevor Chesterfield in *Cric Info*, "and not a lot of it has been easy to handle." In 1999 Adams replaced Pat Symcox on the South African team, and many labeled the switch—from a white to a black player—politically motivated. "This is a sacrifice," wrote Geoffrey Dean in *Cape Town*, "that smacks of political expediency, for Adams has not been bowling well this season." Adams also received a fine in 2001 when he and several of his teammates were caught smoking marijuana in their hotel room. Adams later apologized for the incident, noting that it would not happen again.

Controversy, however, did little to sidetrack Adams' career. During his first season in 1995/96, the player that many considered "too young" scored 43 wickets in eight matches, the second highest in a debut season by a South African. "He has become a more confident bowler," Hansie Cronje told Chesterfield. By 2000, Adams had become a central player on the South African cricket scene. "He has his control back and we

are learning all the time," said Cronje. "He has really come along and is now an integral part of our bowling attack." Although an injury to his knuckles temporarily sidelined Adams in 2000, causing him to miss a tour of India, he soon returned to the playing field. "This summer…we have seen a more confident Adams emerge from the bowler who many thought would not break through after his extraordinary debut summer four seasons ago…" wrote Chesterfield.

In 2002 Adams scored 100 wickets, becoming the seventh South African to achieve this distinction. The same year he was named—along with Steve Elworthy, Andrew Hall, Graeme Smith, and Martin van Jaarsveld—one of the outstanding cricket players of the 2001/2002 season. "The five were chosen for their spirited and impressive performances," noted a United Cricket Board of South Africa (UCBSA) Media Release, "in a year during which the South African team suffered heavy defeats…. Adams, Hall, and Smith were chosen specifically because they sparked a turnaround against the Australians after coming into the national team midway through the home series."

Adams continued to excel as a player in 2003. In October of 2003, he collected a career high seven-wickets against Pakistan in the First Test, leading to South Africa's victory in the match. "A lot of people back home had written me off as an international," Adams told the *Birmingham Post*. "They also questioned my inclusion in the team for the tour, so I feel really good about my performance today. I just stuck to the basics." With his distinct style, even temper, and ability to bowl and bat, Adams' future in cricket looks bright.

Sources

Books

Abrahams, Eugene, *Paul Adams*, Viva Books, 1999.

Periodicals

Birmingham Post, October 20, 2003, p. 26.
Birmingham Evening Mail, October 20, 2003, p. 42.
Cape Town, January 2, 1999.
Cape Times, January 13, 2005.

On-line

"Paul Regan Adams," *Cric Info*, http://usa.cricinfo. com/db/PLAYERS/RSA/A/ADAMS_PR_030022 34/ (January 3, 2005).

Other

UCBSA Media Release, October 7, 2002.

—Ronnie D. Lankford, Jr.

Juan Atkins

1962—

Musician

Atkins, Juan, photograph. AP/Wide World Photos. Reproduced by permission.

Juan Atkins is generally recognized as one of the creators of techno music, which spawned a whole group of genres now known as electronica, and he was probably the first person to apply the word "techno" to music. His novel electronic soundscapes influenced nearly every genre of music that came after. Yet except for followers of electronic dance music, few music fans recognize his name. Despite recognition in the form of an exhibition at the Detroit Historical Museum, he remains among the most obscure of modern musical pioneers.

Techno music originated in Detroit, Michigan, and it was there that Atkins was born on September 12, 1962. Fans worldwide associate the music with Detroit's often bleak landscape, littered with abandoned buildings and other relics of the roaring 1920s and the golden age of the automobile. Atkins himself shared his impressions of Detroit's desolate core with techno historian Dan Sicko: "I was smack in the middle of downtown, on Griswold. I was looking at this building and I see the faded imprint of American Airline [a logo], the shadow after they took the sign down. It just brought home to me the thing about Detroit—in any other city you have a buzzing, thriving downtown."

But the true beginnings of techno took place a half hour's drive to the southwest in Belleville, Michigan, a small town near an interstate leading to Detroit's central city. Atkins and his brother were sent there to live with his grandmother after his grades dropped in Detroit, in the hopes of removing him from the city's violence. As a junior high and high school student in Belleville, Atkins met Derrick May and Kevin Saunderson, both techno pioneers. The trio made trips into Detroit for parties on the weekends. Later they became known as the "Belleville Three," with Atkins, according to Sicko, receiving special mention as "Obi Juan."

Influenced by "Electrifying Mojo"

Atkins's father was a concert promoter, and there were various musical instruments around the house while he was growing up. He became a fan of a Detroit radio disc jockey named the Electrifying Mojo (Charles Johnson), one of a rare breed of "freeform" DJs on American commercial radio whose shows mixed genres and forms. Electrifying Mojo wove various kinds of music around the 1970s funk of artists such as

At a Glance . . .

Born on September 12, 1962, in Detroit, MI; son of a concert promoter. *Education:* Attended Washtenaw Community College, Ypsilanti, MI.

Career: Musician, 1981–; Deep Space Soundworks, co-founder (with Kevin Saunderson and Derrick May),1981; Music Institute club, Detroit, MI, owner, 1981; Metroplex record label, founder, 1985.

Awards: ArtServe Michigan Governor's Awards, International Achievement Award, 2004.

Addresses: *Agent*—Just Say Agency, 2331-D2 East Avenue S, £122, Palmdale, CA 93550.

George Clinton, Parliament, and Funkadelic (which had some Detroit roots of its own), becoming one of just a few American DJs who played the experimental electronic dance music of the German ensemble Kraftwerk on the radio. "If you want the reason [techno] happened in Detroit," Atkins told the *Village Voice,* "you have to look at a DJ called Electrifying Mojo: he had five hours every night, with no format restrictions. It was on his show that I first heard Kraftwerk."

In the early 1980s, Atkins became the artist who found an American middle ground between Kraftwerk's electronics and funk's big bass lines and distinctive atmospheres. He played keyboards as a teenager, but he was a DJ and sound manipulator from the beginning, experimenting at home with a mixing board and a cassette tape player. After finishing high school, Atkins studied at Washtenaw Community College near Ypsilanti, not far from Belleville. It was through a friendship with a fellow student, Vietnam veteran Rik Davis, that Atkins began to learn about electronic sound production; Davis owned a spread of then-innovative equipment including one of the first sequencers (a device allowing the user to organize electronic sound) released by the Roland corporation. "He was very isolated," Atkins told the *Village Voice.* Soon Atkins' collaboration with Davis gave rise to a new music.

"I was around when you had to get a bass player, a guitarist, a drummer to make records, ..." he told the *Village Voice.* "I wanted to make electronic music but thought you had to be a computer programmer to do it. I found out it wasn't as complicated as I thought." Atkins joined with Davis (who called himself 3070), and the pair billed themselves as Cybotron, a name they chose from a list of futuristic compound words that they had compiled and called "the grid." The two released a single "Alleys of Your Mind," in 1981, and it sold

around 15,000 copies in the Detroit area after the Electrifying Mojo aired it on his radio program. A second release, "Cosmic Cars," did equally well, and the duo's sales got the notice of the West Coast independent record label Fantasy. Atkins and Davis hadn't sought a record deal, and in fact, Atkins told Dan Sicko, "We didn't know anything about [Fantasy's interest] until one day we opened the mailbox and found a contract."

Track Title Gave Genre Its Name

In 1982 Cybotron released "Clear," a recording with a distinctive cool tone that would later mark it as an electronic music classic. "Clear" had almost no text, and techno as it developed would use words mostly rhythmically or decoratively (when it used words at all). The following year Atkins and Davis released "Techno City," and listeners began to use the record's title to describe the musical genre of which it was a part. The term was probably inspired by futurist Alvin Toffler's book *The Third Wave* (1980), which used the term "techno rebels" and which Atkins had read in a high school class in Belleville. Atkins received a second jolt of creative inspiration from the 1982 rap hit "Planet Rock," one of the first rap records to incorporate high-tech electronics.

Atkins and Davis split up over creative differences, with Davis wanting to push their music in more of a rock-oriented direction. Davis eventually drifted into obscurity, but Atkins took steps to popularize the new music he was making. Joining with May and Saunderson, he formed a collective enterprise, Deep Space Soundworks, which had begun as a DJ group headed by Atkins and in turn launched a downtown Detroit club called the Music Institute. A second generation of techno DJs, including Carl Craig and Richie Hawtin (also known as Plastikman), began to hold forth at the club, and techno even found a place on Detroit public radio affiliate WDET on a program called *Fast Forward.*

In the middle and late 1980s, Atkins used the name Model 500. His recordings from this time, such as "No UFO's" (1985) and the evocative "Night Drive" (which featured Atkins's whispered narration of a drive around Detroit's freeway system), are often considered techno classics. Economical and polished, they inspired younger electronic musicians, especially after techno became popular in Europe (where its profile was always higher than in the United States) and began to make its mark on nightclubs in England, Germany, and Belgium among other countries. Atkins in 1985 formed a label of his own, Metroplex, releasing his own recordings as well as those of younger Detroit musicians. He had envisioned the label, Derrick May told author Dan Sicko, as early as age 17. Some of Atkins's own 1980s work was collected in the 1990s on the *Classics* album released by Belgium's R&S label.

Techno shaped a new kind of nightclub experience in the United States especially in England, where Atkins and Saunderson found themselves in demand. Techno music was certainly intended for dancers, but its beats weren't the sensual pulsations of disco and its successors; instead, Atkins's music had a mechanistic, modernistic quality that stimulated blissful feelings rather than sheer sexuality. At dance events called "raves," which could last all night, dancers might charge themselves up with fast dance tracks and then cool down with slower, dreamier ones in different rooms of the same building. After making the first of many European trips in 1988, Atkins provided the evening's soundtrack for many a British nightclub patron. The cool quality of Atkins's music, famously described by May (as quoted in the *Village Voice*) as "like George Clinton and Kraftwerk stuck in an elevator," helped inspire the new genre of ambient techno as composers and DJs combined techno music with the intentionally plain "ambient" sounds of avant-garde musician Brian Eno.

Produced Remixes in England

The late 1980s were probably the high point of Atkins's fame, and in England he was invited to do remixes of hits by top acts such as the Style Council, the Tom Tom Club, and the Fine Young Cannibals. He cut back his activities in the early 1990s somewhat, although he released several recordings on which he billed himself as Infiniti. A series of European reissues of his earlier work stimulated his creative juices anew, and he returned to the recording studio, now working in the more expansive album format. The 1995 Model 500 album *Deep Space* was really Atkins's solo CD debut. He released new albums under the names Infiniti (*Skynet*, 1998, on Germany's Tresor label) and Model 500 (*Mind and Body*, 1999, on Belgium's R&S).

Through all this, Atkins was only moderately well known, even in his Detroit hometown. But the Detroit Electronic Music Festival, held annually along Detroit's riverfront, showed the impact of Atkins's creation as a crowd of an estimated one million people turned out to hear his musical descendents make people dance with nothing more than an array of electronic gear. Atkins himself performed at the festival in 2001, and in an *Orange County Register* interview quoted on the Jahsonic Web site he reflected on techno's ambivalent status as African-American music. "I gotta believe that if we were a bunch of white kids, we'd be millionaires by now, but it may not be as racial as one may think," he said. "Black labels don't have a clue. At least the white guys will talk to me; they aren't making any moves or offers, but they say, 'We love your music and we'd love to do something with you.' But blacks don't even know who we are."

In 2001 Atkins also released the *Legends, Vol. 1* album on the OM label. Scripps Howard News Service writer Richard Paton observed that the album "finds

him not resting on past achievement, but still mixing pumping, well-crafted sets," as quoted in the *Cincinnati Post*. Atkins continued to perform on both sides of the Atlantic, moving to Los Angeles in the early 2000s. He was prominently featured in "Techno: Detroit's Gift to the World," a 2003 exhibition mounted at the Detroit Historical Museum, and the year 2005 saw him performing at the Necto club in Ann Arbor, Michigan, not far from Belleville.

Selected discography

Singles

(As Cybotron, with Rick Davis) "Alleys of Your Mind," 1981.
(As Cybotron, with Rick Davis) "Cosmic Cars," 1981.
(As Cybotron, with Rick Davis) "Clear," 1982.
(As Cybotron, with Rick Davis) "Techno City," 1983.
(As Model 500) "No UFO's," 1985.
(As Model 500) "Night Ride," 1985.

Albums

Enter, Fantasy, 1983.
Classics (compilation), R&S, 1995.
Infiniti Compilation, Tresor, 1995.
(As Model 500) *Deep Space,* R&S, 1995.
(As Infiniti) *Skynet,* Tresor, 1998.
(As Model 500) *Mind and Body,* R&S, 1999.
Legends: Vol. 1, OM, 2001.

Sources

Books

Sicko, Dan, *Techno Rebels: The Renegades of Electronic Funk,* Billboard Books, 1999.

Periodicals

Associated Press, January 17, 2003.
Cincinnati Post, August 9, 2001, p. 20.
Grand Rapids Press, May 29, 2001, p. B4.
Guardian (London, England), November 22, 2003, p. 31; July 24, 2004, p. 32.
Village Voice, July 20, 1993, p. SS18; September 11, 2001, p. 126.

On-line

"GearTalk: Juan Atkins," *For Men,* http://formen.ign.com/news/36668.html (January 16, 2005).
"Juan Atkins," *All Music Guide,* www.allmusic.com (January 16, 2005.
"Juan Atkins," www.scaruffi.com/vol15/atkins.html (January 16, 2005).
"Juan Atkins: Biography," *Jahsonic,* www.jahsonic.com/JuanAtkins.html (January 15, 2005).

"Model 500," *R&S Records,* www.rsrecords.com/rsp _m500.htm (January 16, 2005).

"Detroit Techno: Race, Agency, and Electronic Music in Post-Industrial Detroit," *Michigan Journal of History,* www.umich.edu/~historyj/papers/fall2003/ tausig3.html (January 16, 2005).

—James M. Manheim

Tyra Banks

Model, actress

1973—

Tyra Banks has parlayed her supermodel status into film, television, and music; her career is proceeding well according to her ambitious plans. A hit on the runways of top designers since the early 1990s, Banks's career segued first into television and later into film, when she was cast in a leading role in the 1995 film *Higher Learning*, written and directed by John Singleton. With the help of a supportive family, Banks has successfully managed her fame in positive ways, and has chosen roles and collaborations with other African-American arts professionals who seek to portray their community in a diverse, multifaceted way. With her hit show *America's Next Top Model* and her budding pop music career, along with her continued modeling, Banks was poised to reap the benefits of superstardom.

Grounded in Family Love

Tyra Banks was born in Los Angeles December 4, 1973, to Carolyn and Don Banks. Her mother was a medical photographer at NASA's Jet Propulsion Lab, while her father is a computer consultant. They divorced when Tyra was six, although the relationship between parents and children—including Tyra's older brother Devin—remained amicable. Growing up, she would often parade around the family's Inglewood duplex in her mother's high heels and long robes, play-acting at being a model. Her view of the profession came largely from watching the weekly CNN program *Style with Elsa Klensch*, and later the MTV feature *House of Style* starring Cindy Crawford. In more serious moments, Banks entertained the idea of going to veterinary school. Yet her unusual looks sometimes made life difficult, as she told *GQ* writer James Ryan. "People called me Olive Oyl, Lightbulb Head, and Fivehead, because my forehead was so big," Banks recalled.

Banks attended Immaculate Heart High School, a rigorous Catholic girls' school in the Los Feliz section of Los Angeles, where classmates also teased her because of her increasing height (5'11") and weight (around 125 lbs). She told the *Chicago Tribune* that her most humbling experience in life was losing the prom queen crown to a girl she described as the smartest in her class. After graduating, she decided to try modeling on a lark, thinking it might be a good way to do some traveling. Since her mother was a photographer, putting a portfolio together was not a problem. Banks took her book to agencies, but, as mother Carolyn London-Johnson recalled for *People* magazine writers Tom Gliatto and Bryan Alexander, "The market for black models was not very good. They would say, 'We have this many black girls already.'"

After encountering one too many dead ends, Banks decided to go ahead with her backup plan to start college and study film. Accepted at Loyola Marymount University in Los Angeles, Banks was walking down the street two weeks before classes started when a model scout from France spotted her. The scout offered her immediate work for the upcoming fall haute couture shows in Paris, and Banks accepted. "Her sensual lope and sleek, space-age frame gave her instant catwalk charisma," *People* described the model in its "Fifty

At a Glance . . .

Born on December 4, 1973, in Los Angeles, CA; daughter of Don Banks (a computer consultant) and Carolyn London-Johnson (a business manager).

Career: Model, 1991–; actress, 1993–; Tygirl, Inc., founder and CEO, 1995–.

Memberships: none.

Awards: none.

Addresses: *Home*—Los Angeles, CA.

Most Beautiful Women" issue. Designer Todd Oldham likened Banks to "an antelope. She was just born with grace."

Entranced the Paris Runways

Within Banks's first week in Paris, other designers were so entranced by her presence on the runway that she was booked for an unprecedented 25 shows—a record in the business for a newcomer. Next, Banks was offered lucrative contract deals, where the real money in the modeling industry lies. She was the first African American woman on the cover of *Sports Illustrated*'s high-profile swimsuit issue; American designer Ralph Lauren wanted her for another one of his lush, multipage ad campaigns; and cosmetics giant Cover Girl made her the second African American to be offered a long-term deal with them.

Yet Banks's early days in the modeling business were difficult for her, despite a naturally exuberant and flexible demeanor. Subtle racism within the industry was partly responsible; from the start, Banks was called the "new Naomi Campbell," in comparison to the more experienced supermodel who had been the star woman of color on the runways for some years. Campbell, known for her diva-like behavior, was incensed, and managed to get Banks barred from appearing in a Chanel show after refusing to speak to her on several other occasions. "No model should have to endure what I went through at 17," Banks told *Essence* writer Deborah Gregory. "It's very sad that the fashion business and press can't accept that there can be more than one reigning black supermodel at a time."

Banks discussed the racism in the modeling industry with *Cosmopolitan* writer Jamie Diamond in 1993. "I've had bookers tell me, 'You've got light skin and green eyes. You're easy to sell.'" She admitted to relaxing her hair and having hair extensions done "because that's what 'beautiful' is supposed to look like—and that's how I make my living." Nevertheless, success does not insulate Banks from random acts of racism in everyday life. When she and a friend went to a New York City newsstand to purchase a magazine whose cover the model graced, the proprietor yelled at the two women and ordered them out of the store. When her friend pointed out the issue and Banks's image, he responded by saying "I don't care. You all look alike."

Spotted by Influential Director

The difficulties engendered by her daughter's new profession helped convince Carolyn London-Johnson to heed Banks's urgings and get involved. She quit her job and moved to Paris for a time to become her full-time manager, an arrangement that has suited them well. Banks's father handles her finances, and the supermodel daughter did not move out of her mother's house until she was 21. A magazine cover for *Essence* in June of 1993 sparked the next big move in Banks's career. John Singleton, director of the Academy-Award-nominated *Boyz 'N the Hood*, spotted the magazine and thought she would be perfect for an as-yet-uncast role in his next film. After mutual friends introduced them, Singleton attended one of Banks's appearances on the runway. He was entranced. They struck up a friendship that blossomed into romance.

Meanwhile, Banks had been cast in an occasional recurring role on the NBC-TV sitcom *The Fresh Prince of Bel-Air*, starring former hip-hop star and feature-film actor Will Smith. Banks portrayed Jackie Ames, a love interest of Smith's title character. The acting experience made it easier when Singleton and the producers of his upcoming film *Higher Learning* asked her to read for the role of Deja, a star athlete at the film's fictional university. Some assumed that she had gotten the role because of her relationship with Singleton, the film's director, but Banks told *Entertainment Weekly* reporter Tim Appelo that "John said, 'Read for it, but if you're bad, you don't get it. I'd look like I'm thinkin' with my you-know-what.'" Her performance at the audition made an impact, however, and she won the role. *Higher Learning* won kudos from critics for its performances. Although Banks and Singleton eventually parted ways, Banks had established her acting career.

After the success of *Higher Learning*, Banks bought herself a five-bedroom abode in Los Angeles. She has also endowed her alma mater, Immaculate Heart, with a scholarship for African American girls. "I was very privileged that my mother and father sent me to private school," Banks told Gregory in *Essence*. "I want other African-American girls who can't afford it to experience that kind of education." Although still modeling, she pursued her career on the screen with diligence, starting by reading up on the history of the film industry. Banks told *Essence*'s Gregory that she had planned on a career in film prior to even thinking about modeling, but realized that the yoke of Supermodel would be a hard one to shed. "Even when I'm 50 and no longer modeling, everyone will still refer to me as 'Tyra the model.' Once a model, always a model."

Yet being an African American model in an industry dominated by Caucasians has been difficult. "It's long overdue that black models receive the same benefits as white models," she told *Essence*'s Gregory. "But I still don't make as much as the white supermodels do." Rather than waiting for the industry to catch up, Banks made her own plans for a multifaceted career. She formed a corporation in 1991—Tygirl, Inc.—to manage her career, and declined further involvement in *The Fresh Prince of Bel Air*, in part because "everybody started coming up to me on the street and calling me Jackie Ames," she told Ryan in *GQ*. "I felt like I didn't want to get stereotyped into that character." The actor declined a role as a one-night stand with Tom Cruise's character in the 1993 film *The Firm*, primarily because of the one-dimensional, decorative nature of the character. "I don't want roles that scream, I AM SO PRETTY!," Banks told *People* magazine's Gliatto. Another rule? She freely admitted an important one to Appelo in the *Entertainment Weekly* article: "I'm not takin' off my clothes."

Started a Televised Model Hunt

Over the next decade, Banks took her career in many different directions. She wrote a beauty book that preached about the necessity of recognizing one's own inner and outer beauty. She continued to take roles in films. While she played a doll magically given life in the made-for-television movie *Life-Size,* for the most part Banks remained true to her desire not to take roles that simply relied on her looks. In *Coyote Ugly* she played a law student named Zoe, and she faced the murderous Jason in *Halloween: Resurrection.* But Banks focused much more on her own image. Taking cues from the success of reality television programming, Banks created *America's Next Top Model* in 2003. The program follows the ups and downs of a group of models as they compete for the chance to win a modeling contract. Among the show's panel of experts, Banks is portrayed as a powerful gatekeeper to the world of high fashion and glamour. According to *New Yorker* television critic Nancy Franklin, "the aspiring models view her both as the bearer of a magic ticket out of poverty, obscurity, stripping, and waitressing and as a comforting, maternal, Oprah-like figure." The show was hailed in 2005 as UPN's most desirable show. Television analyst Carolyn Finger told *Television Week* that "It's the one show that universally it can be said any network would like to have."

Among her other ventures, Banks planned to record music and launch herself as a pop diva. In addition she was preparing to launch her own talk show. *Television Week* noted that "Banks' planned talk show is considered one of the highest-profile pieces of development for syndication in 2005." Unlike her unique modeling show, which has since encouraged other similar shows, Banks understood that her talk show would be one among many. But, as she told *Television Week,* "there is a void right now for a talk show headed by someone of my generation…. I haven't seen it done how we're doing it. And I hope that will pay off." Only time will tell. However, Warner Bros. Domestic Television Distribution President Dick Robertson is banking on Banks. He told the *Hollywood Reporter:* "If there's ever a future Oprah, she could be the one."

Selected works

Books

(With Vanessa Thomas Bush) *Tyra's Beauty Inside & Out*, HarperPerennial, 1998.

Films

Higher Learning, 1995.
Life-Size, 2000.
Coyote Ugly, 2000.
Halloween: Resurrection, 2002.

Television

The Fresh Prince of Bel-Air, 1990.
America's Next Top Model, 2003–.
The Tyra Banks Show, 2005.

Sources

Periodicals

Chicago Tribune, August 6, 1995, p. C14.
Cosmopolitan, September 1993.
Detroit News, June 1, 1995, p. C3.
Entertainment Weekly, January 13, 1995, p. 3.
Essence, February 1995, p. 60.
GQ, June 1995, p. 176.
Hollywood Reporter, September 30. 2004, p.3.
Jet, February 13, 1995, p. 30.
New Yorker, March 14, 2005, pp. 143-44.
New York Times, August 4, 2000.
People, April 11, 1994, p. 57; May 9, 1994, p. 118; January 23, 1995, p. 33; March 7, 2005, p. 38.
Television Week, January 10, 2005, p. 49; January 31, 2005, p. 12.

—Carol Brennan and Sara Pendergast

Romare Bearden

1912-1988

Artist

A master of technique best known for his collage and photomontage compositions, esteemed artist Romare Bearden consistently depicted African-American culture and experience in his work. His oeuvre reflects the influences of various art traditions and reveals themes common to many different cultures—themes of death, the family, religious ritual, and the beauty of natural landscapes. Bearden also touched on aspects of jazz and city life through his works, and he was noted for his portraits of women in their many roles: mothers, lovers, gardeners, conjurers, healers, and even prostitutes, as in the "Storyville" series of bordello scenes.

Collage, a term taken from a French word meaning to glue or assemble, was brought into the realm of modern European art by the Cubists, followers of an abstract, fragmented style of art. The collagist combines pieces of painted paper, pictures from newspapers and magazines, and colored paper into a distinctive piece of art. Bearden's style of photomontage is based on the collage method but involves photographs and techniques from film documentary.

In Germany immediately after World War I, the Dada artists emerged, overturning traditional values in art and developing the type of photomontage used by Bearden. One Dada artist in particular, Hannah Hoch, used fragments of photographs and pictures from magazines in her work. While Hoch's collages reflect a sense of discontinuity, Bearden's speak of the continuity of artistic tradition. Beginning in the 1960s, Bearden used collage and film documentary techniques to explore—in terms of his own African-American experience—universal themes common to all cultures.

As a *New York* magazine contributor noted, "In collage, Bearden found a way to speak to people who know something about art as well as to people who don't."

"Memory and Metaphor: The Art of Romare Bearden, 1940-1987" was a major retrospective show containing nearly 150 works from Romare Bearden's half-century career in the visual arts. Beginning at the Studio Museum in Harlem in 1991, the show traveled through 1993 to major museums in Chicago, Los Angeles, Atlanta, Pittsburgh, and finally the National Museum of American Art in Washington, D.C. In reviewing the exhibit, Robert Hughes wrote in *Time* magazine, "Romare Bearden...was one of the finest collagists of the 20th century and the most distinguished black visual artist America has so far produced."

Other reviewers have been equally enthusiastic about Bearden's importance. Michael Brenson wrote in the *New York Times* that Bearden was "a remarkably complex and generous artist who should now be given the most concentrated consideration." A *Newsweek* critic suggested that "Bearden constructed a visual narrative of the black American experience that is finally the equal of the same epic tale told in music and literature." And twenty years earlier, Carroll Greene wrote in the exhibit catalog for Bearden's major exhibition at New York's Museum of Modern Art that his work was "an affirmation, a celebration, a victory of the human spirit over all the forces that would oppress it."

At a Glance . . .

Born Romare Howard Bearden on September 2, 1912, in Charlotte, NC (some sources give 1911 or 1914 as Beardon's year of birth, but the Register of Deeds in Charlotte, NC, lists his exact date of birth as September 2, 1912); died of bone cancer, March 12, 1988, in New York City; ashes taken to property on St. Martin, French West Indies; son of Richard Howard and Bessye (Johnson) Bearden; married Nanette Rohan (organizer of New York's Chamber Dance Company), c. 1954. *Education*: New York University, B.S., 1935; studied under George Grosz at the Art Students League in New York, 1936-37; studied art at the Sorbonne, Paris, 1950-51. *Military Service*: U.S. Army, 1942-45; served in all black 372nd Infantry Regiment.

Career: Artist. Department of Social Services, New York City, caseworker, 1938; worked and painted in New York for five years following World War II, showing with the Samuel Kootz Gallery; studied art in Paris, 1950-51; returned to New York, gave up painting briefly to compose music, but soon returned to the visual arts. Harlem Cultural Council, art director, beginning in 1964; Cinque Gallery, New York City, cofounder and director, beginning in 1969.

Awards: Award from National Institute of Arts and Letters, 1966, and American Academy of Arts and Letters, 1970; Guggenheim fellowship, 1970; Ford Foundation grant, 1973; Medal of Arts, 1987.

An only child, Romare Howard Bearden was born on September 2, 1912, in the house of his great-grandfather in Charlotte, North Carolina. His father played piano, and both his paternal grandfather and great-grandfather did paintings and drawings. The family moved to New York City when Bearden was three or four years old. His father, Richard Howard Bearden, worked as a sanitation inspector for the city's Department of Health. His mother, Bessye, the first president of the Negro Women's Democratic Association, served as New York correspondent for the *Chicago Defender*, a regional black newspaper.

Bearden attended various schools in New York, but he finished high school in 1929 in Pittsburgh, where his maternal grandmother lived. Although he had taken a few informal drawing lessons from a sickly boyhood friend in the mid-1920s, Bearden was not very involved with the arts in high school. Following his graduation,

he played semiprofessional baseball for a short time in Boston. He then returned to New York in the early 1930s to attend college. Planning to enter medical school, he majored in mathematics at New York University, receiving his bachelor's degree in science. But Bearden's interest in cartooning was also renewed during his college years. He drew for the university's humor magazine *NYU Medley*, and by his senior year, he had become the magazine's art editor.

After graduating from college, Bearden went to the Art Students League in 1936 and 1937 to study with George Grosz, a German artist known for his satirical drawings and caricatures. He studied with Grosz for two years and took a studio at 33 West 125th Street to paint. Bearden realized at once that he did not want to imitate the works of white artists. He joined the 306 Group, a group of black artists that met at the studios of Henry Bannarn and Charles Alston. The 1930s were an exciting time for modern art, and Bearden was exposed to a range of influences. He was particularly interested in Cubism, Futurism, post-Impressionism, and Surrealism. While studying at the Art Students League, Bearden exhibited early figurative paintings at the Harlem YWCA and the Harlem Art Workshop.

By 1938, Bearden realized he couldn't live by painting alone, so he took a job in the Department of Social Services as a caseworker and painted in his spare time. Creating art that he could feel emotionally, he did a series of paintings largely on Southern themes executed on heavy brown wrapping paper, the least expensive material available. His work of the time was done in a Cubist style, featuring rich colors and simple, planar forms. Bearden had his first one-person show at Ad Bates's Harlem studio in 1940. In his statement for the show, Bearden wrote: "I believe that art is an expression of what people feel and want…. In order for a painting to be 'good' two things are necessary: that there be a communion of belief and desire between artist and spectator, [and] that the artist be able to see and say something that enriches the fund of communicable feeling and the medium for expressing it."

Bearden was drafted into the U.S. Army in 1942 and served until May of 1945. His first one-person show at a major New York gallery came in the fall of 1945 at the Samuel Kootz Gallery, where he showed regularly from 1945 to 1950. The show consisted of Bearden's "Passion of Christ" series, abstract paintings that serve to represent the history of human suffering. "He Is Risen" was acquired by New York's Museum of Modern Art, and the show received a favorable review in the *New York Times*.

After World War II, Bearden resumed his duties as caseworker. His paintings were increasingly abstract, a style that *Newsweek* called "a stained-glass…brand of cubism." Bearden's one-person shows continued at the Kootz Gallery, and he was regularly included in major group shows of contemporary American art, including those at the Whitney Museum in New York and the Art

Institute of Chicago. Literary influences were evident in his series of paintings based on works by Spanish poet Federico Garcia Lorca, French satirist Francois Rabelais, and ancient Greek poet Homer, and in 1948 he painted 16 variations on Homer's *Iliad* and *Odyssey*.

Perhaps it was a sense of alienation that caused Bearden to leave the United States for Europe in 1950. Under the GI Bill, he went to Paris to study at the Sorbonne for two years. While there, he met modern artists such as Pablo Picasso, Georges Braque, and Fernan Leger, as well as Jean Helion and the Romanian sculptor Constantin Brancusi. When he returned to New York, he gave up painting and devoted himself to writing songs. According to some sources, he may have suffered a breakdown in the early 1950s. Nevertheless, he worked his way back into painting by studying and copying the works of old masters as well as those of modern artists like Picasso and Henri Matisse.

Around 1954 Bearden took a studio above the Apollo Theater and created abstract paintings that were heavily influenced by Chinese painting. He developed an interest in Chinese techniques, studied them thoroughly, and recorded his involvement with the tradition of Chinese painting in a book, *The Painter's Mind*, which he wrote with his friend and fellow artist, Carl Holty. From 1956 to 1961, Bearden's paintings grew increasingly personal in nature. An *Artnews* reviewer described a 1960 show of Bearden's large, lyrical abstractions by saying, "Thinned, cool-colored paint is splattered, splotched, blotted and matched to create a romantic and controlled aura of corrosion, growth and agitation."

The early 1960s were another period of transition for Bearden, this time from painting to collage. He executed a series of black and white compositions, experimenting with spatial anomalies and disjuncture. In 1963, a group of black artists began meeting in his Harlem studio. Calling themselves the Spiral Group, they sought to define their roles as black artists within the context of the growing civil rights movement.

As described in *Romare Bearden: Origins and Progressions*, the artist concentrated on "organizing a group project that would express or symbolize some kind of consensus and unity; so he proposed that the group work on a communal collage." The project served to bring a new focus to Bearden's own works, combining photo enlargements and torn-paper techniques in the artistic rendering of childhood memories. In 1964, he began a series of collages based on black urban life, with the overall title "The Prevalence of Ritual." In so doing, Bearden made another transition within collage from abstraction to Cubist figuration.

Bearden's 1964 collages were inspired by techniques of film documentary. He used projected images, abrupt transitions of scale, and cutouts of figures and faces. His subjects included life in Harlem, memories of the rural South, and jazz musicians. Individual titles included "Baptism," "Tidings," "The Conjure Woman," "The Funeral," "The Street—Uptown Looking Downtown," "Train Whistle Blues," and "The Savoy—Grand Terrace Ballroom." An important turning point in Bearden's career occurred when art dealer Arne Ekstrom selected his collages for a show at Cordier & Ekstrom. Included in the show were Bearden's larger photomontages, all done in black and white.

In the collages of the later 1960s, Bearden's colors became richer and his patterns more decorative. He introduced patterns of patchwork quilts, photographs, and pieces of cloth in some works. A growing public interest led to commissions for posters, a mural in Times Square (now removed), and covers for magazines like *Time, Fortune, New York Times Magazine*, and *TV Guide*. He had a solo show at the Corcoran Gallery in Washington, D.C., in 1966, and his work was becoming a major statement in American art.

Analyses of specific collages reveal not only Bearden's mastery of the technique, but also the influences of different art traditions. "Blue Interior—Morning" (1968), for example, was the subject of a *School Arts* review and analysis for the purpose of teaching art appreciation. The reviewer appreciated Bearden's collages as "images of cultural continuity in the voice of his African-American heritage," noting, "They tell us of places and events, public and private rituals and activities from his own memories and personal experience."

"Blue Interior—Morning" shows a family engaged in private domestic rituals and interactions. "The people are portrayed not as isolated individuals, but as interdependent and interconnected with one another," explained the *School Arts* critic. The figures in the collage are depicted in a way that recalls African art traditions, in which the frontal and profile views are done with the head relatively large to the body and the hands large and prominent. Juxtaposed fragments create an African rhythm or polyrhythm through the interplay of stylized and naturalistic forms. The work also reveals the influences of modern European art, especially Cubism and modern abstract art. The use of geometric forms suggests Bearden's love of jazz and his interest in the African-American tradition of quilting.

"Blue Interior—Morning" is actually a photomontage. Bearden has recombined parts of photographs that were originally part of some other image, thus speaking of memory and continuity. As noted in the *School Arts* analysis, "These collaged elements bring their own sense of history to this image." The *New York Times* art critic reaffirmed this point in commenting on another Bearden piece: "In a work like Bearden's "Three Folk Musicians" (1967), heads are pieced together from different people, often different in age, cultures, and style, and drawn from many sources. All of Bearden's men and women carry within them the memory or the actual presence of others."

In his widely acclaimed "Prevalence of Ritual" retrospective at New York's Museum of Modern Art in 1971, many of the works displayed were collage paintings. Writing about the collages in *The Art of Romare Bearden: The Prevalence of Ritual*, M. Bunch Washington found in Bearden's work a truer vision of African-American social reality than ever before: "The social reality, the deceptive, crimson, and pregnant social reality of the sixties, can be seen clearly through these eyes. The eyes of a people and a man unique in the intense, deeply integral quality of their humanity, and, lest we forget in the present din, unique in their suffering, their power."

Bearden was more than a political propagandist, but it is interesting to note that he studied art in the 1930s, a time when social realism was a major force in modern American painting. The social turbulence and civil rights movement of the 1960s seemed to have served as a catalyst for Bearden's art, enabling him to find his truest subjects and the means to render them.

The primary subject of the last 25 years of Bearden's art was the life and culture of African-Americans. His work covered rural themes based on his memories of the South as well as urban life and jazz. In the 1980s, he produced a large body of work featuring compelling images of women. For many years, he spent time annually with his wife on the Caribbean island of St. Martin, adding tropical images to his body of work. According to *New York* magazine, "He discovered a new empathy with Matisse and with the humming colors and overheated emotions of hot climates."

In 1986, Bearden was commissioned by the Detroit Institute of Arts to celebrate their centennial. He executed a mosaic mural, done in mosaic glass, of approximately 10 x 13' and titled "Quilting Time." The work is typical of Bearden in that it is rooted in his memories of his Southern childhood and depicts an important aspect of African-American culture. The brightly colored mosaic shows a group of women making a quilt. The artist's statement on this work states, in part, "It may have come to me in selecting a quilting bee (as these affairs were often called) as my subject that the technique had something to do with my own use of the medium of collage. After all, working in collage was precisely what the ladies were doing."

Bearden's use of mosaic tile late in his career developed from his use of the technique of building his forms with very small pieces of paper, a technique called *tesserae*. Since the paper was so fragile, Bearden began using mosaic tile for his large public artworks.

Bearden received the 1987 Medal of Arts from President Reagan. Less than a year later, he died in New York of bone cancer. In his will, he stipulated his desire to be cremated and his ashes taken to St. Martin in the French West Indies. He left his estate to his wife, Nanette, and also set up a trust fund for the Romare Bearden Foundation to aid in the education and training of talented art students.

Bearden's art has survived him well. The largest retrospective of his works was organized by the National Gallery of Art in 2003. The exhibit included a comprehensive collection of his art, from his most famous collages and photomontages to his lesser-known watercolor, gouache, and oil paintings, illustrations, and his only known sculpture. The exhibit toured the San Francisco Museum of Modern Art, the Dallas Museum of Art, and the Whitney Museum of American Art, in 2004 and the High Museum of Art in Atlanta in 2005. The retrospective did more than simply exhibit Bearden's works, but educated viewers in his technique that came to be called "visual jazz," or artwork that is like music in the techniques used to create it and its visual affect. Recorded commentaries by notable musician Wynton Marsalis and artist David Driskell accompany some of Bearden's works in the exhibit. Both a scholarly book by the exhibition's curator, Ruth Fine, and a children's book by Jan Greenberg were published in 2003 to accompany the retrospective. Bearden had aspired, as quoted by *Insight on the News,* "to establish a world through art in which the validity of my Negro experience could live and make its own logic." The comprehensive exhibition of 130 of his works provides ample proof that Bearden succeeded in turning his knowledge of the African-American experience into art.

Selected writings

(With Carl Holty) *The Painter's Mind: A Study of the Relations of Structure and Space in Painting*, Crown, 1969.
(With Harry Brinton Henderson) *Six Black Masters of American Art*, Doubleday, 1972.

Sources

Books

Bearden, Romare, and Carl Holty, *The Painter's Mind: A Study of the Relations of Structure and Space in Painting*, Crown, 1969.
Fine, Ruth, *The Art of Romare Bearden,* Abrams/National Gallery of Art, 2004.
Greenberg, Jan, *Collage of Memories* (children's book), Abrams, 2003.
Greene, Carroll, Jr., *Romare Bearden: The Prevalence of Ritual*, Museum of Modern Art, 1971.
Patton, Sharon F., *Memory and Metaphor: The Art of Romare Bearden*, 1940-1987, Studio Museum in Harlem/Oxford University Press, 1991.
Romare Bearden: Origins and Progressions, Detroit Institute of Arts, 1986.
Schwartzman, Myron, *Romare Bearden: His Life and Art*, Abrams, 1990.
Washington, M. Bunch, *The Art of Romare Bearden: The Prevalence of Ritual*, Abrams, 1973.

Periodicals

American Artist, September 2004, January 2005.
Art in America, February 1987.
Artnews, February 1960; Summer 1988.
Insight on the News, December 8, 2003.
Instructor, September 1989.
Nation, December 6, 2004.
Newsweek, April 29, 1991.
New York, May 13, 1991.
New York Times, April 19, 1991.
School Arts, January 1990.
Time, June 10, 1991.

On-line

"The Art of Romare Bearden," *San Francisco Museum of Modern Art,* www.sfmoma.org/bearden/index.html (March 9, 2005).

—David Bianco and Sara Pendergast

James A. Bell

1948—

Corporate executive

Bell, James A., photograph. AP/Wide World Photos. Reproduced by permission.

Growing up in the working-class black community of south central Los Angeles, James Bell might have believed that the greatest success he could hope for was to land a steady job with the Post Office, like his father. Yet Bell recognized that an opportunity existed for another kind of future, with more rewarding work and room for advancement. He became one of the few young men from his neighborhood to graduate from college, and went on to positions of increasing responsibility in the business world. After almost thirty years working in the world of business finance, he was promoted to one of the top jobs in a major corporation when he became chief financial officer with aerospace giant The Boeing Company. Then, early in 2005, Bell was appointed interim president and chief executive officer when a scandal took down his predecessor. Despite his ever-increasing business responsibilities, Bell placed great importance on another responsibility of success: supporting and encouraging other African Americans seeking business careers.

Bell was born in Los Angeles on June 4, 1948. His parents, Mamie and Clyde Bell, had come from Oklahoma, seeking the wider opportunities that California seemed to offer African Americans. Clyde Bell worked for the Post Office, and Mamie was a clerk for the County of Los Angeles. They lived and raised their family in the black neighborhood called South Central. Young James spent his youth in the security of his close-knit extended family, enjoying family trips to the park or beach and playing football and baseball with friends.

Bell was an avid reader who liked school and did well in his studies. One of his elementary school teachers, an African American named Mr. Kelly, gave Bell special encouragement by assuring his young black students that they could accomplish anything if they worked hard and had confidence in themselves.

During Bell's junior year of high school in 1965, the arrest of a black driver by California Highway Patrol officers sparked five days of intense rioting in Watts, a black neighborhood in Los Angeles. The riots went on for six days and, when they were over, thirty-four people were killed and hundreds injured. The neighborhood was devastated by fires set by rioters. Though the civil rights movement had previously seemed far away to a schoolboy in southern California, the Watts riots

At a Glance . . .

Born James Aaron Bell on June 4, 1948, in Los Angeles, California; married Mary Howell August 22, 1981; two children: Sean and Champagne. *Education:* California State University at Los Angeles, BA, accounting, 1971.

Career: Rockwell International Corporation, Atomics International Accounting Organization, accounting, corporate audit, cost policy, and cost estimating, 1972-86, director of accounting, 1986-92; Rockwell International Corporation, Space Station Electric Power System Program, director of business management, 1992-96; Boeing Company, vice president of contracts and pricing, 1996-2000, senior vice president of finance and corporate controller, 2000-03, acting chief financial officer, 2003-04, executive vice president and chief financial officer, 2004-05, interim president and chief executive officer, 2005–.

Selected Memberships: Los Angeles Urban League; Urban League of Chicago; New Leaders for New Schools; Joffrey Ballet; World Business Chicago.

Addresses: *Office*—Boeing World Headquarters, 100 N. Riverside, Chicago, IL 60606.

brought the anger and bitterness of the black community very close to James Bell. Though he recognized the feelings of frustration and despair that lay behind the rioters, he felt that they had only succeeded in burning down their own neighborhood. He determined to look for more constructive approaches to change in his own life.

Another major influence in Bell's early life came when he was elected to the office of student body president during his senior year of high school. As part of the student government, he participated in student council events with other schools, where he met students whose experience and expectations were quite different from his own. For the first time, Bell was exposed to other students who assumed they would attend college and go on to rewarding careers. In his own neighborhood, many young African Americans assumed that the best career they could hope for was a secure job. Bell, however, had done a variety of part-time jobs, from cleaning players' shoes at the golf course, to cleaning office buildings, to working in the Post Office, and he had not enjoyed them. Not wanting to settle for a secure but boring job that offered little

hope of advancement, James Bell decided to go to college.

His grades were good enough to earn him a partial scholarship to California State University at Los Angeles. The scholarship paid his tuition for the first year, and Bell continued to work to pay for the rest of his college education. He chose accounting as his major, because he felt it was a concrete business skill that would allow him to get a good job upon graduation.

During his senior year of college, the Rockwell International Corporation sent recruiters to the CSU campus. Based in southern California, Rockwell was a large corporation with many sections, including an aerospace and defense division. After speaking to the recruiters, Bell went to Rockwell to explore the possibility of employment, though he did not plan to apply for a job. To Bell's surprise Rockwell offered him a position in their Atomics International Accounting Organization, and he joined the company in 1972.

His first year at Rockwell did not go smoothly. Bell found it difficult to make the transition from the life of a student to a stressful business career. His first performance appraisal was full of negative feedback about his work. However, some of his more experienced supervisors and co-workers took an interest in the young accountant, and helped him adjust to his new career. With the advice and support of these mentors, Bell made an important change in his attitude. Rather than merely going to work each day, he began to pursue a career.

Bell worked at Rockwell for twenty-four years. He performed various functions in the accounting department, including work with accounting, corporate audits, cost policy making, and cost estimating. Beginning in 1984, he supervised the team responsible for combining the financial activities of the Atomics International and Rocketdyne Divisions of the Rockwell Corporation.

In 1996, the Boeing Company bought the aerospace and defense division of Rockwell. Boeing, based in Seattle and Chicago, had expanded from its roots as an airplane manufacturer into a large, multi-faceted corporation. Bell moved smoothly into the new company, becoming vice president of contracts and pricing. He continued to advance his career at Boeing, combining his financial expertise with excellent management skills. When he became corporate controller in 2000, he was also required to develop company processes for following the many rules about how businesses must report their finances to the government.

In 2003 Bell was promoted to acting chief financial officer at Boeing when a scandal involving then-CFO Mike Sears rocked the company. Bell's performance was so strong—and the trust in him so complete—that in 2004 the position was made permanent. Boeing president and chief executive officer Harry Stonecipher spoke of Bell's qualifications in a much-quoted press release from the Boeing Web site, "James Bell is a superior financial leader," Stonecipher said. "He is a proven, highly skilled manager who has intimate knowledge of our strategy and champions fiscal transparency. James will be a key member of our leadership team."

Bell was lifted even higher in the company early in 2005, when yet another scandal rocked the company. Early in March, the corporate board asked for the resignation of Harry Stonecipher when it was discovered that he had had an adulterous relationship with a Boeing executive, thus violating the company's code of conduct. Bell was immediately named interim president and chief executive officer. It was not immediately known how soon the board expected to make a permanent appointment.

In addition to advancing his executive career, Bell has continued to value his relations with his own close-knit family. He places great importance on education for young African Americans and works with an organization called New Leaders for New Schools to help train and develop more black school principals. He also works as a mentor within the Boeing organization, encouraging blacks in their career development, much

as he was encouraged during his early years at Rockwell.

Sources

Periodicals

Black Enterprise, April 2004.
Chicago Tribune, January 7, 2004.
Seattle Times, November 25, 2003; January 7, 2004; March 7, 2005; March 8, 2005.

On-line

"Biographies: James A. Bell," *Boeing,* www.boeing.com/companyoffices/aboutus/execprofiles/bell.html (March 7, 2005).
"Boeing Names James Bell Chief Financial Officer," *Boeing,* www.boeing.com/news/releases/2004/q1/nr_040106a.html (December 15, 2004).

Other

Information for this profile was obtained through an interview with James Bell on December 15, 2004.

—Tina Gianoulis

Jayson Blair

1976—

Writer

Blair, Jayson, photograph. New York Times/Getty Images.

Jayson Blair became embroiled in one of the most devastating scandals in American journalism when his employer, the esteemed *New York Times,* revealed that he had plagiarized several news stories from other sources, or filed stories from the field while actually holed up in his New York City apartment. Blair became one of the most reviled figures of 2003 for his transgressions, but later wrote a memoir of the downward spiral that led him to create his masterful web of deceit.

Born in 1976, Blair grew up in northern Virginia, the son of a federal employee and a schoolteacher. A newshound from an early age, he wrote for his school paper at Centreville High School in Clifton, and also worked for a community newspaper while still in his teens. He went on to the journalism program at the University of Maryland's College Park campus, where his talents propelled him to the editorship of its student newspaper, the *Diamondback.* During his undergraduate days, he landed prestigious journalism internships at both the *Boston Globe* and the *Washington Post.*

Joined Staff of the New York Times

The *New York Times* was the holy grail for all print-journalism aspirants, and Blair won a summer internship there in 1998. He was offered an extended stint when his term was up, but told his bosses that he needed to head back to Maryland to finish some courses in time for his December graduation date. In June of 1999 Blair returned to New York City to take an entry-level writing job with the *Times.* It seemed the human resources department there never bothered to verify his credentials, for it was later revealed that Blair had never actually graduated from the University of Maryland.

Assigned to the police beat during his first months at the *Times,* Blair was soon promoted to an intermediate reporter position in November of 1999 and became a business writer for the paper's Metropolitan section after that. His correction rate—the number of errors in his reporting discovered after publication—was higher than average for a cub journalist, and he was warned on several occasions to be more careful in his reportage. Nevertheless, he was a gifted writer with a quick grasp of the human-interest angle in any story. In January of 2001 he was made a full-time staff reporter.

Blair detailed these first years at the *Times* in his 2004 memoir, *Burning Down My Masters' House: My Life*

At a Glance . . .

Born in 1976 in Virginia; son of Thomas Blair (a federal employee) and a teacher. *Education:* Attended the University of Maryland, College Park, 1994-98.

Career: Journalism intern at the *Boston Globe, Washington Post,* and *New York Times; New York Times,* reporter, 1999-2003.

Addresses: *Office*—c/o New Millennium Entertainment, 301 North Canon Dr., Ste. 214, Beverly Hills, CA 90210. *Home*—Brooklyn, NY.

at *The New York Times.* He wrote of the heavy drinking and drug abuse he engaged in after the workday was over, and the pressure he felt in the highly competitive atmosphere. His error rate continued to prove worrisome, even after a January 2002 stint in a rehabilitation clinic. Three months later, he was the subject of an e-mail that his Metro desk editor, Jonathan Landman, sent to the *Times*'s managing editor, Gerald Boyd. Landman voiced concerns about Blair's professional integrity and state that "we have to stop Jayson from writing for the *Times,*" Landman declared, according to the 7,000-word *mea culpa* that the paper published when Blair's deception came to light.

Covered D.C.-Area Sniper Shootings

Blair was moved to the sports desk, a less risky area for a reporter who seemed to need some managerial supervision, but then the Washington, D.C.-area sniper story broke in the fall of 2002. Because the suburban region was where he grew up and he knew it well, he was sent there along with a slew of other National desk reporting staffers to cover the story. Blair filed numerous front-page articles about the mysterious killings and the apprehension of suspects John Muhammad and Lee Malvo. But some of his claims earned the ire of local and national law-enforcement authorities, and his veracity was questioned. Blair defended his stories in meetings with his editors, but began to succumb to increasing internal pressure.

Despite his workplace problems, Blair was allowed to remain on the National desk after the sniper story quieted down, and after March of 2003 began filing stories about the war in Iraq from the perspective of military families awaiting word of missing or injured loved ones. In one of his reports he recounted a visit to a military hospital; another appeared to have centered around a visit to the home of 18-year-old Private

Jessica Lynch, who had been captured by Iraqi forces and then dramatically rescued. However, he had been in neither place.

Blair remained in Brooklyn, but he continued to tell his editors that he was on the road chasing stories. Oftentimes, his bosses and colleagues had a hard time reaching him via his cell phone number, and no one at the paper thought to examine his expense-account reports, in which journalists are reimbursed for costs like car-rental fees and meals while reporting from the field. It was an April 18 edition of the San Antonio *Express-News* that finally exposed Blair's immense string of deceptions at the *Times.* An *Express-News* reporter, Macarena Hernández, had written a story about a missing U.S. soldier from Texas and the anguish his mother was experiencing. Eight days later a similar story appeared in the *New York Times,* with Blair's byline. The *Express-News* editor, like most journalists, read the *Times* daily, and she was surprised by the parallels between the stories. The *Times* editors were contacted, and Blair was called in for heated meetings that stretched over two days. Though he claimed to have visited the soldier's home in Los Fresnos, he could not produce any other proof save for his handwritten notes.

Incited Maelstrom of Controversy

Blair resigned from the *Times* on May 1, and ten days later the paper published a massive front-page story that detailed his plagiarism in some three dozen stories. A pariah, he landed on the cover of *Newsweek* and stayed inside his apartment while the journalistic debate raged. Many were stunned that nation's most prestigious newspaper could have harbored a charlatan reporter for so long, and others called it a setback for the concept of affirmative action. Though Blair may have obtained the job because he was African American in a time when American newspapers were ardently committed to diversifying their workforce, foes of preferential hiring practices claimed that he was protected and even promoted despite his poor job performance.

What became known as "L'Affaire Blair" incited a rebellion of sorts among the paper's extensive editorial staff. Many *Times* journalists were already unhappy with executive editor Howell Raines, on board since 2001, and had many criticisms about the newspaper's coverage and operations under his watch. On May 14, staffers assembled in a movie theater in Times Square, the Manhattan landmark whose very name was a nod to the venerable newspaper, and Raines and Boyd were excoriated by their staff. "You have a right to ask if I, as a white man from Alabama with those convictions, gave [Blair] one chance too many," Raines told his employees that day, according to a *New York Observer* article by Sridhar Pappu. "When I look into my heart for the truth of the matter, the answer is yes."

Weeks later, both Raines and Gerald Boyd resigned, and the *Times* installed a public editor to monitor its coverage and accuracy.

Blair finally surfaced in late May, giving an interview to Pappu for the *New York Observer.* He answered several challenging queries with a feistiness that bordered on the defensive. "There are senior managers at *The New York Times* who want African-American reporters to succeed," Blair said about the affirmative-action debate, "and there are hundreds of white junior managers who resent that and don't." He also commented on a recently published novel at the time, *The Fabulist,* written by another disgraced reporter named Stephen Glass. Glass's book was a thinly veiled account of his tenure at the *New Republic* before he was fired for plagiarizing sources and fabricating quotes. Glass was white, and Blair fumed in the *New York Observer* interview, "I don't understand why I am the bumbling affirmative-action hire when Stephen Glass is this brilliant whiz kid, when from my perspective—and I know I shouldn't be saying this—I fooled some of the most brilliant people in journalism," he said. "He [Glass] is so brilliant, and yet somehow I'm an affirmative-action hire. They're all so smart, but I was sitting right under their nose fooling them."

Blair landed a $150,000 contract to write his own book, and the nonfiction *Burning Down My Masters' House* appeared in March of 2004. A *Black Issues Book Review* critique from Wayne Dawkins warned readers to be cautious, however. "Consider every detail with skeptical eyes," Dawkins counseled. "He has lied in elaborate ways that most people will not comprehend, so how can we know that he has not conned us now?" Other reviews were far more scathing in their assessments, and on his press tour Blair faced the wrath of many professional journalists irate that he had managed to tarnish the profession so devastatingly. Interviewed by *Washington Post* media writer Howard Kurtz on CNN, Blair conceded his tale was a tough one

for most to forgive. He blamed substance abuse, the pressure to succeed, and the bipolar disorder with which he was later diagnosed after his *Times* tenure dissolved in ignominy, but noted that these were, in the end, insufficient factors. "Even though I do explain what's going on with me and, you know, what was going on with me during the time in my book, an important thing to remember is that ultimately I was never so impaired that I didn't understand the difference between right and wrong, and I made bad decisions. And I have to take—and I am taking—full responsibility for those decisions."

Selected writings

Burning Down My Masters' House: My Life at The New York Times, New Millennium Press, 2004.

Sources

Periodicals

America's Intelligence Wire, March 2, 2004.
Black Issues Book Review, May-June 2004, p. 52.
Nation, June 30, 2003, p. 10.
Newsweek, May 19, 2003, p. 40.
New York Observer, May 25, 2003, p. 1.
New York Times, May 11, 2003, p. A1.
Nieman Reports, Fall 2003, p. 25.
Time, May 19, 2003, p. 56.

On-line

"Lessons from the Times Blair Affair," *Business Week Online,* www.businessweek.com/bwdaily/dnflash/may2003/nf20030514_4334_db009.htm (January 16, 2005).

—Carol Brennan

George Branham III

1962—

Professional bowler

In 1993 George Branham became the first African American to win a Professional Bowlers Association (PBA) title. He had bowled since the age of six and joined the PBA at age 24. In 17 years as a professional bowler, Branham won five major titles, including the sport's highest honor, the Tournament of Champions. He also rolled 23 games with a perfect score of 300 and earned $747,138 in prize money. When he retired from the game in 2004, he remained one of the world's top contenders and was still the only black bowler to become a PBA champion.

Began Bowling as a Young Boy

George Branham III was born on November 21, 1962, in Detroit, Michigan, to Betty and George Branham II. He started bowling at six when his father, an amateur league bowler, introduced him to the sport. By the time the family moved to southern California, Branham had become an avid bowler, though as a student at Sun Valley's Polytechnic High, he kept his hobby quiet. "No one in school knew I bowled, because when you're not a bowler, you don't want to hear about bowling," he told *Sports Illustrated*. Instead he joined Polytechnic's basketball team. Playing guard, Branham entertained thoughts of earning a basketball scholarship. When he stopped growing at five feet ten inches, he gave up that dream and turned back to his first love, bowling.

Branham's bowling heroes when he was a teen were top PBA players, such as Mark Roth. As he watched them on television, he realized that he wanted to pursue a professional bowling career. He had been coached by his father since he was a child and by the time Branham was 17, both men had realized that Branham was indeed good enough to become a professional. That realization was cinched in 1983 when he won the Southern California Junior Bowler of the Year tournament. The following year, at the age of 23, he joined the PBA and went on his first professional tour.

Became First Black to Win PBA Title

A professional bowler's life is led on the road, traveling to and from the various tournaments that lead up to championship title games. Branham told *Sports Illustrated* that he would, "eat, sleep, and drink bowling." Despite his dedication, Branham's first two years on the PBA tour were uneventful. He competed in tournaments but rarely finished high enough to be noteworthy. That changed in 1986 when he defeated his childhood bowling hero Mark Roth to win the Brunswick Memorial World Open in Chicago. The win made Branham the first African American to win a PBA championship. He went on to finish out 1986 with $59,000 in tour winnings.

In 1986 Branham had begun to appear on televised tournaments and by 1987 he had set a PBA record for the most consecutive wins to start a career on television, with a total of eight. They included another PBA title, the AC Delco Classic, in 1987. After the high of that win, Branham sunk into a six-year drought. "I was consistently cashing, but I was never winning," Branham told *Sports Illustrated*. In 1991 he earned

At a Glance . . .

Born November 21, 1962, in Detroit, MI; married Jacquelyne Phend, 1990; children: Hadley.

Career: Professional Bowlers Association, professional bowler, 1984-2002.

Memberships: Professional Bowlers Association, 1984-2002.

Selected awards: Brunswick Memorial World Open, 1986; AC/Delco Classic, 1987; Baltimore Open, 1993; Firestone Tournament of Champions, 1993; Cleveland Open, 1996.

Addresses: *Home*—Indianapolis, IN.

$63,990. In 1992 that figure dropped to $45,770. He continued, "that got frustrating after a few years. I knew I had to change something, but what thing? Then I realized maybe I just had to wait my turn." It was not an easy wait. When a bowler is not winning, sponsorships dry up and the bowler is left footing their own expenses, including travel, hotel, and tournament fees. "When you go on tour, it's easy to get down on yourself," Branham told *The Record* in 1993; "...it gets tough when you go a few weeks without making any money."

Branham channeled his frustration into weightlifting and put on 20 pounds of muscle. He also left California and settled in Indianapolis. There he met Jacquelyne Phend. When she found out that Branham was a professional bowler, she was surprised. He recalled to *Sports Illustrated* that her reaction was, "You can make money doing that?" The couple married in 1990 and eventually had one daughter, Hadley.

Won Bowling's Top Title

In 1993 Branham returned to the ranks of tournament champions when he won the Baltimore Open, his third PBA title. During the 42-game tournament Branham bowled an average 231 points per game. The win qualified him for the Tournament of Champions held in Fairlawn, Ohio. The tournament is professional bowling's most prestigious title, on par with tennis's U.S. Open or auto racing's Indianapolis 500. In the first two rounds he averaged 238 in eight games including one 300 point finish, securing the lead qualifier spot. When he advanced to the final rounds, he only needed one game to cinch the title. He earned it with a 227 to 214 win. Branham pocketed $60,000 in prize money. He

also went on to win the post-title "King of the Hill" match. It added $5,000 to Branham's winnings, bringing his 1993 earnings to $107,000, a career high.

"Obviously this is the biggest title of my life," Branham told *The Record* after winning the Tournament of Champions. "This is the result of six years hard work on my game and my life." Branham's win was also big news for black history—he was the first African American to win the PBA's top title. However in interviews Branham preferred to focus on his dedication to the sport, rather than the color of his skin. "I've worked hard and paid my dues, and I see this as a start, not the peak, of my career," he told *Jet*.

Over the next few years, despite playing well, titles eluded Branham. He averaged 244 points in the first six games of the 1994 Quaker State Open, emerging as an early leader. However, he was later bowled out of the competition. In 1995 he rolled two 300 games in a row and had a string of 27 consecutive strikes during the Peoria Open. Again he did not reach the winner's circle. It was not until 1996 that Branham pulled out of his losing streak and won the Cleveland Open. The win earned him his fifth PBA title as well as a check for $16,000. Unfortunately this would be his last major win. After a good showing in the 1997 PBA National Championships in Toledo, Ohio, Branham and his career gutter-balled. Once again, he entered a bleak period of constant touring and few wins. In an interview on the PBA Web site Branham pointed to problems with the organization as a partial explanation for his inability to win big. "I think it had a lot to do with what the tour was going through. It was kind of falling apart. So was I." It was a difficult time for Branham. "I was worrying about what I was going to do if the tour folded," he told the *Las Vegas Review-Journal*. "I was 38 with no college degree. It would have been like starting all over again."

Things seemed to be looking up for Branham in 2002 when he played in the Orleans Casino Open in Las Vegas. Branham's parents had retired there several years earlier and were on hand to watch Branham bowl. Playing under their watchful eyes, he also had to ward off worry. "Mom's always so nervous," he told the PBA Web site. "I tell her—calm down or you're going to have a heart attack. Just clap when I strike." She had a lot of reason to clap early on during the tournament. Branham took the first game of the tournament with a win of 245 to 238 over Parker Bohn. He went on to beat Bohn in the next two games. The three-game sweep shook up the professional bowling world as Bohn was the top-ranked bowler at the time. It also gave Branham hope. "I feel like I'm ready to win," he told the *Las Vegas Review-Journal*. "I would like to make it to the show (top five)." Despite his impressive debut in the tournament, he did not make it to the top five.

Later in the year Branham entered the PBA Banquet Classic, but a lower back injury forced him to withdraw mid-tournament. He bowled one more season as a professional before retiring from the tour at the end of 2003. Branham returned full-time to his family in Indianapolis and began to nurture dreams of opening his own bowling center. Whenever his name appeared in print it was always with the notation that he was the first African American to win a PBA championship. A less-noted fact was that, as of the close of 2004, he was also the only African American to hold that distinction. In a rare comment on professional bowling and race, Branham told *The Record* in 1993, "We can always use a little more color on the tour." What the tour could really use is another African-American champion, letting the "only" be erased from Branham's name and the history books.

Sources

Periodicals

Jet, June 7, 1993.
Las Vegas Review-Journal, January 23, 2002.
The Record (Bergen County, NJ), May 2, 1993.
Sports Illustrated, May 3, 1993.

On-line

"Parents Give Branham Boost; Shafer Still Alive," *Professional Bowlers Association,* www.pba.com/news/default.asp?ID=478&Type=0 (December 22, 2004).

—Candace LaBalle

Patrick "Sleepy" Brown

1970—

Vocalist, songwriter, producer

When Patrick "Sleepy" Brown contributed the "I love the way you move" refrain to rap duo OutKast's 2004 hit "The Way You Move," it was only the latest in a series of irresistible hooks, steeped in classic Southern soul, that he had added to the recordings of rappers at work in the fertile music scene of Atlanta, Georgia. Many listeners assumed that such hooks had been sampled from the 1970s works of Marvin Gaye, Curtis Mayfield, or other classic soul vocalists, when in fact Brown had composed them from scratch. As part of the Organized Noize production team and of the looser creative collective known as the Dungeon Family, Brown was one of the hidden forces behind the success of Atlanta-based urban musicians in the late 1990s and early 2000s. He made several attempts to break out as a solo artist on his own and, after several hit singles, seemed ready to emerge with the release of his *For the Grown and Sexy* album in 2005.

Born in 1970, Brown told an Africana Web site interviewer that he, like OutKast's Big Boi (Antwan Patton), had grown up in Savannah, Georgia. The two planned an album together called the *West Savannah Project*. His father, saxophonist and vocalist Jimmy

Brown, Patrick "Sleepy", photograph. Sandra Rose/Getty Images.

Brown, played in the 1970s band Dazz, and Brown absorbed the desire to perform from him. Brown was old enough to remember 1970s vocalists like Gaye and Barry White, but as a teenager in the early days of rap he had another favorite. "I was a big fan of Big Daddy Kane, and he always looked like he was asleep," Brown told *USA Today*. "So I was like, 'What could be cooler than that?' So I decided to call myself Sleepy because that stood for the coolest of the cool for me."

Formed Organized Noize Production Group

Brown moved to Fayetteville, Georgia, near Atlanta, where Big Boi had also taken up residence. In the early 1990s, both gravitated toward Atlanta, where a creative arts and music scene was beginning to blossom around the city's Little Five Points neighborhood, among other places. Brown, who played keyboards and wrote songs, caught the attention of Atlantan Wade, who brought Ray Murray on board, and the trio began billing themselves as Organized Noize, giving production help to other Atlanta artists and sometimes performing as backup musicians or vocalists.

At a Glance . . .

Born Patrick Brown, 1970; raised in Savannah, GA; married 1995.

Career: Organized Noize (production trio), Atlanta, cofounder, early 1990s; Society of Soul (musical group), cofounder, 1996.

Awards: Grammy nomination (as producer, with Organized Noize) for Record of the Year for TLC's "Waterfalls," 1995.

Addresses: *Label*—DreamWorks/Universal Music Group, 2220 Colorado Avenue, Santa Monica , CA 90404. *Web*—www.sleepybrown.com.

By 1995 Brown and his comrades in Organized Noize had scored several triumphs. They produced the hit song "Waterfalls" by the all-female group TLC, earning a Grammy nomination for record of the year the following spring. Another Organized Noize production was Goodie Mob's "Cell Therapy," which topped rap charts in the fall of 1995. Brown's personal breakthrough was a section of OutKast's "Player's Ball," from the duo's hit album of the same name. Brown's contribution, which he both wrote and sang, sounded as though it had been sampled from a recording by the philosophical 1970s soul singer Curtis Mayfield.

All these recordings had serious ideas and diverged from the violent themes popular among urban music audiences in the mid-1990s, which was much to Brown's liking. "To me, music from the heart is better than music from the pocket," he explained to the *Atlanta Journal-Constitution*. "Just sampling something and throwing somebody on the track works for some people. Yeah, you get rich. Get paid. Get your cars. Get your crib. But music from the heart always stays with you. Through the years."

Performed on OutKast Releases

Brown led a group of musicians who played on OutKast's *Southernplayalisticadillacmuzik* album, and that group took the name Society of Soul and in 1996 released an album, *Brainchild*. One song from the album, "E.M.B.R.A.C.E.," got some radio airplay, but *Brainchild* failed to break out from the crowd of Atlanta releases vying for national attention. A solo Sleepy Brown release, 1998's *Vinyl Room*, met the same fate despite positive write-ups in music publications. Organized Noize formed a label and released albums by such acts as Kilo, Cool Breeze, and Witchdoctor, finding only moderate success despite distribu-

tion backing from the large Interscope label. The production crew continued to work with OutKast on their *Stankonia* album and found success in the soundtrack field, providing music from the 2000 remake of the 1970s hit *Shaft*.

By 2001 Organized Noize, OutKast, and Goodie Mob had become known as the Dungeon Family, and Brown had become credited more often for the hooks he added to others' recordings. Those included the 2001 single "Crazy" by child star turned teen rapper Lil' Bow Wow. But things really began to turn around in the fall of 2003 with the release of "The Way You Move" as the first single from OutKast's double *Speakerboxxx/The Love Below* album, an innovative collection of diverse material that brought Atlanta hip-hop to a new commercial level. The song juxtaposed unusual rapped rhymes with Brown's classic soul hook, and it rose to the top chart levels in early 2004.

"Big Boi was actually going to give me that song for my album," Brown told *USA Today*. "But once (then-Arista president) Antonio 'L.A.' Reid heard the song, everything changed." Brown did not have a label deal at the time, but the hit raised his profile and he was soon signed to the DreamWorks label, which in turn was absorbed by his former distribution partner Interscope. Brown had another hit with "I Can't Wait," included on the soundtrack of the film *Barbershop 2* and featuring OutKast in a guest role for a change. The romantic song was complemented by a video that depicted Brown as a fashionably dressed robber.

Sported Sunglasses

Indeed, Brown toned down the baggy pants and flamboyant jewelry known as "bling bling" favored by other hip-hop stars; his tailored look (accessorized by carefully chosen sunglasses) as well as his music recalled the soul music figures of the 1970s. "Everybody is getting older and things are getting more sophisticated," Brown told *USA Today*. "It's no longer all about the jerseys. Brothers are keeping it hip-hop with suit jackets and nice shirts." Brown built his popularity further with a featured guest appearance on "Blueberry Yum-Yum" by the chart-topping rapper Ludacris.

With a fresh image and several years spent building a familiar yet new sound, Brown seemed ready for stardom as his album *For the Grown and Sexy* received the finishing touches in early 2005. The album had originally been titled *Phunk-O-Naut*, but was restocked with more mainstream material after the success of "I Can't Wait" and given a new title, reflecting the same duality between experimental and mainstream instincts visible in OutKast's music. Regardless of the album's eventual fortunes, Brown had already had a big part in shaping one of contemporary hip-hop's most vital scenes, and he planned to continue his work as a producer. "I was just waiting for my time to come," he told *USA Today*. "Now the window has come, I'm climbing through it."

Selected discography

(With Society of Soul) *Brainchild,* 1996.
Vinyl Room, 1998.
For the Grown and Sexy, DreamWorks, 2005.

Sources

Periodicals

Atlanta Journal-Constitution, November 14, 1005,
    p. D1; January 5, 1996, p. P5; December 28, 2001,
    p. P3; August 1, 2004, p. MS6.
Billboard, August 23, 2003, p. 37.
USA Today, March 8, 2004.

On-line

"The Africana QA: Sleepy Brown," www.africana.
    com/articles/qa/mu20040525sleepy.asp (January
    17, 2005).
"Organized Noize," All Music Guide, www.allmusic.
    com (January 17, 2005).

—James M. Manheim

Reuben Cannon

1946—

Casting agent

Cannon, Reuben, photograph. Ana Elisa Fuentes/Getty Images.

Despite growing up in an inner-city Chicago housing project, Reuben Cannon knew his future lay in the entertainment industry. With luck, pluck, and a lot of hard work, Cannon broke into the competitive field and became the first African-American casting director in Hollywood—and one of the most successful casting agents ever. He helped launch the careers of Oprah Winfrey, Bruce Willis, Danny Glover, Michael J. Fox, and many more. He has worked with legends like Maya Angelou, Spike Lee, and Steven Spielberg. More recently he has founded a new movement in black film—that of financing black films with black investors. "African Americans don't get the respect that they deserve in Hollywood," Cannon told *Contemporary Black Biography (CBB)*. "What people respect is product. So we have to make our own product to get the respect we deserve."

Began Working at Age Eight

Reuben Cannon was born on February 11, 1946, in Chicago, Illinois. Until he was eight, he lived in a two-story duplex with his three siblings and his parents.

Then his father died. "I remember my mother saying to me, 'Junior, you have to be the man of the house now,'" Cannon told *CBB*. "To me, the man of the house meant work, so I went to work." He did what he could—shined shoes, delivered groceries. "I remember being really proud to be a provider even thought it cost me part of my childhood," he told *CBB*. When the family moved into a housing project, Cannon began delivering papers. On his route were several successful businesses run by black men, including Johnson Publishing, run by publishing magnate John Johnson. "Even though I was living in the projects, I saw successful black men professionally conducting themselves," Cannon told *CBB*. "They became my role models."

Cannon also found inspiration onstage. "My father could play guitar and sing, so as I was imitating him, I started singing and then I started entering talent shows and winning," he told *CBB*. "Being on stage and having the audience appreciation, it really inspired me and set my career path. I remember thinking, wouldn't it be great if I could find a way to make a living doing this. It was always a fantasy of mine—to find a way to provide entertainment." After graduating high school

At a Glance . . .

Born on February 11, 1946 in Chicago, IL; married Linda Elsenhout; children: Tonya, Reuben Jr., Christopher, Sydney. *Religion:* Christian.

Career: Universal Studios, Universal City, CA, mail room clerk, 1971-72, casting director trainee, 1972-74, casting director, 1974-78; Warner Brothers, Hollywood, CA, head of television casting, 1978-79; Reuben Cannon & Associates, Los Angeles, CA, president, 1979–.

Memberships: Los Angeles Urban League, board of directors; Casting Society of America; Motion Picture Academy of America.

Awards: Humanitas, Film Award, for *Dancing in September*, 2001; The Chrysler Group, Behind the Lens Award, 2002; Morehouse College, honorary doctorate, 2002; Casting Society of America, Artios Award, for *The Bernie Mac Show*, 2002; West Angeles Church, Man of the Year, 2005.

Addresses: *Office*—Reuben Cannon & Associates, 5225 Wilshire Blvd., Suite 526, Los Angeles, CA 90036.

Cannon held a series of blue collar jobs. Finding a job was never a problem for Cannon. He explained on the *History Makers* Web site, "…if you want a job, go to the place you want to work the day after payday. Because someone's gonna go out and party the night after they get paid and they're not gonna show up the next day."

After stints at a printing press, as a bus boy, and in a steel factory, Cannon landed the job that helped launch his career in entertainment. He became a meter reader. "I had to go into dingy basements with rats," Cannon told *CBB*. "I had a friend who had moved out to California and he told me that if I wanted to work in entertainment I had to go out there and get a job with a studio. But I had never left Chicago. I was afraid to leave my family, all I knew. But after the horror of those basements, I knew I had to go." Cannon saved $500 and bought a one-way ticket to Los Angeles.

Went from Mail Clerk to Casting Director

In November of 1971 Cannon had an interview with

Universal Studios. Though he was told there were no jobs, he applied his job-landing theory and proceeded to stake out the studio's employment office everyday until December 31st. "And finally the theory worked," Cannon told *CBB*. "Some guys didn't want to work New Year's Eve so I got a temporary job bagging mail. That turned into full-time work." It was Cannon's dream come true. "On my mail route there was Alfred Hitchcock, there was Paul Newman. And then I would go to the sound stage and there was Quincy Jones scoring *Ironside*. I mean there was Edith Head in the back in the wardrobe department," Cannon told *History Makers*. "I mean I was in heaven."

"The mailroom was, and still is, considered training ground for executives," Cannon told *CBB*. "You were required to wear a suit and tie." As he distributed mail throughout Universal, Cannon got to know every department and most of the key players. Soon he landed a job interview with Ralph Winters, the head of casting. Cannon recalled that meeting to *History Makers*. "[Winters] said, 'I've seen you deliver mail here 'cause you're in this department. And, you know, everyone in this department likes you.'" Winters, who studied astrology, then analyzed Cannon's sign and determined that Cannon's calling was religion. Cannon told *History Makers* that his reply to Winters was, "You know, I believe my ministry will be here in entertainment." The response impressed Winters and he decided to hire Cannon over two more qualified applicants.

Less than a year after arriving in Los Angeles, Cannon became the first black casting director trainee in the entertainment industry. Initially he worked as the assistant to Winters' secretary. "But I was also available to assist everyone in the casting department," Cannon told *CBB*. "It was a learning ground for me." He supplemented this training with a strict diet. "Twenty hours of television a week, two films a week, and two plays a week for seven years," he told *History Makers*. He did this so "that when I sat in a room with a producer and director that no one in that room knew more about actors than I did," he confided to *History Makers*. His hard work paid off and by 1974 Cannon had become a casting director at Universal.

Founded Successful Casting Agency

At Universal, "*Ironside* was the first show I cast on my own," he told *CBB*. Cannon also worked on *The Rockford Files* and *Beretta*. In 1978 he left Universal to become head of television casting at Warner Brothers. His first big job there was to cast *Roots II: The Next Generation*, the sequel to the groundbreaking 1977 miniseries. "It was my first mini-series and there was a lot of pressure for it to live up to the original." The program was a hit and it won several awards, including an Emmy Award for Best Supporting Actor for Marlon Brando, who was cast by Cannon. However, this was not the highlight of Cannon's time with

Warner Brothers. "My proudest moment there was being able to help integrate the industry," Cannon told *CBB*. "I was the first black casting director in all of Hollywood and until I got to Warner, I was the only one. I knew if things were going to change, it would have to start with me." As head of casting Cannon was able to hire his own assistants. He chose talented African Americans such as Eileen Knight, who later went on to become a powerful casting director in her own right.

In 1979 Cannon opened Reuben Cannon and Associates. "I said, 'If I am as good as people say, I should go independent,'" he told *CBB* of his decision to found his namesake casting agency. He was that good and soon he landed a major client, Stephen J. Cannell Productions. Cannon cast several shows for Cannell, including *The A-Team*, *Riptide*, *Hardcastle & McCormick*, and *Hunter*. Cannon also worked on shows for other clients. Cannon is credited with giving Bruce Willis his first big break when he cast the actor in the hit show *Moonlighting*.

Cannon continued casting hits into the 1990s with *Star Trek: The Next Generation*, *Matlock*, and *Touched by an Angel*. In 2002 he won an Artios Award for best casting for *The Bernie Mac Show*. Artios is the awards wing of the Casting Society of America. Cannon followed up that success with casting credits on *Half and Half* and *The Parkers*. Cannon also cast dozens of films. In 1985 he teamed with director Steven Speilberg on the acclaimed film *The Color Purple*. His casting of Oprah Winfrey in the film helped solidify her early career. He also cast *Who Framed Roger Rabbit?*, *The Josephine Baker Story*, *Desperado*, and *What's Love Got to Do with It?*

Found Success in Film Production

In 1986 Cannon turned his talents to producing when he was hired to co-produce the television series, *Amen*. In 1989 he produced the mini-series *The Women of Brewster Place*. It spawned a television show of the same name, which Cannon also produced. The series, shot in Chicago, gave Cannon the opportunity to work back in his hometown for the first time. "It was an honor for me," he told *CBB*.

In 1995 the Million Man March brought hundreds of thousands of African-American men to Washington, D.C. The march was a moving display of black solidarity and a public commitment on behalf of the men to family and community. A director friend suggested Cannon make a film about a group of black men traveling by bus from Los Angeles to the march. "I liked the idea because it would show diversity among black men," Cannon told *CBB*. "So I decided to call Spike Lee and he said he would direct if I raised the money independently. We decided that the money should come from black men." Cannon contacted 15 promi-

nent black businessmen and raised $2.4 million to make 1996's *Get on the Bus*. Even before filming was complete, Columbia bought the picture for $3.5 million, ensuring all the investors a solid return.

Cannon used this model of financing to produce *Dancing in September*, *Women Thou Art Loosed*, based on the inspirational best-selling book of the same name by Reverend T. D. Jakes, and *Diary of a Mad Black Woman*, scheduled for released in February of 2005. He also produced two more films, using traditional financing through studios: *Down in the Delta*, directed by legendary author Maya Angelou, and *Love Don't Cost a Thing*.

Began Black Independent Film Movement

The financing of *Get on the Bus* launched a new era for Cannon. "It was always my intention to use the movie to inspire young brothers and sisters to take responsibility for making their own films," Cannon told *Black Enterprise*. Traditional Hollywood funding has been based on profit potential, a model that often left black films unmade. "There are a lot of stories out there about African-Americans that aren't being told because the studios have so many preconceptions about what will sell and what won't," Cannon told *The Star-Ledger*. "[Get on the Bus] couldn't have been made through the normal channels. You can't go in and pitch your story as, 'A movie about a bunch of black men who get on a bus and just talk for two hours.' They'd send you right out the door."

To be successful Cannon had to offer investors more than just a good reason to finance the film. He also had to offer a solid business plan. "There is always risk, you know, in investing in a film, but we minimize the risk by keeping the budget low and adding these elements, elements meaning that it will usually be a name that will assure some type of sale," Cannon told Tavis Smiley in a sound clip on the *National Public Radio* Web site. For that reason, Cannon looked for good stories, solid actors, and skilled writers and directors. The formula worked for *Women Thou Art Loosed*. "[It] was made for $1.3 million and so far it has grossed $7 million," Cannon told *CBB*.

Cannon believed that the idea of blacks financing black films marked a new movement. "I think of myself as the Marcus Garvey of Hollywood," Cannon told *CBB*, referring to the early twentieth century orator who called for blacks worldwide to embrace their African history and culture with pride. Cannon has already won converts. Director John Singleton, a friend and former intern of Cannon, decided to finance *Hustle and Flow* with $3.5 million of his own money. Paramount later picked up the film for $9.5 million. Cannon predicted such success back in 2004 when he told Smiley, "Hollywood is not going to change, but we can change how we do business in Hollywood."

Sources

Periodicals

Black Enterprise, December 1, 1996.
The Star-Ledger (Newark, NJ), October 16, 1996.

On-line

"Reuben Cannon," *The History Makers,* www.thehis torymakers.com/biography/biography.asp?bioindex =98&category=entertainmentMakers (February 9, 2005).
"Reuben Cannon: Making *Woman Thou Art Loosed."* *NPR* (October 4, 2004), http://www.npr.org/tem plates/story/story.php?storyId=4059523 (February 9, 2005).

Other

Additional information for this profile was obtained through an interview with Reuben Cannon on January 14, 2005.

—Candace LaBalle

Keshia Chanté

1988—

Musician

Canada's Keshia Chanté is a teen pop star—but her background does not fit the typical pattern of other young performers who have emerged in recent years in either Canada or the United States. "She was not a contestant on either *American Idol* or *Canadian Idol*," noted the *Edmonton Sun*. "She is not a former star of a popular children's television show, she was not a model, did not hook up with a former member of a boy band, did not participate in a reality show of any kind, was not written up in National Enquirer and was not a member of the Mickey Mouse Club."

All of the *Edmonton Sun*'s examples referred to other teen successes, but Chanté earned her spot on Canadian music charts the old-fashioned way—she stayed cool under pressure and impressed influential people in the music industry with her voice and look. Born Keshia Chanté Harper on June 16, 1988, she was raised in the Canadian national capital of Ottawa. Her father was of Trinidadian background, and although Chanté stayed on good terms with him, she was raised mostly by her mother, Teresa Agnelo. The first hint of Keshia's talent came at a very early age, when she began singing along to a tape her mother was playing on a car stereo.

Sang at Black History Month Event

"I didn't take it seriously," Agnelo told the *Ottawa Citizen*. "I play a lot of music in my car, and one day, this girlfriend with us nudged me and said, 'Does she do this all the time?' I was, like, 'Yeah, she does it all the time.'" Soon after that, when Chanté was six, her mother signed her up to perform rapper Tupac Shakur's "Dear Mama" at a Black History Month event at Ottawa's Carleton University. Her mother made a printout of the lyrics. "I already knew the words but she wanted to make sure I knew how to pronounce them correctly—she had to leave out the bad words," Chanté recalled to the *Ottawa Citizen*.

Chanté went on stage without being afraid, and the experience instilled in her a desire for a musical career. "I've always been 'when I get older I'm going to sing. I'm going to dance and sing,'" Chanté explained to the *Ottawa Sun*. "I wasn't really focused on being famous. I was like 'I'm going to have a song on the radio.'" Her mother taught her to be comfortable in front of a camera by videotaping her daily. Though Chanté never took voice lessons, she did start writing songs. And she kept performing in talent shows and schools around Ottawa and its eastern suburb of Orleans, where she attended St. Peter's Catholic high school.

One person who noticed her talents was Ottawa DJ Trevor Mason, who sent a tape of Chanté's singing to BMG Canada executive Ivan Berry. When Chanté was 14, Berry called her at home and asked her to sing something into the receiver of the phone. Not really aware of who he was, she launched confidently into the R. Kelly hit "I Believe I Can Fly." "It's important for people who have that dream and they get that shot to not hesitate, to not ask 'Oh what song should I sing? What should I do?' None of that," Chanté told the *Edmonton Sun*.

At a Glance . . .

Born Keshia Chanté Harper on June 16, 1988; raised in Ottawa, Ontario, Canada area.

Career: Singer, 2002–.

Awards: Canadian Urban Music Awards for best new artist, video of the year, and fan's choice, 2004.

Addresses: *Label*—Sony BMG Music (Canada) Inc., 190 Liberty St., Suite 100, Toronto, ON M6K 3L5, Canada. *Web*—www.keshiachante.com.

Impressed Executive by Phone

Her phone performance earned her an in-person audition with label executives in Toronto, and for that one performance Chanté felt nervous. She apparently did well, though, for she soon had a contract with the label. One factor that worked in her favor was her resemblance to former teen star Aaliyah, who had recently died in Caribbean plane accident. Attending St. Peter's on weekdays, Chanté traveled to Toronto on weekends to begin recording for BMG Canada's Vik-music imprint. In 2004 she and her mother moved to the Toronto suburb of Brampton so that she could be closer to Toronto's recording studios, but both mother and daughter were adamant that she stay in high school rather than dropping out or hiring a private tutor.

Chanté's first single revived the old pop genre of the answer song; her "Shook (The Answer)" was a response to "Shook," a recording by Toronto R&B star Shawn Desman. It was Desman who wrote much of the material on Chanté's debut album. "Shook (The Answer)" and another hit single, "Unpredictable," were included on Chanté's debut CD, *Keshia Chanté,* which was released in June of 2004. That month Chanté turned 16. The album, once released, spawned two more Canadian hits, the street-themed "Bad Boy" and a composition co-written by Chanté herself, "Let the Music Take You."

Won Urban Music Awards

With this string of hits, Chanté steamrollered the competition at Canada's Urban Music Awards in October of 2004. She won awards in all three categories in which she had been nominated, including best new artist, video of the year (for "Bad Boy"), and the fan's choice award. That fall, Chanté gained exposure to a spectrum of fans beyond Canadian teens with an appearance singing "O Canada" at the Grey Cup, the championship game of Canadian professional football. She had already sung the anthem on baseball's Opening Day at the stadium of the Toronto Blue Jays. In November of 2004 she shared a stage with vocalist-keyboardist Alicia Keys and U2 leader Bono at Toronto's UrbanAIDS benefit, and the following January she appeared on an all-star CBC network musical extravaganza designed to raise money for South Asian tsunami relief.

The only obstacles in Chanté's way seemed to be the relatively small size of the urban music market in Canada, and the fact that Chanté, unlike Canadian teenager Avril Lavigne, hadn't yet shows signs of breaking out in the United States. Yet Chanté seemed to have the charisma to make a wider breakthrough happen; she is a friendly, articulate, mile-a-minute talker, who is well-liked by media writers. More than 1,000 people turned out to see her at a Toronto mall in September of 2004. In November she made her first U.S. television appearance, on Black Entertainment Television's "Rated Next" program. She seemed to be coping well with the whirlwind pace of fame, finishing her school homework in the early hours of the morning after answering fan mail. "It feels really natural now," Chanté was quoted as saying in the *Portage Daily Graphic* after winning her three Urban Music Awards. "I feel like this is where I'm supposed to be."

Selected discography

Albums

Keshia Chanté, BMG Canada, 2004.

Sources

Periodicals

Canada NewsWire, January 11, 2005.
Edmonton Journal, September 2, 2004, p. C5.
Edmonton Sun, December 16, 2004, p. 49.
Maclean's, December 22, 2003, p. 59; June 21, 2004, p. 67.
Ottawa Citizen, October 20, 2004, p. E6. *Ottawa Sun,* June 19, 2004, p. 29; November 19, 2004, p. 69.
Philadelphia Inquirer, November 1, 2004.
Portage (Manitoba) Daily Graphic, October 22, 2004. p. Entertainment-6.
Toronto Sun, June 27, 2004, p. S18.

On-line

Keshia Chanté, www.keshiachante.com (January 17, 2005).
"Keshia Chanté," www.maplemusic.com/artists/kch/bio.asp (January 17, 2005).

—James M. Manheim

Dave Chappelle

1973—

Actor, writer, comic

From a very early age, Dave Chappelle could make people laugh. Chappelle realized the power of his natural talent and made some very serious goals for his art. As a teenager, he crafted his standup comedy act out of the realties of his life growing up black in the capital city of the United States. Racism and racial division became his main targets, and he approached them with an outrageous irreverence that often shocked his audiences into shouts of laughter. Though Chappelle has worked toward recognition and success, he has continually refused to tone down his style or dilute his outspoken African-American point of view in order to make his comedy "more acceptable." As a result, he has gained fame and success on his own terms, and has become especially popular with young audiences who appreciate Chappelle's sly social commentary and aggressively satiric style.

Born David Chappelle on August 24, 1973, in Washington, D.C., he grew up in the city and the nearby suburb of Silver Springs, Maryland. Summers were often spent in Yellow Springs, Ohio with his father who was a professor at Antioch University. He enjoyed the peaceful rural atmosphere of Yellow Springs, and as an adult, his home on an Ohio farm would become a family refuge from the more hectic entertainment worlds of New York and Los Angeles.

Chappelle was only 14 when he first performed his standup comedy act in public venues in Washington. His mother, a Unitarian minister, was very supportive of her son's talent and frequently accompanied him as a chaperone when he performed in nightclubs and bars. After a few years on stage, Chappelle began to

win comedy contests, and by the time he was a senior in high school, he was traveling to comedy jobs on the road, excused from school by the principal so that he could pursue his career.

After his graduation from high school, Chappelle made a bargain with his parents. Instead of going to college right away, he would go to New York to work on his comedy act. If he did not succeed after one year, he would consider college. While working with other comics in the Washington area, Chappelle had learned a lot about the comedy clubs of New York, and he had grown to feel that he had to go there to become a real success in comedy.

Chappelle took two different approaches to developing his art as a performer and breaking into the national comedy scene. Other comics had advised him that the Boston Comedy Club in Greenwich Village was a good place for younger comedians, so he began performing there to build his reputation in the city. His plan worked well, and within weeks he was not only performing regularly at the Boston, but at comedy clubs all over New York.

However, Chappelle was not content just working the club circuit. He wanted to keep an edge of street-wise spontaneity in his work. To do this, he went, quite literally, out on the street and performed comedy in the parks and sidewalks of the city, alongside other street performers. There he met Charles Barnett, a street comedian who became his good friend and mentor. Working on the streets taught Chappelle confidence and honed his fast-paced aggressive style. He was impressed by the courage and skill of street comics like Barnett, who had the nerve and skill to capture the attention of passers by, but whose work was seen by so few. When Charles Barnett died of AIDS, Chappelle planned someday to make a film about his mentor, with himself portraying Barnett.

Just before the end of his first year in New York, Chappelle performed at the Montreal Comedy Festival. His success at that large event left no doubt that he was destined for a career in comedy. His dedication and nerve were tested during the early 1990s when he was booed off the stage during his standup comedy debut at the famous Apollo Theater in Harlem. However, in 1992 he won critical and popular acclaim for his television appearance in *Russell Simmons' Def Comedy Jam* on HBO. His popularity began to rise, and he became a regular guest on late-night television shows such as *Politically Incorrect*, *The Late Show With David Letterman*, *The Howard Stern Show,* and *Late Night With Conan O'Brien*.

In 1993 Chappelle landed his first film role: the Mel Brooks comedy *Robin Hood: Men in Tights*. He had small roles in several other films, but it was his role as the nasty comic Reggie Warrington in Eddie Murphy's 1996 film *The Nutty Professor* that brought him to the attention of Hollywood.

Suddenly Dave Chappelle was in demand for character roles, and he did several films in the next few years. In 1998, he co-wrote his first film, *Half Baked*, a tribute to Cheech and Chong, a comedy duo who had made a series of recreational-drug-related slapstick comedies during the late 1970s and 1980s. Though *Half Baked* enjoyed some success, Chappelle was disappointed with his first experience in filmmaking. He felt that the studio had weakened the film by trying to make it more acceptable to conservative audiences. He did not like losing control over his work, and this experience would influence his later choices.

Chappelle had dabbled in developing television pilots beginning in the early 1990s. After creating more than ten, one pilot, called *Buddies*, was picked up by ABC in the early 1990s. But as Chappelle recalled to *60*

Minutes, as quoted on the CBS Web site: "It was a bad show. It was bad. I mean when we were doing it, I could tell this was not gonna work." Indeed, it aired for only 13 episodes before cancellation. As his comic popularity continued to rise, Chappelle attracted network attention. The FOX television network offered to build a situation comedy around Dave Chappelle's comedy in the late 1990s. Chappelle was interested, but when network executives began to suggest adding white characters to the cast in order to broaden the show's appeal, the comic withdrew from the deal. As much as possible, he would always refuse to compromise his principles or his comedy.

Chappelle continued to write and perform in films as well as on stage. In 2000 he did a very successful one-man show for HBO called *Dave Chappelle: Killin' Them Softly*. In 2003 he was offered a chance to do television on his own terms. Comedy Central, a comedy network, offered Chappelle his own show. *Chappelle's Show*, a half-hour program, repeated several times each week, featured Chappelle and a cast of regulars and guests performing satirical skits. Cable television proved to be a more comfortable location for Chappelle's outrageous comedy, and the show soon developed a devoted following. Though no topic was safe from Chappelle's sharp satire, racism remained a major focus of his biting humor. His first show, for example, featured Chappelle playing a blind leader of a white supremacist movement who does not realize that he is black. Each half hour was packed with skits like "Race Draft," in which members of different races get to claim celebrities as their own, and "Ask a Black Dude," in which whites ask show regular Paul Mooney questions about being black.

Though *Chappelle's Show* is designed for hilarity, a very serious political message underlies the show's attacks on racism and bigotry. Even the musical guests reflect the show's hard-hitting social critique, by focusing on hip-hop artists, whose music contains pointed political messages and appreciation of black culture. Critics recognize the similarities between Chappelle's comedy and that of comedian Richard Pryor during the 1970s. Pryor's wife spoke for her ailing husband on *60 Minutes,* saying that Pryor approves of Chappelle's work and has "passed the torch" to him. Chappelle's respect for Pryor showed in his response: "That's a lot of pressure. He was the best, man. For him to say that is, you know, that's something, I don't even know if I'll attempt to live up to that."

Despite his modesty, in the early 2000s Chappelle seemed well on his way to such super stardom. The DVD of the 2003 season of *Chappelle's Show* quickly became the best selling DVD of all time, surpassing the popular *Simpsons* cartoon show. In 2004 Comedy Central signed Dave Chappelle to a two-year contract to continue his show.

Selected works

Films

Undercover Blues, 1993.
Robin Hood: Men in Tights, 1993.
Getting In, 1994.*Comedy: Coast to Coast,* 1994.
The Nutty Professor, 1996.
Joe's Apartment, 1996.
Bowl of Pork, 1997.
The Real Blonde, 1997.
Damn Whitey, 1997.
Con Air, 1997.
You've Got Mail, 1998.
Woo, 1998.
Half Baked, 1998.
Blue Streak, 1999.
200 Cigarettes, 1999.
Screwed, 2000.
Undercover Brother, 2002.

Television

Def Comedy Jam, 1992.
Dave Chappelle: Killin' Them Softly, 2000.
Chappelle's Show, 2003–.
Dave Chappelle: For What It's Worth, 2004.

Screenwriting

The Dana Carvey Show, 1996.
The Dave Chappelle Project, 1997.
Damn Whitey, 1997.
(With Neil Brennan) *Half Baked,* 1998.
Dave Chappelle: Killin' Them Softly, 2000.
Chappelle's Show, 2003–.
Dave Chappelle: For What It's Worth, 2004.

Sources

Periodicals

Jet, August 23, 2004, p. 37.

On-line

Dave Chappelle, www.davechapelle.com (January 21, 2005).
"Chappelle: 'An Act of Freedom,'" *60 Minutes,* www.cbsnews.com/stories/2004/10/19/60II/main650 149.shtml (February 8, 2005).
"Chappelle's Show." *Comedy Central,* www.comedy-central.com/tv_shows?chappellesshow (January 21, 2005).
"Interview with Dave Chappelle." *mulDoomstone Interviews,* www.deathvalleydriver.com/muldoomst one/Chappelle.html (January 28, 2005).

—Tina Gianoulis

Shirley Chisholm

1924-2005

Politician, writer, educator

In becoming the first black, as well as the first woman, to ever seek a major political party's nomination for the U.S. presidency, former New York congresswoman Shirley Chisholm demonstrated that aspirations for the nation's executive office need not be the exclusive domain of white males. Chisholm's unsuccessful 1972 campaign for the Democratic presidential nomination—largely viewed as more symbolic than practical—was intended to both break ground and prove a point. "I ran because someone had to do it first," she stated in *The Good Fight*, her candid recounting of the campaign. "In this country everybody is supposed to be able to run for President, but that's never been really true. I ran because most people think the country is not ready for a black candidate, not ready for a woman candidate." By staying in the race all the way to the Democratic National Convention, Chisholm hoped to set an example for other nontraditional presidential candidates. "The next time a woman runs, or a black, a Jew or anyone from a group that the country is 'not ready' to elect to its highest office, I believe he or she will be taken seriously from the start. The door is not open yet, but it is ajar."

Chisholm's reputation as a trailblazer for minorities in politics, however, is more lastingly illustrated by her tenure in Congress. The first black woman ever elected to the U.S. House of Representatives, Chisholm served from 1969 to 1982 as congresswoman from New York's 12th District, which comprised a largely black constituency in her home city of Brooklyn. Chisholm soon became famous for her candid and strongly held viewpoints as well as her refusal to be undaunted by the status quo of the congressional power structure. "Since I went to the House of Representatives in 1969, I have grown to detest many of the white Northern liberals who are always ready with rhetoric about equal opportunity in jobs and education,
when the time comes to put the heat on, in committee and on the floor, and *do* something, like passing an amendment or increasing an appropriation, too many of these white knights turn up missing," she wrote in *The Good Fight*. Criticizing what she called a media-driven image or "mold" that often predetermines candidates for public office, Chisholm suggested, "Could it be that the persistence of poverty, hunger, racism, war, semiliteracy and unemployment is partly due to the fact that we have excluded so many persons from the processes that make and carry out social policies?"

Chisholm was born Shirley Anita St. Hill in 1924 in Brooklyn. Her early schooling took place on the Caribbean island of Barbados, where she and her two sisters were sent to live with their grandmother because of family financial difficulties. "Years later I would know what an important gift my parents had given me by seeing to it that I had my early education in the strict, traditional, British-style schools of Barbados," Chisholm stated in her 1970 autobiography *Unbought and Unbossed*. "If I speak and write easily now, that early education is the main reason." In 1934, the daughters were rejoined with their parents, who were still struggling financially in the midst of the Great Depression but nevertheless provided a rich family life. Chisholm's father was an avid reader who introduced the youngster to the teachings of early black nationalist leader Marcus

At a Glance . . .

Born Shirley Anita St. Hill on November 30, 1924, in Brooklyn, NY; died on January 3, 2005, in Ormond Beach, FL; daughter of Charles and Ruby St. Hill; married Conrad Chisholm (divorced, 1977); married Arthur Hardwick, Jr., 1977 (died, 1986); children: none. *Education*: Brooklyn College, BA, cum laude; Columbia University, MA. *Politics*: Democrat.

Career: Mount Calvary Child Care Center, New York City, teacher for seven years during the 1940s; member of New York State Assembly, 1964-68; U.S. House of Representatives, Washington, DC, Democratic congresswoman from 12th New York District, 1969-82; ran for Democratic party nomination for U.S. presidency, 1972; Mt. Holyoke College, South Hadley, MA, Purington Professor, 1983-2004(?); writer; lecturer. Visiting scholar, Spelman College, 1985. Cofounder, National Political Congress of Black Women; member of advisory council, National Organization for Women; honorary committee member, United Negro College Fund.

Memberships: League of Women Voters, National Association for the Advancement of Colored People (NAACP), National Board of Americans for Democratic Action, Delta Sigma Theta.

Awards: Woman of the Year award, Clairol, 1973, for outstanding achievement in public affairs; recipient of numerous honorary degrees.

Garvey, while her mother emphasized the importance of her daughters' receiving quality educations. An excellent student in high school, Chisholm received scholarship offers to Vassar and Oberlin colleges, but enrolled in the more financially accessible Brooklyn College.

At Brooklyn College, Chisholm decided to pursue a career in teaching. Her political awareness as a black—which had been fostered by her father—was heightened when she became a member of the Harriet Tubman Society. "There," as she wrote in *Unbought and Unbossed*, "I first heard people other than my father talk about white oppression, black racial consciousness, and black pride." Although she was assured by both professors and fellow students that she possessed ideal qualities for a political career, Chisholm continued her studies in education. She graduated with

honors in the early 1940s, and subsequently worked for seven years as a teacher at a child care center in New York City. At the same time, she pursued her master's degree in early childhood education at Columbia University, where she also met her future husband, Conrad Chisholm.

During the 1950s, Chisholm became involved for the first time with political campaigning when she worked to elect a black underdog lawyer, Lewis S. Flagg, Jr., to a district court judgeship in New York. In 1960, she helped form the Unity Democratic Club, an organization that sought to promote and elect candidates for New York State's 17th Assembly District. Deciding to run herself for the 17th District representative seat, she won a landslide victory in the fall of 1964 after a long and grueling campaign. Chisholm served on the New York legislature for the next four years and gained a reputation as a competent and effective lawmaker. She helped introduce bills to assist disadvantaged students in obtaining quality education and to secure unemployment insurance for domestic employees.

Chisholm's political aspirations broadened in the late 1960s with the creation of New York's 12th Congressional District. She decided to pursue the new congressional seat in spite of sparse campaign funds and entered a heated primary race against a much-favored Democratic party candidate, William Thompson. Her hard work, combined with a low voter turnout, resulted in a slim primary victory and helped carry her in the fall election against Republican opponent James Farmer. Chisholm proved to be a determined and outspoken representative who was especially vocal in her support of programs and policies that benefited disadvantaged groups. During her tenure, she served on the Veterans' Affairs Committee, the Education and Labor Committee, and the influential House Rules Committee.

Three years into her congressional career, Chisholm further distinguished herself by becoming the first black woman to seek a major political party nomination for the presidency. Although many political observers considered her chances for victory remote, Chisholm nonetheless pressed ahead, and at the final Democratic convention tally, she received a total of 151 votes. In *The Good Fight* she assessed the possible long-range effects of her campaign: "The United States was said not to be ready to elect a Catholic to the Presidency when Al Smith ran in the 1920s. But Smith's nomination may have helped pave the way for the successful campaign John F. Kennedy waged in 1960. Who can tell? What I hope most is that now there will be others who will feel themselves as capable of running for high political office as any wealthy, good-looking white male."

Chisholm retired from public office in 1982, wanting to spend more time with her ailing second husband Arthur Hardwick, who had been critically injured in an automobile accident. At the time of her retirement from Congress, Chisholm expressed her frustration with both the male-dominated power structure on Capitol Hill as well as the social policies of President Ronald Reagan's administration. In her typically direct manner, she stated in a 1982 *Glamour* article that one of the major problems in the United States was a "scarcity of people in power who are sensitive to the needs, hopes, and aspirations of the various segments of our multi-faceted society. We have become too plastic; we have become too theoretical.... We need individuals who are compassionate, concerned, committed." Commenting on the necessity of more women pursuing political careers, Chisholm added, "Men don't seem to have time for complexity.... They really do not give enough attention to the areas of conservation and preservation of human resources."

Her retirement from Congress did not cast Chisholm into oblivion. She remained extremely active, serving as Purington Professor at Massachusetts' Mt. Holyoke College. There she taught politics and women's studies throughout the 1980s. She also remained involved in U.S. politics, co-founding in 1984, the National Political Congress of Black Women, which in 1988 sent a delegation of over 100 women to the Democratic National Convention. Chisholm also participated in the presidential campaigns of black candidate Jesse Jackson. "Jackson is the voice of the poor, the disenchanted, the disillusioned," she was quoted as saying in *Newsweek*, "and that is exactly what I was."

Chisholm moved to Florida in 1991 and eased into less strenuous retirement. After suffering many strokes, Chisholm died at age 80 on January 1, 2005, in her Florida home. She will be remembered well. Her career, especially her struggle for political power, was brought vividly to life in the documentary, *Chisholm '72: Unbought and Unbossed.* Producer Shola Lynch compiled newsreels and fresh interviews to highlight Chisholm's run for the presidency, even including interviews with Chisholm in her old age. In the documentary, Chisholm explained that despite her many historic "firsts" she would like to be remembered differently: "When I die, I want to be remembered as a woman who lived in the 20th century and who dared to be a catalyst of change," Chisholm noted in the film, according to the *Seattle Post-Intelligencer.* "I want to be remembered as a woman who fought for change in the 20th century." National Public television aired the documentary in February to commemorate Chisholm's

life. Hopefully, the world will remember her as she saw herself; according to *Newsweek* her preferred epitaph would be "Shirley Chisholm had guts."

Selected writings

Unbought and Unbossed, Houghton, 1970.
The Good Fight, Houghton, 1973.

Sources

Books

Scheader, Catherine, *Shirley Chisholm: Teacher and Congresswoman*, Enslow, 1990.

Periodicals

Essence, August 1982.
Glamour, November 1982.
Houston Chronicle, January 9, 2005.
Jet, January 24, 2005.
Newsweek, November 14, 1983; May 21, 1984; January 17, 2005.
Seattle Post-Intelligencer, February 3, 2005.
Time, June 21, 1982.
Variety, February 9, 2004.

On-line

"About Shirley Chisholm," *PBS,* www.pbs.org/pov/pov2005/chisholm/about_chisholm.html (March 9, 2005).
"*Chisholm '72: Unbought and Unbossed,*" *Black Sky Media,* www.chisholm72.net (March 9, 2005).
"Shirley Chisholm," *AfricanAmericans.com,* www.africanamericans.com/shirleyChisholm.htm (March 9, 2005).
"Shirley Chisholm's 1972 Presidential Campaign," *Jo Freeman,* www.jofreeman.com/polhistory/chisholm.htm (March 9, 2005).

Other

Chisholm '72: Unbought and Unbossed (film), REALside Productions, 2004.

—Michael E. Mueller and Sara Pendergast

Sam Cornish

1935—

Poet, educator

An underappreciated figure of the Black Arts movement of the 1960s and 1970s, poet Sam Cornish wrote about the urban African-American experience in a voice just as tough and realistic as that of any other black poet of the time. His poems, however, replace the enthusiastic self-expression and the experimental African-American idioms of much modern black poetry with a terse, precise style that at times found more admirers among white readers and publishers than among blacks. In a poem about the assassination of Dr. Martin Luther King ("Death of Dr. King," 1971), Cornish depicted rage not in mounting cascades of language but in a devastating quick brushstroke: "we are mourning // our hands filled with bricks // a brother is dead."

Samuel James Cornish was born on December 22, 1935, in Baltimore, Maryland. He spent much of his life in the city, returning there even after beginning to find work and publication opportunities in the Boston area. After his father's death, he and his brother Herman Jr. were raised by his mother and grandmother. "These women raised us on two things: chicken and God," Cornish wrote in his autobiographical prose poem "Winters" (included in *Generations,* 1971). After one semester at Baltimore's Douglass High School, he dropped out. He later attended Booker T. Washington High School in Baltimore and took courses at Goddard College in Vermont and Northeastern University in Boston. For the most part, however, he was self-educated.

Worked at Baltimore Library

From 1958 to 1960 Cornish served in the United Stated Army Medical Corps. He returned to Baltimore and began to get acquainted with other creatively inclined people and to write poetry seriously himself, issuing his first small collection of poems, *In This Corner,* around 1961. His best-known publication, *Generations,* began life as a single poem in the early 1960s, grew to a 16-page pamphlet that Cornish published himself in 1964 (using the publisher name Beanbag Press), and finally became a full-length book. In 1965 Cornish began working at Baltimore's public library, the Enoch Pratt Free Library, as a writing specialist. He worked with children in that job, co-editing a magazine of children's writing called *Chicory* and compiling an anthology called *Chicory: Young Voices from the Black Ghetto* that the library issued through its 1960s-era Community Action Program.

Cornish continued to have a strong interest in the creative lives of children and wrote several children's books, including *Your Hand in Mine* (1970), which *Black World* called "a gem," noting that "the book is about a little boy who might have been Sam himself." By that time, Cornish had issued several more small volumes of poetry, known as chapbooks, under his Beanbag Press imprint. Traveling frequently between Baltimore and Boston, Cornish worked in several bookstores and at an insurance office in the Boston area and did editorial work for what was then the U.S. Office of Education in Washington. After marrying

At a Glance . . .

Born on December 22, 1935 in Baltimore, MD; married Jean Faxon, 1967. *Education:* Attended Goddard College, Plainfield, VT, and Northeastern University, Boston. *Military Service:* U.S. Army Medical Corps, 1958-60.

Career: Enoch Pratt Free Library, Baltimore, writing specialist, 1965-66, 1968-69; *Chicory* (children's magazine), editor; bookseller, 1966-67; CARE, U.S. Office of Education, Washington, DC, editorial consultant, 1967-68; Highland Park Free School, Roxbury, MA, teacher, 1969-early 1970s; Fiction and Literature Bookstore, Brookline, MA, operator; Education Development Center, Newton, MA, staff adviser and consultant on children's writing, 1973-78; Edmondson High School, Baltimore, and Coppin State College, teacher, mid-1970s; Massachusetts Council on the Arts and Humanities, literature director; Emerson College, Boston, MA, instructor of Afro-American Studies, late 1970s-2004.

Awards: National Endowment for the Arts grant, 1967, 1969.

Addresses: *Home*—Brighton, MA. *Office*—c/o Department of English, Emerson College, 100 Beacon Street, Boston, MA 02116.

Jean Faxon (who had edited the first edition of *Generations*) in 1967, he returned to the Enoch Pratt Free Library for a year in 1968-69. In 1969 he took a post as a creative writing instructor at the Highland Park Free School in the Boston ghetto of Roxbury.

Although his poetry had attracted national attention as early as 1967, when he won a National Endowment for the Arts grant, Cornish's breakthrough occurred with the publication of the full-length *Generations* in 1971. The mostly short poems in that volume were organized into five sections ("Generations," "Slaves," "Family," "Malcolm," and "Others") that interwove Cornish's own family experiences with those of figures from African-American history. "Cornish shows that America has always been a land of crisis and social chaos," noted Jon Woodson in a *Dictionary of Literary Biography* essay. "His work is an individual's record of tragic events."

Work Published by Church-Owned Press

Generations was issued by Beacon Press, a Boston publishing house owned by the predominantly white Unitarian Universalist Church. The book was well reviewed by a variety of critics nationwide, but Cornish remained somewhat outside of the large group of black poets of the time who chose publishers from within the African-American community. He named black writer Amiri Baraka as an influence, but also the reserved white Bostonian Robert Lowell. Yet Cornish's poems often had a steely tone informed by the black militancy of the time, and his depictions of slavery in the first part of *Generations* were sharp and unforgettable. He wrote several poems from the perspective of famous figures of the pre-Civil War era, and in his poem "Frederick Douglass" he has the famed abolitionist leader recall his mother's childhood, during which "white fingers walked into her mouth // to count the teeth and raise the price."

Cornish continued to draw creative energy from his dual residency in Boston and Baltimore, returning to his hometown in 1973 to teach writing at Edmondson High School and Coppin State College. His next full-length book of poetry, *Sometimes*, was published that year; it depicted New England scenes while touching humorously on the racial divide in a poem called "Vermont Where White Students, Poets and Radicals Live and Expect to Meet Blacks Skiing Cross-Country." By the late 1970s he had returned to Boston and taken a staff job at the Education Development Center in the Boston suburb of Newton. He later became an instructor in the Afro-American Studies department at Boston's Emerson College, and taught there until his retirement in 2004.

Wrote Poems about Musicians

Issuing new poetry volumes in 1978 (*Sam's World*), 1993 (*Folks Like Me*), and 1996 (*Cross a Parted Sea*), Cornish continued to write prolifically, penning the memoir *1935* (published by Boston's Ploughshares Press in 1990) as well as several children's books including *Grandmother's Pictures* (1974). His later poetry continued to take up the themes of personal and group history that had appeared in *Generations*. "Brown Bomber," from *Cross a Parted Sea*, recalled "Joe Louis fighting // from radio to radio" during Louis's celebrated heavyweight boxing championship fights of the late 1930s. Cornish also wrote a series of poems about great musicians from the African-American tradition: ragtime composer Scott Joplin, classic blues vocalist Bessie Smith, and modern rhythm-and-blues great Ray Charles.

By the 1990s Cornish was beginning to become more widely recognized. An essay in *Contemporary Literature* in 1992 explored *Generations* and argued for its place in the list of great works of black poetry in the 1960s and 1970s. Cornish himself exerted influence as a critic, writing freelance reviews in the 1990s for a variety of Boston publications. Cornish summed up his own style for *Contemporary Poets* by saying that "I try to use a minimum of words to express the intended thought or feeling, with the effect being starkly frank at times." His poems had appeared in a spate of anthologies of black writing in the 1970s, and by the early twenty-first century he seemed a promising candidate for inclusion in the curricula of African-American literature classes of the future.

Selected writings

People Beneath the Window, Sacco Publishers, 1962 (reprinted 1987).
Generations, Beanbag Press, 1964; enlarged edition, Beacon Press, 1971.
(Editor, with Hugh Fox, and contributor) *The Living Underground: An Anthology of Contemporary American Poetry,* Ghost Dance Press, 1969.
Winters, Sans Souci Press, 1968.
Sometimes: Ten Poems, Pym-Randall Press, 1973.
Sam's World: Poems, Decatur House, 1978.

Songs of Jubilee: New and Selected Poems, 1969-1983, Unicorn Press, 1986.
1935: A Memoir, Ploughshares, 1990.
Folks Like Me, Zoland Books, 1993.
Cross a Parted Sea: Poems, Zoland Books, 1996.

Sources

Books

Contemporary Poets, 7th ed., St. James, 2001.
Dictionary of Literary Biography, Volume 41: Afro-American Poets Since 1955, Gale, 1985.

Periodicals

Black World, July 1970, p. 50.
Contemporary Literature, Winter 1992, p. 665.

On-line

"Sam Cornish," *Biography Resource Center,* www.galenet.com/servlet/BioRC (January 18, 2005).

—James M. Manheim

Ellis Cose

1951—

Journalist, writer

Ellis Cose was a Chicago newspaper columnist before he was old enough to vote, and from that brilliant beginning has gone on to build successful careers in three related fields. A respected journalist, Cose has worked as reporter and columnist for several major newspapers and went on to become editor of the *New York Daily News*'s editorial page and contributing editor to *Newsweek*; he is the author of a number of well-received, bestselling books; and he has also served with government and university think tanks as an expert in journalism and the politics of energy. Honored with several journalistic awards, including a lifetime achievement award from the New York Association of Black Journalists, Ellis Cose has secured a place among the leaders of his profession.

Cose was born in Chicago on February 20, 1951, the son of Raney and Jetta Cose. He grew up in one of Chicago's high-rise public housing projects—an environment notorious for perpetuating crime and stunting lives—and he might well have remained there if not for the political upheavals and rising black consciousness of the 1960s. By the time Cose reached high school the civil rights movement and Vietnam War had given a political edge to his youthful dissatisfactions, and after demonstrating an early interest in mathematics, he found his voice as a writer. As he told *Publishers Weekly* in a 1992 interview, "In the midst of everything blowing up, the big riots and [Martin Luther] King [Jr.] getting killed [in 1968], I got this notion that I had something worthwhile to say."

Like many other budding authors, however, Cose found his high school English classes more of a hin-

drance than a help to his development. After drifting through three years of indifferent work, in his senior year Cose met a teacher named Mrs. Klinger who encouraged him to write about whatever interested him. In short order, Cose turned out two hundred pages of essays on a variety of social and racial topics, so impressing Klinger that she forwarded his work to Gwendolyn Brooks, the famed black poet laureate of Illinois. Brooks congratulated Cose on his precocious talent and invited him to join her circle of writers, an honor for which the rebellious Cose had little use. "I'm seventeen in with these guys in their thirties and forties," he recalled in *Publishers Weekly*. "I didn't stay very long." More to his taste was a novel he completed soon thereafter and sold to a small publishing firm; the publisher promptly went bankrupt, however, and Cose went off to the University of Illinois at Chicago to study psychology.

While a student, Cose contributed regularly to the university newspaper, sharpening his skills as a political commentator. On a momentary inspiration he sent a collection of his work to Ralph Otwell, managing editor of the Chicago *Sun-Times*. Otwell liked what he saw and asked Cose to write a column for the paper's school edition. In 1970, when Cose was still only nineteen years old, Otwell and *Sun-Times* editor Jim Hoge invited him to contribute a column to the regular edition of the *Sun-Times*, making him the youngest columnist in the history of Chicago newspapers.

The exalted position brought with it a huge responsibility for Cose, who suddenly found himself a major spokesperson for Chicago's black population at a time

Born on February 20, 1951, in Chicago, IL; son of Raney and Jetta (Cameron) Cose; married Lee Llambelis (attorney); children: Elisa Maria. *Education*: University of Illinois at Chicago, BA, 1972; George Washington University, MA, Science, Technology and Public Policy, 1978.

Career: *Chicago Sun-Times*, columnist and reporter, 1970-77; Joint Center for Political Studies, Washington, DC, senior fellow and director of energy policy studies, 1977-79; *Detroit Free Press*, Detroit, MI, editorial writer and columnist, 1979-81; resident fellow at National Academy of Sciences and National Research Council, 1981-82; special writer for *USA Today*, 1982-83; president of Institute for Journalism Education, University of California at Berkeley, 1983-86; Gannett Center for Media Studies fellow, Columbia University, New York City, 1987; *New York Daily News*, editorial page editor, 1991-93; *Newsweek*, contributing editor, 1993–.

Selected awards: Illinois United Press International, first place award, 1973; Stick-o-Type Award from Chicago Newspaper Guild, 1975; Lincoln University National Unity Award for best political reporting, 1975 and 1977; New York Association of Black Journalists, Lifetime Achievement Award, 2002; National Association of Black Journalists, Best Magazine Feature Award, 2003; New York Association of Black Journalists, Awards for best commentary and magazine features, 2003; Maynard Institute for Journalism Education, Vision Award (first recipient of the newly inaugurated annual award), 2004.

Addresses: *Office*—Newsweek, 251 W. 57th St., New York, NY 10019; *Web*—www.elliscose.com.

during which time he completed both his bachelor's degree and a master's from George Washington University in science, technology, and public policy.

In 1977 Cose was named senior fellow and director of energy studies at the Joint Center for Political Studies in Washington, D.C. Energy and the politics of its distribution became matters of great concern for Americans after the oil crisis of 1973-1974, and Cose spent much of the later 1970s researching and writing about the politics of energy. The fruit of this labor took the form of several books, culminating in the 1983 publication of *Decentralizing Energy Decisions: The Rebirth of Community Power*.

In *Decentralizing Energy Decisions*, Cose addresses the growing awareness by Americans of the country's critical shortage of energy sources. The frustration and helplessness felt by many consumers following the 1973 oil crisis prompted a wave of resolutions calling for energy management on the level of local communities, together with a general sentiment that "small is better" in all aspects of economic and social life. Cose describes the efforts of communities both large and small to remedy what he calls the "loss of control many Americans feel over important parts of their lives." He analyzes the contradictions inherent between the desire for local control of resources and the realities of modern energy production and distribution, and he concludes that while local empowerment is possible and in some cases a reality, few communities are willing to pay the price for such control. As the author succinctly put it in his book, community activists need "to realize that even a 'quiet revolution' is not free." After his stint at the Joint Center for Political Studies, Cose resumed his career in journalism as a columnist and editorial writer for the *Detroit Free Press* between 1979 and 1981. He later joined the staff of the newly created *USA Today* as a special reporter on management and labor issues, remaining there until 1983 when he was named president of the Institute for Journalism Education at the University of California at Berkeley.

Cose's three-year tenure at the institute led to the 1989 publication of *The Press: Inside America's Most Powerful Newspaper Empires—From the Newsrooms to the Boardrooms*, his first book to receive widespread notice. In this ambitious book Cose attempts to chronicle the changes at five of the leading U.S. newspapers between the early 1960s and late 1980s. (The five papers studied are the *New York Times, Los Angeles Times, Washington Post*, and the Knight-Ridder and Gannett chains.)

The Press focuses on a period during which these mostly family-owned newspapers came under increasing pressure from business advisers to diversify and enlarge their non-news holdings—to become more like other large corporations and less like the traditional ideal of an independent, "above the fray" observer of the national scene. Cose provides thumbnail sketches

of extreme social tension. While radical black organizations such as the Black Panthers were attacking the foundations of the so-called "establishment," Cose was given the task and honor of articulating the needs of black people in the pages of one of the establishment's leading journals, all while completing his degree in psychology at the University of Illinois. It was the kind of pressure-filled situation journalists thrive upon, and Cose proved to be a born journalist. He continued writing columns for the *Sun-Times* for seven years, of each of the paper's origins as background for his tale of boardroom battles and generational change and for the most part concludes that the papers have avoided the conflicts of interest possible in diversified asset holdings by confining their growth to the media business.

Following a year with the Gannett Center for Media Studies at Columbia University, Cose spent several years researching and writing another substantial book, *A Nation of Strangers: Prejudice, Politics, and the Populating of America.* Here Cose provides a history of America's ambivalent attitude toward the waves of immigration that have contributed to its population during the last three centuries. The United States was created by immigrants, as Cose points out, yet each generation of citizens has feared and opposed the arrival of certain groups of later immigrants. At various times, Americans have been worried about the increasing numbers of Catholic, Irish, Jewish, Chinese, and Hispanic individuals in this country, to name only a few of the religious and ethnic groups singled out for hostility. As Cose wrote in the epilogue to *Nation,* "For while it is true America's history is one of absorbing successive waves of immigrants, it is also a history of intermittent outbreaks of anti-immigrant hysteria." Cose decries the existence of such discrimination but sees little hope that it will soon end.

In August of 1991 Cose became editor of the *New York Daily News* 's editorial page and soon became chairman of the editorial board at the paper. He moved on in 1993 to accept a contributing editor position with *Newsweek,* where he has continued to report on matters of social and racial consequence in America and beyond.

His journalistic career affords him constant stimulation, an energizing "hustle-bustle" of daily news, but he has continued his authorship of powerful book-length social commentaries on race and social relations. He even expanded some of his journalistic reports into book-length ponderings of particular topics. Published in 2004, Cose's book *Beyond Brown v. Board: The Final Battle for Excellence in American Education* provided a base for a *Newsweek* cover story on the U.S. Supreme Court's historic school desegregation decision in 1954 and its aftermath as seen in the challenges faced by American educators into the new millennium.

Cose's reputation as a keen observer of the human and political experience of black Americans was solidified in his books *The Rage of a Privileged Class, The Envy of the World: On Being a Black Man in America, Bone to Pick: Of Forgiveness Reconciliation, Reparation and Revenge. The Rage of a Privileged Class,* an examination of the difficulties middle-class blacks have succeeding in America, became a bestseller. *The Envy of the World: On Being a Black Man in America* offers case studies that illustrate how prejudice shapes the experience of black American males.

And *Bone to Pick: Of Forgiveness Reconciliation, Reparation and Revenge* details opposing arguments aimed at addressing social justice throughout the world. Recurring topics in his books about social justice are reconciliation, revenge, and forgiveness. At the dawn of the new millennium, Cose was primed to offer more insightful commentaries on society, for not only were his journalistic works and books highly praised by critics, he also proved himself to be a skillful and thus sought after speaker and appeared regularly on television shows and radio programs.

Selected writings

Energy and the Urban Crisis, Joint Center for Political Studies, 1978.
(Editor) *Energy and Equity: Some Social Concerns,* Joint Center for Political Studies, 1979.
Decentralizing Energy Decisions: The Rebirth of Community Power, Westview, 1983.
The Press: Inside America's Most Powerful Newspaper Empires—From the Newsrooms to the Boardrooms, Morrow, 1989.
A Nation of Strangers: Prejudice, Politics, and the Populating of America, Morrow, 1992.
The Rage of a Privileged Class, HarperCollins, 1993.
A Man's World : How Real Is Male Privilege—And How High Is Its Price?, Harper Collins, 1995.
Color-Blind : Seeing Beyond Race In A Race-Obsessed World, HarperCollins, 1997.
(Editor) *The Darden Dilemma : 12 Black Writers On Justice, Race, And Conflicting Loyalties,* Harper-Perennial, 1997.
The Best Defense, HarperCollins, 1998.
The Envy of the World: On Being a Black Man in America, Washington Square Press, 2002.
Beyond Brown v. Board: The Final Battle for Excellence in American Education, Rockefeller Foundation, 2004.
Bone to Pick: Of Forgiveness Reconciliation, Reparation and Revenge, Atria Books, 2004.

Sources

Periodicals

Black Enterprise, July 2004.
Newsweek, June 3, 1985.
Publishers Weekly, March 23, 1992.
Time, November 27, 1989.

On-line

"Black Men in America," *National Public Radio: Weekend Edition,* http://www.npr.org/templates/story/story.php?storyId=1140451 (March 9, 2005).
Ellis Cose, www.elliscose.com (March 9, 2005).
"Ellis Cose: Enduring Hardship and 'A Bone to Pick,'" *National Public Radio: Tavis Smiley Show,* http://

www.npr.org/templates/story/story.php?storyId=1
8 68738 (March 9, 2005).

—Jonathan Martin and Sara Pendergast

Sylvester Croom

1954—

College football coach

Croom, Sylvester, photograph. AP/Wide World Photos. Reproduced by permission.

When Sylvester Croom Jr. became head football coach at Mississippi State University (MSU) late in 2003, the history books beckoned. Croom was the first African American tapped to lead a Southeastern Conference (SEC) school in its 71-year history. National media swooped down on the story and much was made about the progress of racial equality in the Deep South. Croom wanted none of it. In an oft-quoted statement made at his first MSU press conference, he said loudly, "I am the first African-American coach in the SEC, but there ain't but one color that matters here and that color is maroon." Mississippi's school color would be Croom's focus, no matter what history had to say.

Found Refuge from Racism in Football

Sylvester Croom was born on September 25, 1954, in Tuscaloosa, Alabama, the son of a schoolteacher and a preacher. Segregation and racism were the norm for he and his brother Kelvin. "When you were in your black neighborhood and your black churches, that wasn't a problem," Croom told the *Milwaukee Journal Senti-*

nel. "When you needed to get some food, stop for gas, that's when it hit you in the face." Despite the injustices, the Croom boys kept their heads high, their anger at bay. It is what their parents Louise and Sylvester Sr. had taught them. "Our motto always was that color doesn't matter, it's the people who matter," Louise Croom told the *New York Daily News.* "There are bad black people, and there are bad white people." After becoming one of the first black students at Tuscaloosa Junior High, Croom joined the football team. Following a game with an all-white team, Croom was taunted and chased by an angry mob. Teachers and parents from Tuscaloosa, both black and white, surrounded Croom, ushering him to safety.

Football was always Croom's preferred refuge. He and his brother spent hours playing in the backyard and practicing slow motion plays in the living room. Louise recalled to the *New York Daily News* that she would tell Croom, "You don't need to play football; you might get killed." His standard reply was, "If I die playing football, I die happy." As Croom grew into a 6-foot, 230-pound offensive lineman, racial barriers around him were falling. The year he was born the Supreme

Court decision *Brown v. the Board of Education* made segregation in public schools illegal. When he was ten, the Civil Rights Act of 1964 prohibited discrimination based on race in nearly all areas of public life. Yet in the South, old habits died hard, and even as Croom was integrating local Tuscaloosa schools, the Ku Klux Klan was on the rise. Once, while Croom hosted a meeting of the Tuscaloosa High Key Club at his home, a cross was set on fire not far from his front door.

Became Alabama Champion as Player and Coach

Despite the racial turbulence, Croom stayed focused on football and dreamed of playing for Tuscaloosa's University of Alabama. The Crimson Tide was the top-ranked football program in the nation. It was also all white. The coach at the time was Paul "Bear" Bryant, and to the football-crazed masses of the Deep South, he was both a hero and a legend. After losing miserably to a California team led by a star running back who was black, Bryant decided to integrate his team in 1970. No fuss, no fight, he just did it. Croom joined the Crimson Tide when he became a freshman at Alabama in 1971.

Croom quickly distinguished himself on the gridiron. He played on three SEC championship teams and was a starting center on the 1973 national championship team. During his senior year he was named team captain and was selected a 1974 Kodak All-American player. His devotion to the game caused the Alabama athletic staff to create the Sylvester Croom Jr. Commitment to Excellence Award. It also earned him a spot with the NFL's New Orleans Saints. Just before leaving Alabama Coach Bryant stopped Croom in the hallway. Croom told *The Sun Herald*, "He says, 'Croom, if you don't make it in pro football, I want you to come back and coach for us.'"

Croom and his wife—high school sweetheart Jeri—moved to New Orleans with all they owned in the back of a van. They would barely have time to unpack. Croom was cut from the Saints after his first game. Back in Tuscaloosa he enrolled in the master's program for educational administration at Alabama and joined Bryant's coaching team. From 1977 to 1986 Croom coached Alabama's linebackers. During Croom's tenure the Crimson Tide won two national championships and went to ten bowl games.

Spurned by Alabama after Stellar NFL Career

In 1987 Croom joined the NFL again, this time as running backs coach for the Tampa Bay Buccaneers. He held that position for three years before taking on the same role with the Indianapolis Colts. In 1992 he joined the San Diego Chargers, again as a running backs coach. He helped drive the Chargers to two conference championships and to the 1995 Super Bowl. In 1997 Croom joined the Detroit Lions as offensive coordinator. There he coached Barry Sanders as Sanders made NFL history rushing for 2,063 yards in a single season. Under Croom, the Lions were second in the league in offense. "[Croom] just got better and better," former Lions coach Bobby Ross told *The Sporting News*. "He conceptually had the big picture." In 2001 Croom joined the Green Bay Packers as running backs coach and by 2003 the Packers ranked number one in the NFL for rushing.

In 2003, the head coaching spot at the University of Alabama became vacant. With Alabama history plus 17 years in the NFL, Croom seemed perfect for the job. It came down to him and Mike Shula, another former Alabama player. However, only Croom had collegiate coaching experience. He was also a Tuscaloosa native and a favorite for the position. When he was passed over for Shula, who was white, disappointment shrouded Alabama. "It angered more than just African-Americans," an assistant Alabama athletic director told *The New York Times*. "It went way, way beyond race. People had made some decisions about who would be the best person for the job." Croom gave up hopes of coaching college ball. "I was done," he told *New York Daily News*. "Because I thought if that was going to ever happen in this conference it would have to be a former player going back to his alma mater. That's what I thought. If you're not willing to hire a guy of color who played for you, coached for you, grew up in your hometown, then surely nobody else is going to give him a chance."

Hired as Head Coach at Mississippi State

Another chance did come, however, when the head coach of Mississippi State University (MSU) resigned. MSU wanted Croom, but he was not so sure. Burned by the Alabama incident, he was also wary of being hired only as an enticement to black football recruits. "After our first interview, I made it very clear that if that's what the expectations were, then they needed to look for another coach," Croom told the *Knight-Ridder/Tribune News Service*. He continued, "But, during that second interview, they made me feel I was the best coach available. That was important to me."

In December of 2003, Croom signed on as head coach of the MSU Bulldogs, a Division 1-A team. In doing so he became the first African-American coach in the SEC. Though his appointment brought national press to MSU, Croom dodged the spotlight. "I'm going to let everyone else focus on it," he told *The Sun Herald*. "I really don't have time." He continued, "I've been in that situation, where I'm 'the first,' or 'the only.' Maybe all of that was part of being preparation for this, I don't know. Right now I've got to think about a coaching staff, about these players, about the job at hand."

It was a big job. The Bulldogs had won just eight games in the previous three years. MSU was also awaiting NCAA sanctions in response to recruiting violations committed by Croom's predecessor. However Croom's most pressing problem was discipline—or lack of it. Croom wasted no time laying down ground rules. Athletic director Larry Templeton recalled Croom's first meeting with the team to the *Knight-Ridder/Tribune News Service*. A few players showed up late, one let his cell phone ring, another was busy writing something down. "Sly went over there and stood in front of him and said, 'Son, when I talk, I expect every eye in this room on my two eyes.' For the next 20 minutes you could hear a pin drop." Before long Croom was checking up on his players' classroom attendance and enforcing early morning runs on players who broke rules. He dropped the team's top rusher from the roster when he refused to shape up. The players got the message real quick. "He was very blunt," a senior player told *The Sporting News*. "He told you what it is, and what it's going to be."

Began Slow Drive to Revive Bulldogs

Croom made his coaching debut in September of 2004 at a home game against Tulane. The Bulldogs won 28-7 in front of 50,000-plus ecstatic fans, many in t-shirts proclaiming "Maroon is all that matters." Fans left that game feeling that just maybe Croom was the salvation the beleaguered team needed. Reality set in, however, as the Bulldogs lost the next five games, including an embarrassing home loss to a lower division team. Yet, no one had expected a program as wrecked as Mississippi's to turn around in one season. "We're not looking for a quick fix," Croom told *The Miami Herald*. "We're building a foundation. We're trying to win games now, but how we do things now will establish things for a long time."

The following month Mississippi scored an upset victory over 20th-ranked University of Florida with a 38-31 win. "I've been in a lot of big games in my career, but this was the biggest win," Croom said in *Sports Illustrated*. The Bulldogs also won their next game, 22-7 over Kentucky. However, the game everyone was waiting for was Mississippi versus Alabama. "To me, it meant the culmination of a lifetime dream," Croom told The *New York Times*. "I stood on the same sidelines as Coach Bryant although it was the other side of the field. I'll take it any way I can get it." The players were not immune to the excitement. "Coming into the game, everybody was talking about how they wanted to win for Coach Croom," a player added. Though they rushed for a season high 225 yards, the Bulldogs lost 14-30. They also lost the last two games of the season, finishing with a 3-8 record.

Despite the losing season, MSU administration extended Croom's contract through 2008. Templeton said in an article on Mississippi's *NBC 4* Web site that the contract recognized "the outstanding job that coach Croom has done in just one year." Perhaps more gratifying to Croom were the grade point averages earned by his players. In December of 2004, MSU football players posted their highest GPAs in three years. "I am pleased with the progress our players have made in the classroom," Croom told the *Mississippi State University Athletics* Web site. "It is obvious that they are taking pride in doing the right things on and off the field. There is a commitment on their part to becoming the complete person." That is just the sort of commitment Croom has long believed in. "My ultimate goal will involve how the players perform, in class, on the field. I know I'm going to be judged on wins and losses," he told *The Sun Herald*. "My yardstick, my true yardstick, is seeing these young men being successful. That's what it's all about for me."

Sources

Periodicals

Knight Ridder/Tribune News Service, August 3, 2004.
Miami Herald, October 23, 2004.
Milwaukee Journal Sentinel, October 22, 2004.
New York Daily News, December 8, 2003; September 5, 2004.
New York Times, July 18, 2004; November 7, 2004.

Sporting News, August 23, 2004.

Sports Illustrated, November 1, 2004.

Sun Herald (Biloxi, MS), December 2, 2003; December 30, 2003.

On-line

"Mississippi State Extends Croom," *NBC 4,* www. nbc4.tv/cfoot545/4003535/detail.html (December 28, 2004).

"MSU Football Team Posts Three-Year Grade-Point High," *Mississippi State University Athletics,* www. mstateathletics.com/0,5604,1_27_0_64826,00.ht ml (December 28, 2004).

—Candace LaBalle

Fred D'Aguiar

1960—

Writer

Poet, playwright, and novelist Fred D'Aguiar prefers to be described simply as a writer. He was born in London but grew up in Guyana and belongs to a second generation of Caribbean-British writers. His work is often highly politicized, addressing a sense of divided or dual identity. In his early poetry in particular D'Aguiar attempts to reconcile his early experiences in Guyana with his adult life in 1970s urban Britain. Although already an award-winning poet, during the 1990s D'Aguiar established himself as an important British novelist. His first novel, *The Longest Memory* (1994), won the Whitbread Prize for a first novel and has been compared favorably with Toni Morrison's *Beloved*, but it brings a distinctively British sensibility to the subject of slavery and its historical legacy. D'Aguiar's clean, almost underwritten prose style reflects his beginnings as a poet. This, along with his versatility and his ability to combine the British written tradition with the oral Caribbean tradition, have earned him a reputation as one of the finest British writers of his generation.

Born in London on February 2, 1960, D'Aguiar moved to Guyana not long before his second birthday, where he lived with one of his grandmothers and extended family in a village called Airey Hall, forty miles from the capital, Georgetown. He returned to England at the age of twelve in 1972 and credits an inspiring English teacher, Geoffrey Hardy, with introducing him to contemporary poetry through the influential anthologies released by Penguin and through the "Liverpool Poets," Adrian Henri, Brian Patten, and Roger McGough. He admired songwriters such as Bob Dylan and Joni Mitchell, but his lyrical influences also extend to reggae and calypso, in particular the Trinidadian calypso singer Lord Kitchener. D'Aguiar began publishing poetry in school magazines and local newspapers while he was still a teenager, but when he left school he trained to be a psychiatric nurse; he continued working as a nurse while he attended the University of Kent at Canterbury, where he majored in African and Caribbean studies. He graduated with honors in 1985.

D'Aguiar has claimed that the atmosphere of racial tension in London during the 1970s was what made him a political writer and has mentioned in particular an anti-racist rally he attended where one of the protesters, Blair Peach, was killed. His first book of poetry, *Mama Dot* (1985), recalls his time in Guyana, with the Mama Dot of the title being a combination of his two grandmothers. As with *Airy Hall* (1989) the poems in *Mama Dot* combine elements of the Guyanese vernacular of his childhood with more conventional British English. D'Aguiar is part of a generation of black British writers who have reinvented British literary style since the 1980s and these two collections of poems mark his beginnings as an influential member of that group. Both collections won awards, *Mama Dot* the Malcolm X Poetry Prize and a Poetry Book Society recommendation, and *Airy Hall* the Guyana Prize for Poetry.

While D'Aguiar has been very successful as a writer, he is also an educator, having held the prestigious Judith E. Wilson Fellowship at Cambridge University (1989-90) and, from 1990-92, the position of Northern Arts Literary Fellow at the University of Newcastle upon Tyne. During the late 1980s and early 1990s D'Aguiar

At a Glance . . .

Born on February 2, 1960, in London, England. *Education:* University of Kent at Canterbury, UK, BA (honors) in African and Caribbean Studies, 1985.

Career: Trained and worked as a psychiatric nurse before attending university; London Borough of Lewisham, writer-in-residence, 1986-87; Birmingham Polytechnic, writer-in-residence, 1988-89; Cambridge University, Cambridge, England, Judith E. Wilson Fellow, 1989-90; Northern Arts Literary Fellow, 1990-92; Amherst College, Amherst, MA, visiting writer, 1992-94; Bates College, Lewiston, ME, assistant professor of English, 1994-95; University of Miami, Coral Gables, FL, professor of English, 1995-2004; University of Newcastle upon Tyne, Professor of Creative Writing and Postcolonial Literature, 2005–.

Awards: Minority Rights Group award, 1983; T. S. Eliot Prize, University of Kent, 1984; Greater London Council (GLC) literature award, 1985; Malcolm X Prize for poetry, for *Mama Dot,* 1989; Guyana Prize for Poetry, for *Airy Hall,* 1989; Book Trust (London, England), David Higham Prize for Fiction, for *The Longest Memory,* 1995; Whitbread First Novel Award, for *The Longest Memory,* 1995.

Addresses: *Agent*—David Higham Associates, 5-8 Lower John Street, Golden Square, London W1F 9HA. *Office*—School of English Literature, Language, and Linguistics, Percy Building, University of Newcastle upon Tyne, Newcastle upon Tyne, NE1 7RU United Kingdom.

wrote several plays that were broadcast on BBC radio and television. He moved to the United States in 1992 and worked at several American colleges, becoming professor of English at the University of Miami in 1995. His move to the United States coincided with his emergence as a novelist, as he published his first novel, *The Longest Memory*, in 1994 to great acclaim, winning the 1995 Whitbread Prize for best first novel.

The Longest Memory is an unconventional novel. Set on a Virginia slave plantation, it switches from past to present and back again and is narrated by several different characters in their own voices. The deliberate circularity of the narrative suggests the impossibility of future generations ever "recovering" from slavery's

legacy. After such a dramatic debut it was almost inevitable that D'Aguiar's second novel, *Dear Future* (1996), would not be received so well; its contemporary themes of globalization and the after-effects of colonization were perhaps also less attractive to readers. *Feeding the Ghosts* (1999) returned more directly to the subject of slavery, but in a more poetic and metaphoric style than his earlier work.

In 1998 D'Aguiar published *Bill of Rights*, a long narrative poem about the Jonestown massacre in Guyana in 1978, and a book that re-established him as a poet with a powerful political voice. It was followed in 2000 by *Bloodlines*, another long narrative poem in the form of a novel, this time about a black slave and her white lover. *Bethany Bettany*, published in 2003, is seen by critics as a return to the form of *The Longest Memory*. The novel tells the story of a five year-old girl left to look after herself by her mother after her father dies. She has been seen as a symbol of Guyana searching for an identity as it emerges from between two cultures.

In publicity material prepared for *Bethany Bettany*, D'Aguiar describes himself as a product of the three countries in which he has lived: "My origin is not in itself of interest, except to say that Guyana, London and now the United States provide a curious cocktail of ethnicity, history and Conradian horror unmatched by any other triple mix of sovereign states." Perhaps because it deals with issues of race and identity more familiar to American readers, D'Aguiar's work since the 1990s has not received a high level of exposure in the British media. Yet his work has been of a consistently high quality and wide influence, having helped pave the way for better known younger writers such as Zadie Smith. In 2005 he returned to Britain to take up a post as professor of creative writing and postcolonial literature at the University of Newcastle upon Tyne.

Selected writings

Novels

The Longest Memory, Pantheon, 1994.
Dear Future, Pantheon, 1996.
Feeding the Ghosts, Ecco, 1999.
Bloodlines, Chatto and Windus, 2000.
Bethany Bettany, Chatto and Windus, 2003.

Plays

1492 (radio play), BBC Radio 3, 1992.
Sweet Thames (television play), BBC2, 1992.
Rain (television play), BBC2, 1994.
A Jamaican Airman Forsees His Death, Methuen, 1995.

Poetry

Mama Dot, Chatto and Windus, 1985.
Airy Hall, Chatto and Windus, 1989.

British Subjects, Bloodaxe, 1993.
Bill of Rights, Chatto and Windus, 1998.

Sources

Periodicals

African American Review, Fall 1998, p. 506.
Economist, February 24, 1990, p. 92.
Los Angeles Times Book Review, March 5, 1995, p. 6; February 4, 1996, p. 11.
Nation, January 13, 1997, p. 32.
New Statesman and Society, November 12, 1993, p. 37; September 2, 1994, p. 37.

New York Times Book Review, May 7, 1995, p. 26; March 24, 1996, p. 28; November 10, 1996, p. 56.
World Literature Today, Fall, 1999, p. 796.

On-line

"Fred D'Aguiar," *Biography Resource Center*, www. galenet.com/servlet/BioRC (January 26, 2005).
"Fred D'Aguiar," *Caribbean Poetry Web*, www.hum boldt.edu/~me2/engl240b/student_projects/dagu iar/daguiartoc.htm (January 26, 2005).
"The Poetry Kit Interviews Fred D'Aguiar," *The Poetry Kit*, www.poetrykit.org/iv/daguiar.htm (January 26, 2005).

—Chris Routledge

James E. Davis

1962-2003

Politician

New York City councilman James E. Davis died in a bizarre city hall shooting in 2003 that caused panic in the municipal building as well as the activation of an emergency-event plan for Lower Manhattan. The Brooklyn Democrat was gunned down by a political rival, with whom he was trying to forge a more productive working relationship. It was a tragic end for the irascible Davis, a political newcomer who had made his name leading anti-violence initiatives in the city.

Davis was born in 1962 and grew up in Brooklyn. His father was a corrections officer, while his mother Thelma worked as a registered nurse. He graduated from Tilden High School in 1980 and seemed to drift for a time. His political activism began, he once said, when two white police officers used undue force against him during a 1983 incident. After earning a degree from Pace University, he became a corrections officer as his father had been, and joined the New York City Transit Police department in 1991. Two years later, he moved on to the New York Police Department (NYPD) itself, where he trained recruits at the police academy.

Along the way, Davis also became an ordained minister and ran a ministry out of his home to help New York teens. Out of that group came "Love Yourself, Stop the Violence," an anti-violence group he founded in 1990. Davis led an annual "Stop the Violence" march in New York City that helped establish his name in the community. The group also launched various campaigns to raise awareness of gun violence, one of them a challenge to retailer Toys 'R' Us to urge it to stop selling realistic-appearing toy guns.

Davis made a few unsuccessful bids for municipal office before he became a district leader with the Brooklyn Democratic Party organization. In 2001 he ran for an open New York city council seat from the 35th Council District in Brooklyn, and bested six other candidates at the polls. Quickly gaining a reputation as a maverick who regularly challenged the status quo—even within his own party—Davis regularly engaged in heated political battles with rivals, and sometimes with perceived rivals as well. He once allegedly threatened to investigate the child-support payment record of a potential political challenger, but observers of New York City politics usually noted in newspaper reports that such tactics had a long history in all five boroughs. In Brooklyn, he was a popular figure and approachable public servant. "He had become a player in a City Council that for the first time in generations was without entrenched veterans," noted a *New York Times* report, and "was developing a reputation among his constituents for delivering on his promises and had worked hard to win over his most bitter opponents."

A political novice and onetime male model named Othniel Askew emerged as a potential rival in Davis's 35th District as his 2003 re-election campaign gained steam. Askew had none of the social-activist background upon which Davis had built his own career, and police had even been called to his residence when Askew allegedly chased his male partner, who was naked, out onto a Manhattan street one day in 1996. But on July 23, 2003, Davis came to City Hall with Askew in tow. The pair bypassed the metal detectors

At a Glance . . .

Born on April 3, 1962 in New York, NY; died of gunshot wounds on July 23, 2003, in New York, NY; son of a corrections officer and Thelma Davis (a registered nurse). *Education:* Pace University, B.A., 1989. *Politics:* Democrat.

Career: New York City, corrections officer, 1989-91; New York City Transit police officer, c. 1991-93; New York City Police Department, academy instructor, 1993-2001; ordained minister and founder of the community group Love Yourself, Stop the Violence, 1990; Brooklyn Democratic Party, district leader; New York city council, elected representative of 35th district, 2001-03.

that all attendees to city council meetings were required to pass through thanks to a wave from Davis, who was exempt from the daily search because he was an elected official. Davis brought Askew onto the floor of the city council chambers, where the meeting was slated to begin soon, in order to introduce him to a council member from the Bronx, Larry B. Seabrook. "He said this guy was going to run against him and had decided not to run against him," Seabrook told *New York Times* writers Randal C. Archibold and Winnie Hu. "And now they were going to work together."

After that, both Davis and Askew headed to the balcony. Just as the meeting was about to start with roll call, ten shots rang out. Mayhem erupted, with city council members and their staffers ducking for cover. Many initially believed it was perhaps another attack on the city, so soon after the events of September 11, 2001; nearby, Mayor Michael R. Bloomberg was prevented from leaving his office for safety reasons once he heard of the incident. From the floor, a plainclothes NYPD officer, who served as part of the security detail for council president Gifford Miller, shot Askew and killed him. Emergency personnel and a flood of police officers arrived on the scene, and Davis was taken down the steps of City Hall on a stretcher. A photograph of this part of the scene became the front-page leader for the city's newspapers that day. Subsequent police work revealed that Askew had told others that

Davis had pressured him to drop out of the race, possibly by threatening that he would "out" Askew, who was gay, to his family. Once the two began working together earlier that week, however, observers recounted that Askew appeared excited to be working in a political atmosphere, and seemed to have pressured Davis for a permanent post on his staff.

The slain council member was honored by some 3,000 mourners during a funeral at the Elim International Fellowship Church in the Bedford-Stuyvesant section of Brooklyn. Speakers included Mayor Bloomberg and the Reverend Al Sharpton, the latter receiving a number of thunderous ovations for his lead eulogy. Commenting on the media frenzy that surrounded the shooting, Sharpton pointed out that violence regularly touched the lives of many New Yorkers. "We've been scrubbing blood off of stairs for years," Sharpton told a crowd that included Davis's friends, family, and teenagers he worked with in his Stop the Violence group, as well as some of New York City's most powerful political figures, according to a *New York Daily News* report. "But it didn't matter to folks until it went in the Hall. That makes them uncomfortable."

In November of 2003, Davis's brother Geoffrey ran for his city council seat, but lost to a third-party candidate. By then, NYPD officers were a permanent fixture at city council sessions, and everyone was required to pass through the metal detectors in the building, even elected officials. Mayor Bloomberg remembered Davis as a rising new voice in city politics, and paid tribute to his spirit at the funeral. "He was never shy about expressing himself," the *New York Daily News* quoted Bloomberg as saying. "His great strength was that he told it like he saw it."

Sources

Periodicals

Knight-Ridder/Tribune News Service, July 29, 2003.
New York Daily News, July 23, 2003; , p. B3.
New York Times, June 16, 2002, p. 26; July 24, 2003, p. A1; July 25, 2003, p. A1; July 30, 2003, p. B3; August 1, 2003, p. B1; August 20, 2003, p. B3; November 7, 2003, p. B4; August 14, 2004, p. B3.
New Yorker, August 4, 2003, p. 22.
United Press International, July 24, 2003.

—Carol Brennan

Ossie Davis

1917-2005

Actor, director, producer, writer

With the build and vitality of an NFL lineman, Ossie Davis hardly looked like the grand old man of black theater. Known to younger audiences as Ponder Blue on television's *Evening Shade* and as "the mayor" in filmmaker Spike Lee's *Do the Right Thing*, Davis made his Broadway debut in *Jeb* in 1946. He directed the landmark film *Cotton Comes to Harlem* in 1970 and wrote and starred in *Purlie Victorious*, the 1961 play that was eventually revived as the smash Broadway musical *Purlie*. Enthralled with his art, Davis worked until the day he died in 2005.

Grew Up Poor in the South

Raiford Chatman Davis was born on December 18, 1917, in tiny Cogdell, Georgia. His name was officially registered as "Ossie" when a clerk misheard Davis' mother pronounce her newborn son's initials "R. C." Laura Davis did not correct the clerk, according to the *Sarasota Herald Tribune*. The oldest of five children, he grew up in a family of poor but inspired preachers and storytellers, an environment that provided him good grounding for the stage. "Acting and preaching are essentially the same—unabashedly so," Davis told Florida's *Palm Beach Post*. "The theater is a church and I consider myself as part of an institution that has an obligation to teach about Americanism, our culture and morals."

Though neither his father, Kince Charles Davis, a railway construction worker, nor his mother, Laura, ever learned to read, they nevertheless, through the oral tradition, taught Davis the importance of educa-tion. "I was just caught up in the wonderful stories mom and dad would tell," he told the *Palm Beach Post*. "They weren't children's stories, but humorous tales of their own escapades. They took life and broke it up in little pieces and fed it to us like little birds. I think I always knew what I wanted to do. I went to school to learn to write."

Like many blacks growing up in the 1920s, Davis managed to find good role models despite a resource-poor environment. "My mentors were real and unreal," he told *American Visions*. "My mentors were Brer Rabbit and High John the Conqueror, and even ani-mals to whom I could talk when I was a boy. My mentors were friends who could tell jokes faster than me. Of course, I had organized mentors, too. Regular teachers in school and out. And there were mentors on the stage itself. People like [singers] Paul Robeson, Lena Horne, and [trumpet player] Louis Armstrong."

But while a lack of resources could not prevent him from wanting to learn, they almost prevented him from getting an education. Though Davis's parents were full of pride when he won a scholarship to Tuskegee Institute in Alabama, he had to turn it down because they had no money to pay for his living expenses. In 1935, though, things took a turn for the better; two aunts living in Washington, D.C., agreed to house him while he attended Howard University. "My parents found enough money to buy me lunch one day and I hitchhiked to Washington to live with my aunts and attend Howard University," he told the *Palm Beach Post*. "There I met a number of people who were very important to my career."

At a Glance . . .

Born Raiford Chatman Davis on December 18, 1917, in Cogdell, GA; died on February 4, 2005, in Miami, FL; son of Kince Charles (a railway construction worker) and Laura Davis; married Ruby Ann Wallace (Ruby Dee; an actress) on December 9, 1948; children: Nora, Guy, Lavern (Hasna). *Education*: Howard University, BA, 1939. *Military Service*: US Army, 1942-1945.

Career: Member of Rose McClendon Players, 1938-1941; actor, 1946-2005; director, 1970-2005; social activist, 1917-2005.

Awards: Emmy nomination for performance in *Teacher Teacher*, 1969; NAACP Image Award Hall of Fame, inductee, 1989; Theater Hall of Fame, inductee, 1994; U.S. National Medal for the Arts, 1995; NAACP Image Award, for "Promised Land" miniseries, 1996; New York Urban League Frederick Douglass Award, 2001; Screen Actor's Guild Lifetime Achievement Award, 2001; Kennedy Center Honor, shared with Ruby Dee, 2004.

Began Acting as Research

Chief among Davis's influences at Howard was Alain Locke. Called "the philosophical midwife to a generation of younger artists, writers and poets" by *American Visions*, Locke, a drama critic and professor of philosophy, encouraged Davis, who already wanted to write for the theater, to move to Harlem and join the Rose McClendon Players. Locke suggested that Davis, who had never seen live actors, would benefit from acting and learning what it takes to put on a play. Davis accepted the idea but only as a way to further his writing ambitions. "I never, never intended to become an actor," he told *Newsday*.

Davis arrived in Harlem in 1938 and worked odd jobs while studying acting. It was a difficult period; at times he was reduced to sleeping in parks and scrounging for food. In 1941 he made his stage debut in the McClendon Players presentation of *Joy Exceeding Glory*. When the United States entered World War II, Davis joined the Army. He began his service as a surgical technician in Liberia, West Africa. Later, he was transferred to the Special Services Department, where he wrote and produced stage works to entertain military personnel. Among these was *Goldbrickers of 1944*, which was first produced in Liberia.

After the war Davis returned to Georgia but was soon contacted by McClendon director Richard Campbell, who convinced him to come to New York and audition for *Jeb*, a play by Robert Ardrey. At age 28, Davis won the lead role and made his Broadway debut. He earned favorable reviews as a disabled veteran attempting to succeed as an adding-machine operator in racist Louisiana, but the play itself was panned and lasted only nine performances. Though it bombed at the box office, *Jeb* was far from a total loss; it put Davis on the theatrical map, and it was in the cast of *Jeb* that Davis met Ruby Ann Wallace, whose stage name was Ruby Dee. The two became close and took roles with the touring company of *Anna Lucasta*. They were married on December 9, 1948. "Ruby was my colleague," Davis told *Newsday*, "and then she became my friend and eventually my wife."

After his marriage, Davis continued to appear in plays and, as time progressed, he took roles in television and films. Presentations like *Stevedore* and *No Time for Sergeants* paid the bills while others, like *No Way Out*—the powerful film about racial violence with Sidney Poitier and Ruby Dee—Lorraine Hansberry's *A Raisin in the Sun*, and Kraft Theater's 1955 television presentation of Eugene O'Neill's *The Emperor Jones* provided roles into which Davis could sink his teeth. Later, he remembered what an all-encompassing political and social—as well as professional—life the theater was. "In our day, theater was a serious commitment," he told the *Milwaukee Journal*. "That was the style of the times…. In New York City, you acted in the theater, and afterward, you went to a [civil rights movement] party for a lynching victim later that evening. [Actor Marlon] Brando was in one corner and [actor-director] Orson Welles was in the other corner. It was the same at home. I was born in the South, and my parents were always involved in something, raising money for this cause or that protest."

Noted Poor Treatment of Blacks

Despite some good roles, Davis was not happy with his treatment or that of blacks in general. "I knew I was going to be rejected so I had very low expectations," he revealed in *Blacks in American Film and Television*. "But rejection did sting. In the theater it took a peculiar form—of having to compete with your peers, like I did for *The Green Pastures* on Broadway, to fight to say words you were ashamed of. Ruby and I came along at a time when being black was not yet fashionable. There was little in the theater for us except to carry silver trays."

But Broadway was not the only place in which Davis could exercise his considerable talents. "We have always been involved in black theater, in the way that we saw [it]," Davis told *American Visions*. "Ruby and I took our notebooks and created our own theater. We went out into the marketplace, then to churches, to the schools and did what we could theatrically. Our relationship with black theater has always been continuous.

It is just that we had to sometimes define what it is we meant by black theater." Davis and Dee's commitment to the black community went beyond staging dramas; in 1963 they acted as official hosts for the legendary civil rights March on Washington. Throughout the 1950s and '60s they stayed in constant contact with African-American activists such as Martin Luther King, Jr., and Malcolm X (at whose funerals Davis delivered the eulogy), Paul Robeson, and W. E. B. Du Bois. "Protest invigorated Davis," according to *People*. "Like exercise strengthens the body, struggle strengthens the character," Davis told *People* in a 1998 interview quoted in the magazine's obituary for him.

Davis and Dee made every effort to build a normal family life for their three children, Hasna, Guy, and Nora. Living in a working-class neighborhood of Mount Vernon, New York, they preserved the family unit, which is so often distorted by the pressures of show business. "I think if there is anything to be said, our children were able at all levels and at all times to participate fully in the life we led," Davis told *American Visions*. "We didn't live a life away from them. There wasn't a career outside of the house from which they were barred. We managed to function as a family—with a sense of 'us-ness.'"

Realized His Dream of Being a Writer

Davis, who had never ceased to regard himself primarily as a writer, continued writing and shopping his plays and screenplays to producers throughout the 1950s and 1960s. His play *Alice in Wonder* appeared in New York in 1952. The drama, which recreated the Senator Joe McCarthy era of Cold-War communist-hunting, was revised and expanded the following year as *The Big Deal* but was dimly received. It was not until 1961 that Davis's writing abilities brought him real success. *Purlie Victorious* premiered September 28, 1961, at New York City's Cort Theatre. A comedy about an itinerant black preacher who attempts to claim his inheritance and establish an integrated church, *Purlie Victorious* enjoyed a long and interesting life; it ran more than seven months in New York City and was later revived first as a motion picture called *Gone Are the Days* and then as the Broadway musical *Purlie*. Despite its relatively long run in its first incarnation, *Purlie Victorious* made little money. Whites did not attend it and without white support, a black theater of that era could not succeed in New York.

Davis spent much of the 1960s earning his bread and butter in movies and in episodes of television shows like *The Defenders*, *The Doctors*, *The Fugitive*, and *Bonanza*. It was not the kind of work he relished. "I'm not a great actor," he told *Blacks in American Film and Television*. "I've never devoted myself to my craft with the intensity Ruby has. I've always felt I'd rather be a writer. But we had to make a living." Despite this self-criticism, Pauline Kael, film critic for the *New Yorker*, wrote that Davis, "in such movies as *The Hill* and *The Scalphunters*, brought a stronger presence to his roles than white actors did, and a deeper joy. What a face for the camera. He was a natural king."

As the 1960s progressed, Davis began receiving the kind of attention he deserved; in 1968 his play *Curtain Call, Mr. Aldridge, Sir* was produced at the University of California at Santa Barbara and in 1969, he received an Emmy nomination for his performance in the teleplay *Teacher Teacher*. By 1970 he had become one of the busiest African Americans in the entertainment industry. He made his debut as a film director with *Cotton Comes to Harlem*, adapted Nigerian writer Wole Soyinka's *Kongi's Harvest* for the screen, and his play *Purlie Victorious* returned to Broadway as the musical smash *Purlie*.

Cotton Comes to Harlem was a landmark of black cinema. One of the first black films to make money from a mainstream audience, it opened the way for a wave of pictures about blacks now known as "blaxploitation" films. Unlike that of later, darker movies like *Shaft*, Davis's vision was more comic. Donald Bogle, author of *Blacks in American Film and Television*, attested of *Cotton*, "A joyousness ran through the film that lured audiences around the country into the theaters." Clive Barnes of the *New York Times* called *Purlie*, which opened at the Broadway Theater on March 15, 1970, "by far the most successful and richest of all black musicals," describing the production as "strong" and "so magnificent" and praising "the depth of the characterization and the salty wit of the dialogue."

Through the mid-1970s Davis continued to direct. While his films—*Black Girl*, *Gordon's War*, and *Countdown at Kusini*—were received unevenly, there was a significance to his work that critics could not ignore. Bogle commented that "in a strange way…Davis could be called one of the more serious black directors of his era; political undercurrents [ran] throughout much of his work. He…never settled for simply making a standard action movie…. [He] hoped to take black American cinema into a new, more politically oriented direction [and] for that he has to be commended."

Hit His Stride

Davis spent the remainder of the 1970s pursuing diverse interests. From 1974 until 1978 he and his wife co-hosted the *Ossie Davis and Ruby Dee Story Hour* on radio. In 1976 he appeared in the film *Let's Do It Again*. Also that year, his play *Escape to Freedom: A Play About Young Frederick Douglass* was produced at New York City's Town Hall. In 1981, he and Ruby began appearing in *With Ossie and Ruby* on PBS. Through their company, Emmalyn II Productions, they co-produced the show with two public television stations. The program, which presented a broad mix of material, ran for three years. "It was one of the highlights of our lives because it gave us the opportunity to do shows by authors we respect," Dee told the *Greensboro News and Record*.

With their children, Davis and Dee worked in the context of Emmalyn II through much of the 1980s, producing a variety of programs including *Martin Luther King: The Dream and the Drum* and *A Walk Through History* for PBS. Far from withdrawing from acting, though, Davis continued working on the stage, in film, and on television. In 1986 he starred in a production of Tony Award-Winning American dramatist Herb Gardner's *I'm Not Rappaport* at actor Burt Reynolds's Jupiter Theater in Florida. Davis appeared in Spike Lee's 1988 film *School Daze* and in 1989, he played "the mayor" in Lee's controversial and acclaimed *Do the Right Thing*. It was a role in which he presided not only over the street where the film's action took place but over the coming of age of a new generation of black filmmakers.

When he was past 70 and in the public eye more than ever for his stunning performance as the Good Reverend Dr. Purify in Lee's *Jungle Fever*, as well as for his regular spot as Burt Reynolds's best friend on television's *Evening Shade*, Davis reflected on his career, telling *American Visions*, "I was able to hang on to the gifts of my childhood longer than normal, to daydream, to think of things in the imagination, to play and be a play actor."

In 1992 Davis exercised his gifts as a novelist when he published a story for young adults called *Just Like Martin*. Centered on the activities of a small-town Alabama church congregation during the civil rights movement, Davis's first foray into fiction is "an attempt to recapture some sense of the black church as a political and moral base in the fight against racism," according to *Publishers Weekly* contributor Calvin Reid. Of his decision to move in this direction, Davis told Reid, "I can move between these different disciplines because I am essentially a storyteller, and the story I want to tell is about black people. Sometimes I sing the story, sometimes I dance it, sometimes I tell tall tales about it, but I always want to share my great satisfaction at being a black man at this time in history."

Fondly Remembered

On February 4, 2005, while working on the film *Retirement* in Miami, Florida, Ossie Davis died of natural causes at age 87. His family, friends, and fans gathered by the thousands at a Manhattan church to pay their respects to the acting legend. The funeral was attended by such well-known people as former U.S. President Bill Clinton, Pulitzer Prize winner Maya Angelou, film director Spike Lee, musician Wynton Marsalis, and actors Alan Alda and Burt Reynolds.

Many mourners noted Davis's commitment to his art and his unfailing support of his community. The work of Ossie Davis and his wife Ruby Dee consistently "explored and celebrated the lessons of black history in the United States, making the couple, over the decades, an inspiration and iconic presence in contemporary African American culture," as the Kennedy Center Web site noted. He was remembered as "a giant" and "a noble warrior," according to National Public Radio, and as an "American treasure," by the Actors' Equity Association, according to MSNBC. Harry Belafonte, a family friend for sixty years eulogized Davis, saying, as quoted in the *Houston Chronicle*: "It is hard to fathom that we will no longer be able to call on his wisdom, his humor, his loyalty and his moral strength to guide us in the choices that are yet to be made and the battles that are yet to be fought. But how fortunate we were to have him as long as we did."

Selected works

Books

With Ossie and Ruby: In This Life Together (memoir), William Morrow, 1998.
Just Like Martin (fiction), Simon & Schuster, 1992.

Films

Gone Are the Days, Trans Lux, 1963.
(With Arnold Perl; and director) *Cotton Comes to Harlem*, United Artists, 1970.
(And director) *Kongi's Harvest* (adapted from work by Wole Soyinka), Calpenny Films Nigeria Ltd., 1970.
Harry and Son, 1984.
School Daze, 1988.
Do the Right Thing, 1989.
Grumpy Old Men, 1993.
She Hate Me, 2004.

Radio

The Ossie Davis and Ruby Dee Story Hour, mid-1970s.

Plays

(And director) *Goldbrickers of 1944* (produced in Liberia), 1944.
Alice in Wonder (produced at Elks Community Theater, 1952; revised and produced as *The Big Deal* at New Playwrights Theater, New York City, 1953).
Purlie Victorious (produced at Cort Theatre, New York City), 1961.
Curtain Call, Mr. Aldridge, Sir (produced at University of California at Santa Barbara), 1968.
(With Philip Rose, Peter Udell, and Gary Geld) *Purlie* (produced at Broadway Theater, New York City), 1970.

Escape to Freedom: A Play About Young Frederick Douglass (produced at Town Hall, New York City), 1976.
Langston: A Play, Delacorte, 1982.

Television

The Emperor Jones, 1955.
The Outsider, 1967.
Today Is Ours, CBS-TV, 1974.
Roots: The Next Generation, 1979.
We'll Take Manhattan, 1990.
The Stand, 1994.
Miss Evers' Boys, 1997.
Finding Buck McHenry, 2000.

Other

Ossie Davis performed in over 100 plays, films, and radio programs from the 1940s until his death in 2005.

Sources

Books

Bogle, Donald, *Blacks in American Film and Television*, Garland, 1988.
Funke, Lewis, *The Curtain Rises—The Story of Ossie Davis*, Grosset & Dunlap, 1971.

Periodicals

American Visions, April/May 1992.
Daily News (New York), February 12, 2005.
Greensboro News and Record (North Carolina), August 17, 1989.
Guardian (London), February 8, 2005.
Houston Chronicle, February 14, 2005.
Jet, February 28, 2005.
Los Angeles Times, July 6, 1989.
Milwaukee Journal, June 9, 1991.
Newsday, March 24, 1987.
New York Post, February 13, 2005.
New York Times, June 30, 1989.
Palm Beach Post (Florida), May 10, 1988.
People, February 21, 2005.
Publishers Weekly, December 28, 1992.
Sarasota Herald Tribune, February 20, 2005.
Washington Times, February 14, 2005.

On-line

"Biography: Ossie Davis and Ruby Dee," *Indiana University,* http://newsinfo.iu.edu/news/page/normal/200.html (March 11, 2005).
"Biography: Ossie Davis and Ruby Dee," *Kennedy Center,* www.kennedy-center.org/calendar/index.cfm?fuseaction=showIndividual&entitY_id=12124&source_type=A (March 11, 2005).
"Morning Edition: Ossie Davis and Ruby Dee," *National Public Radio,* www.npr.org/templates/story/story.php?storyId=1119605 (March 11, 2005).
"Ossie Davis Found Dead in Miami Hotel Room," *MSNBC,* http://msnbc.msn.com/ID/6914059/ (March 11, 2005).
"Remembrances: Ossie Davis," *National Public Radio,* www.npr.org/templates/story/story.php?storyId=4486027 (March 11, 2005).

—Jordan Wankoff and Sara Pendergast

Ruby Dee

1924—

Actress, civil rights activist, writer

Actress and social activist Ruby Dee expressed her philosophy in *I Dream a World: Portraits of Black Women Who Changed America*: "You just try to do everything that comes up. Get up an hour earlier, stay up an hour later, make the time. Then you look back and say, 'Well, that was a neat piece of juggling there—school, marriage, babies, career.' The enthusiasms took me through the action, not the measuring of it or the reasonableness."

Dee's performing career has spanned more than 60 years and has included theater, radio, television, and movies. She and her husband, the late actor Ossie Davis, raised three children and were active in such organizations as the National Association for the Advancement of Colored People (NAACP), the Southern Christian Leadership Conference (SCLC), and the Congress of Racial Equality (CORE), as well as supporters of civil rights leaders such as Dr. Martin Luther King and Malcolm X.

Ruby Ann Wallace was born on October 27, 1924, in Cleveland, Ohio. Her parents, Marshall and Emma Wallace, moved the family to New York City in search of better job opportunities, ultimately settling in Harlem. Emma Wallace was determined not to let her children become victims of the ghetto that the area was quickly becoming. Dee and her siblings studied music and literature. In the evening, under the guidance of their school-teacher mother, they read aloud to each other from the poetry of Longfellow, Wordsworth, and Paul Laurence Dunbar. The influence of this education became apparent early in Dee's life, for as a teenager

she began submitting poetry to the *New York Amsterdam News*, a black weekly newspaper.

Her love of English and poetry motivated Dee to study the arts, especially the spoken arts. Her mother had been an elocutionist who, as a young girl, wanted to be in the theater. Fully realizing the value of a good education, Dee decided that the public schools of Harlem, where so many of the black girls were being "educated" to become domestics, were not for her. She underwent the rigorous academic testing required for admittance to Hunter High School, one of New York's first-rate schools that drew the brightest girls. The self-confidence and poise that Dee's mother had instilled in her helped Ruby adjust to her new environment, which was populated with white girls from more privileged backgrounds. A black music teacher, Miss Peace, provided encouragement to the young Ruby, telling her to go as far and as quickly as she could.

While in high school, Dee decided to pursue acting. In an interview with the *New York Times*, she related that this decision was made "one beautiful afternoon in high school when I read aloud from a play and my classmates applauded." After graduation she entered Hunter College. There Dee joined the American Negro Theater (ANT) and adopted the on-stage name Ruby Dee. The struggling theater had little money, so in addition to rehearsing their parts the troupe sold tickets door-to-door in Harlem and performed all the maintenance duties in the theater, located in a basement auditorium of the 135th Street Library. Dee found the work she did with the ANT to be a memorable part of her training. Other young actors who started at the

ANT and eventually became famous include Harry Belafonte, Earl Hyman, and Sidney Poitier.

While still at Hunter College, Dee took a class in radio training offered through the American Theater Wing. This training led to a part in the radio serial *Nora Drake*. When she graduated from Hunter College in 1945, Dee took a job at an export house as a French and Spanish translator. To earn extra income, she worked in a factory painting designs on buttons. Dee knew, however, that the theater was to be her destiny.

In 1946 Dee got her first Broadway role in *Jeb*, a drama about a returning black war hero. Ossie Davis, the actor in the title role, caught Dee's attention. After watching him do a scene in which he was tying a necktie, Dee experienced an awareness that she and Davis would share some type of connection. Critical reviews were good, but the play ran for only nine performances. Dee's intuition, however, proved to be true. She and Davis became close friends and worked

together in the road company production of *Anna Lucasta*. Later they played Evelyn and Stewart in Garson Kanin's *Smile of the World* and were married on December 9, 1948, during a break in rehearsals for that play. (Davis died in 2005.)

Dee's first movie was *Love in Syncopation*, which was released in 1946. In 1950 she appeared in *The Jackie Robinson Story* as the legendary baseball player's wife. Also in that year she appeared in *No Way Out*, the story of a black doctor—played by Sidney Poitier—who is accused of causing the death of his white patient. The film was revolutionary for its time because it was the first American film in which blacks and whites confronted each other in a realistic way.

Over the next decade, Dee appeared in several plays and movies in which she was cast as the consummate wife or girlfriend—patient, always understanding, all-forgiving. Such roles spurred at least one publication to refer to her as "the Negro June Allyson." A few parts helped Dee break free from this stereotyping. Of note is the role of the ebullient Lutiebelle Gussie Mae Jenkins in Davis's 1961 play *Purlie Victorious*. In this satire on black/white relationships, Davis plays the preacher Purlie who, with Lutiebelle's assistance, helps to outwit a white plantation owner. In 1963 this highly successful play was made into a movie titled *Gone Are the Days* and was later musicalized as *Purlie*.

Dee again was typecast as a long-suffering wife and daughter-in-law in the Broadway production of Lorraine Hansberry's *A Raisin in the Sun*. She recreated her role as Ruth Younger in 1963 film version of the play. Donald Bogle, in his book *Toms, Coons, Mulattoes, Mammies, and Bucks*, noted that prior to *A Raisin in the Sun*, Dee's roles made her appear to be "the typical woman born to be hurt" instead of a complete person. Bogle continued, "But in *A Raisin in the Sun*, Ruby Dee forged her inhibitions, her anemia, and her repressed and taut ache to convey beautifully the most searing kind of black torment."

The one role Dee feels put an end to her stereotyped image was that of Lena in the 1970 production of Athol Fugard's *Boesman and Lena*. Fugard, a white South African dramatist, portrays the dilemma of South Africa's mixed race people who are rejected by both blacks and whites. Lena wanders the South African wilderness and ekes out a living with her brutish husband Boesman, played by James Earl Jones. Dee told interviewer Patricia Bosworth in the *New York Times* that "Lena is the greatest role I've ever had." It was also her first theater role since 1966, and she was not sure she could do it. Her husband encouraged her, saying that the part could have been written for her even though Fugard had originally written the role of Lena with a white actress in mind.

Dee immediately felt a bond with Lena. "I relate to her particular reality," she told Bosworth, "because it is mine and every black woman's. I can understand the extent of her poverty and her filth and absolute subjugation.... On one level [Boesman and Lena] represent the universal struggle of black against white, man against woman. But they are also victims of something that is permeating an entire culture."

Dee finally realized that she was being offered a great part at a time when few, if any, good parts were written for black actresses. In the Bosworth interview she revealed, "I have always been reticent about expressing myself totally in a role. But with Lena I am suddenly, gloriously free. I can't explain how this frail, tattered little character took me over and burrowed so deep inside me that my voice changed and I began to move differently.... [I am as] alive with her as I've never been on stage." Critics took note of Dee's performance. Clive Barnes wrote in his *New York Times* review of the play: "Ruby Dee as Lena is giving the finest performance I have ever seen.... Never for a moment do you think she is acting.... You have no sense of someone portraying a role.... her manner, her entire being have a quality of wholeness that is rarely encountered in the theater."

Beginning in the early sixties, Dee made numerous appearances on television including roles in the *Play of the Week* and in such television series as *The Fugitive, The Defenders, The Great Adventure*, and *The Nurses*. On *Peyton Place*, where in 1968-69 she played Alma Miles, the wife of a neurosurgeon, she was the first black actress to be featured on the widely-watched nighttime serial. Her performance in an episode of the series *East Side, West Side* earned her an Emmy nomination. In 1991 Dee's performance in *Decoration Day* won her an Emmy.

Dee and Davis collaborated on several projects designed to promote black heritage in general and other black artists in particular. In 1974 they produced *The Ruby Dee/Ossie Davis Story Hour*, which appeared on more than 60 stations on the National Black Network. In conjunction with the Public Broadcasting System (PBS), they produced the series *With Ossie and Ruby* in 1981. It was work that Dee found particularly satisfying because she got to travel around the country talking to authors and others who could put the black experience in perspective. She believes that the series made black people look at themselves outside of the problems of racism.

Issues of equality and civil rights have long been a concern of Dee's. Her activism can be traced back to when she was 11 years old, and her music teacher lost her job when funds for the Federal Music Program were cut. The teacher, terrified that she could not find another job in the Depression-ridden country, committed suicide. At a mass meeting following the teacher's death, Adam Clayton Powell was the principal speaker, and Dee was chosen to speak in favor of restoring the music program. Several years would pass before Dee became actively involved in civil rights.

The year was 1953, and the cause was Julius and Ethel Rosenberg. The Rosenbergs had been convicted of wartime sabotage against the United States and were scheduled to be executed. Dee's vocal protest of the planned executions was expressed in several interviews with the press. Some accused her of being exploited by the Communists; others were convinced she was a card-carrying member of the party. Dee's notoriety for denouncing the U.S. government's decision to execute the Jewish Rosenbergs eventually parlayed itself into her first non-black part in a play. In *The World of Sholem Aleichem*, Dee played the Defending Angel. This experience helped Dee realize that racism and discrimination were not the exclusive provinces of black people—other races and cultures experienced it also. Dee began to understand how art and life blended together and how all human cultures are interrelated. She was inspired by these events to make a firm commitment to social activism.

Future events solidified this commitment. In September 1963, a bomb was thrown into a Birmingham, Alabama, church. The bomb killed four young black girls as they sat in their Sunday school class. People throughout the country were outraged by this senseless murder. Dee and Davis, along with other artists, formed the Association of Artists for Freedom. The group launched a successful boycott against extravagant Christmas spending and urged people to donate the money to various civil rights groups. Dee and Davis were involved in and supported several other civil rights protests and causes, including Martin Luther King's March on Washington. In 1970 the National Urban League honored them with the Frederick Douglas Award, a medallion presented each year for distinguished leadership toward equal opportunity.

By establishing the Ruby Dee Scholarship in Dramatic Art, Dee put into action her commitment to help others. The scholarship is awarded to talented young black women who want to become established in the acting profession. Both she and Davis donated money and countless hours of time to causes in which they believe. They founded the Institute of New Cinema Artists as a way to train chosen young people for film and television jobs. Their Recording Industry Training Program helps develop jobs for disadvantaged youths interested in the music industry.

Dee has also used her talent to make recordings for the blind and to narrate videocassettes that address issues of race relations. She has reinterpreted West African folktales for children and published them as *Two Ways to Count to Ten* and *Tower to Heaven*. Dee returned to poetry, her early love, to edit *Glowchild and Other Poems* and to collect her poems and short stories in a volume titled *My One Good Nerve*.

Dee's remarkable acting talent has endured over the years. She continued to appear in theater, movies, and television into the 2000s. In 1990 Dee appeared in the television movie *The Court Martial of Jackie Robinson*, playing Robinson's mother Mallie. Writing in *New York*, John Leonard laments that the movie gives Dee too little to do but commends her for "deliver[ing] one fine line" as she reprimands her son, who is about to sabotage his courtship with Rachel. With fervor Dee, in the role of Mallie, states: "I didn't raise my boys to have sharecropper minds!" Leonard attributes the conviction with which Dee played her part to the fact that she played the role of Rachel herself 40 years earlier.

Director Spike Lee cast Dee in the role of Mother Sister—and Davis in the role of Da Mayor—for his controversial 1989 film *Do the Right Thing*. As Mother Sister, Dee plays a widow who lives in a brownstone and spends her time watching the neighborhood through a ground-floor window. In *New Republic* Stanley Kauffmann described Dee as "that fine actress with an unfulfilled career in white America" and described her role in Lee's movie "as a sort of neighborhood Delphic oracle." Davis plays a beer-drinking street philosopher who is in love with Mother Sister.

As racial tension rises in the neighborhood, Mother Sister and Da Mayor are unable to do anything to diffuse it. According to Terrence Rafferty in the *New Yorker*, these two characters "stand for the older generation, whose cynical, 'realistic' attitude toward living in a white society may have kept them from finding ways out of their poverty but may also have helped keep them alive." Lee also cast the pair as the parents of the main character in *Jungle Fever*.

Though she was in her early 80s, Dee played the role of Nanny in the 2005 television production of author Zora Neale Hurston's classic work *Their Eyes Were Watching God*, to great critical acclaim. She was also scheduled to appear in several other movies.

In 1988 *Ebony* featured Dee and Davis as one of "Three Great Love Stories." Explaining the success of their long marriage, Dee told *Ebony*: "The ratio of the good times to the bad times is better than 50-50, and that helps a lot.... We shared a great deal in common; we didn't have any distractions as to where we stood in society. We were black activists. We had a common understanding." Davis added, "We believe in honesty. We believe in simplicity.... We believe in love. We believe in the family. We believe in black history, and we believe heavily in *involvement*."

Selected works

Films

Love in Syncopation, 1946.
The Jackie Robinson Story, 1950.
No Way Out, 1950.
Go, Man, Go!, 1954.
Take a Giant Step, 1959.
Virgin Island, 1960.
A Raisin in the Sun, 1961.
Gone Are the Days, 1963.
The Incident, 1967.

Black Girl, 1972.
Do the Right Thing, 1989.
Jungle Fever, 1991.
A Simple Wish, 1997.
Baby Geniuses, 1999.
Baby of the Family, 2002.

Plays

Jeb, 1946.
Anna Lucasta, 1946.
The World of Sholom Aleichem, 1953.
A Raisin in the Sun, 1959.
Purlie Victorious, 1961.
Boesman and Lena, 1970.
Checkmates, 1988.
(And author) *My One Good Nerve*, 1999.

Television

East Side, West Side, 1963.
The Nurses, 1963.
Peyton Place, 1968-69.
Wedding Band, 1974.
(Co-producer) *The Ruby Dee/Ossie Davis Story Hour*, 1974.
Roots: The Next Generations, 1979.
I Know Why The Caged Bird Sings, 1979.
(And co-producer) *With Ossie and Ruby*, 1981.
Long Day's Journey Into Night, 1983.
The Court Martial of Jackie Robinson, 1990.
Decoration Day, 1991.
The Stand, 1994.
Mr. and Mrs. Loving, 1996.
Promised Land, 1998.
Finding Buck McHenry, 2000.
Their Eyes Were Watching God, 2005.

Writings

(With Jules Dassin and Julian Mayfield) *Uptight* (screenplay; adapted from Liam O'Flaherty's novel *The Informer*), Paramount, 1968.
(Editor) *Glowchild and Other Poems*, Third Press, 1972.
Twin-Bit Gardens (musical play; also known as *Take It From the Top*), produced Off-Broadway at New Federal Theater, 1979.
My One Good Nerve (poetry and short stories), Third World Press, 1986.
(Reteller) *Two Ways to Count to Ten* (juvenile), Holt, 1988.
"Zora Is My Name" (screenplay), *American Playhouse*, PBS, 1990.
(Reteller) *Tower to Heaven* (juvenile), Holt, 1991.
(With Ossie Davis) *With Ossie and Ruby: In This Life Together* (memoir), W. Morrow, 1998.
My One Good Nerve (memoir), J. Wiley and Sons, 1999.

Sources

Books

Black Women in America, Carlson, 1993.

Bogle, Donald, *Blacks in American Film and Television*, Garland, 1988.

Bogle, Donald, *Toms, Coons, Mulattoes, Mammies, and Bucks*, Viking, 1973.

Directory of Blacks in the Performing Arts, Scarecrow Press, 1990.

Fax, Elton C., *Contemporary Black Leaders*, Dodd, 1970.

Lanker, Brian, *I Dream a World: Portraits of Black Women Who Changed America*, Stewart, Tabori, Chang, 1989.

Salley, Columbus, editor, *The Black 100*, Citadel Press, 1993.

Periodicals

Commonweal, January 13, 1989, p. 21; July 14, 1989, p. 403.

Cosmopolitan, August 1991, p. 28.

Ebony, February 1988, p. 152.

Essence, May 1987, p. 28.

Jet, December 5, 1988, p. 55; March 26, 2001.

Library Journal, October 1, 1991, p. 153; January 1992, p. 198.

Nation, July 17, 1989, p. 98.

National Review, August 4, 1989, p. 45.

New Republic, July 3, 1989, p. 24.

Newsweek, July 3, 1989, p. 64.

New York, August 22, 1988, p. 142; October 22, 1990, p. 136; November 26, 1990, p. 165.

New Yorker, July 24, 1989, p. 78.

New York Times, June 23, 1970; July 12, 1970.

People, July 3, 1989, p. 13; March 14, 2005.

Publishers Weekly, June 10, 1988, p. 80; May 17, 1991, p. 63.

School Library Journal, October 1990, p. 76; July 1991, p. 67; March 1992, p. 196.

Washington Post, December 5, 2004.

—Debra G. Harroun and Tom Pendergast

Thomas Covington Dent

1932-1998

Writer, civil rights activist

Thomas Covington Dent, usually known as Tom Dent, was an author, a playwright, a poet, an essayist, a civil rights activist, and an oral historian. He was a leading member of a group of black writers who during the 1950s merged artistic expression with explorations of black identity. Combining the quest for self-identity and cultural identity with a political agenda that challenged racism and the status quo, these writers formed literary and performance-based organizations that developed into the Black Arts Movement. Dent, in all his many endeavors, always projected a forceful image of the black experience.

Dent was born on March 20, 1932 in New Orleans, Louisiana, the oldest of three sons born to Dr. Albert Walter and Ernestine Jessie (Covington) Dent. Dent's family was prominent and socially aware; his father was the president of historically black Dillard University and his mother was a teacher and a concert pianist. His grandfather, Dr. Jesse Covington, was a leader in the Booker T. Washington National Negro Business League and was instrumental in the founding of Riverside General Hospital, the first medical center for blacks in Houston, Texas. His grandmother, Belle Covington, was prominent in early interracial relations and a founding member of the Blue Triangle YWCA. Dent was educated at both public and private schools and graduated from Gilbert Academy, a black college preparatory school in New Orleans, in 1947.

After graduating from high school, Dent enrolled in Morehouse College in Atlanta, Georgia, and earned a bachelor's degree in political science in 1952. During his senior year at Morehouse, Dent served as the editor-in-chief of the school's newspaper, the *Tiger Maroon*. Dent's editorials, which were often socially reflective and sometimes humorous, were his first foray into writing. Although his self-assured embrace of integration—he had been groomed from his youth to become a prominent member of society—would later turn dramatically toward concerns for racial integrity, his sharp wit remained a common character of his writing throughout his lifetime. During his summers off from school, Dent spent time with his maternal grandparents in Houston and worked as a cub reporter for the *Houston Informer*, the oldest continuously published black newspaper in Texas.

From Academia to Activism

In 1952 Dent began graduate studies in international relations at Syracuse University's Maxwell School of Citizenship. Over the next four years Dent became more and more involved in the developing civil rights movement. In 1956 he abandoned his studies before he completed his doctoral degree. From 1957 to 1959 he served in the U.S. Army. On his discharge, he moved to New York, where he became politically and culturally active in the fledgling Black Arts Movement.

From 1959 to 1960 Dent worked as a reporter for the black political newspaper *New York Age*, and then from 1960 to 1961 he served as a social worker for the New York Welfare Department. In 1961 he took a job as a press attaché and public information director of the National Association for the Advancement of Colored People (NAACP), where he assisted Thurgood

At a Glance . . .

Born on March 20, 1932, in New Orleans, LA; died on June 6, 1998, in New Orleans, LA; son of Jessie Covington Dent and Albert Dent; married Roberta Yancy (divorced). *Education:* Morehouse College, Atlanta, BA, 1952; attended Syracuse University, 1952-58; Goddard College, Vermont, MA, 1974. *Military service:* U.S. Army, 1957-59.

Career: *Houston Informer*, cub reporter, 1950-52; *New York Age*, reporter, 1959-60; *On Guard for Freedom* (political newspaper), writer, 1960; New York Welfare Department, social worker, 1960-61; NAACP, New York, press attaché and public information director, 1961-63; *Umbra Magazine*, co-founder and writer, 1962-63; Free Southern Theater, New Orleans, LA, associate director, 1966-70; Mary Holmes College, instructor, 1968-70; *Nkombo* (literary journal), co-editor, 1968-74; Total Community Action, New Orleans, LA, public relations officer, 1971-73; Southern Black Cultural Alliance, co-founder, 1971; Congo Square Writers Union, New Orleans, LA, founder, 1974; *Callaloo* (literary journal), co-founder, 1976; University of New Orleans, instructor, 1979-81; New Orleans Jazz and Heritage Foundation, executive director, 1987-90; Tulane University, guest instructor, 1994.

Selected Memberships: African Literature Association; Oral History Association; Langston Hughes Society; New Orleans Jazz and Heritage Foundation.

Selected Awards: Whitney Young Fellow, 1973-74.

Marshall. In 1960 Dent joined other black writers, including LeRoi Jones and Harold Cruse, in forming On Guard for Freedom, a black nationalist literary organization that became known for staging a highly publicized protest at the United Nations in response to the U.S. Bay of Pigs invasion of Cuba. The organization also produced the publication *On Guard for Freedom*, to which Dent contributed as a writer.

In 1962 Dent helped found the influential Umbra Writers' Workshop, a collective of writers, activists, and artisans from New York's lower east side. The workshop, which integrated the arts and the distinct identity of black America, included such writers as David Henderson, Ishmael Reed, Joe Johnson, Norman Pritchard,

Askia M. Touré, Calvin Herton, and Archie Shepp. Umbra focused primarily on poetry and performance-based arts, and Dent worked with the organization's publication, *Umbra Magazine*, from 1962 to 1963. Umbra disbanded in 1964, mostly over the tensions caused by trying to balance the group's identity as both a literary and activist organization.

Worked with Free Southern Theater

In 1965 Dent returned to New Orleans for a short visit and he never left. He became involved with the black activist Free Southern Theater (FST), a community theater project, which had formed the previous year, and in 1966 he became the associate director, a position he held until 1970. The FST staged the work of black playwrights throughout the South, including Dent's plays *Negro Study No. 34A, Riot Duty, Snapshot,* and *Features and Stuff.* Dent also contributed to FST's literary journal *Nkombo* and served as the co-editor from 1968 to 1974. Like On Guard and Umbra, FST had a blended purpose of advancing both cultural and artistic agendas and provided an outlet for black artists who challenged the status quo and combated racism. Out of FST grew BLKARTSOUTH, a literary workshop co-founded by Dent and Kalamu ya Salaam. Both BLKARTSOUTH and the Southern Black Cultural Alliance, which Dent helped form in 1971, were instrumental in development black theater, especially in the South.

From 1968 to 1970 Dent also taught classes at Mary Holmes College in West Point, Mississippi. In 1969 he joined with Gilbert Moses and Richard Schechner to edit *The Free Southern Theater by the Free Southern Theater.* The book, which included letters, plays, poems, and essays, documented the role and history of the radical black theater. From 1971 to 1973 Dent worked as a public relations officer for the New Orleans-based Total Community Action.

In 1974 Dent was awarded a Whitney Young Fellowship and he earned a master's degree Goddard College in Vermont. In that same year he founded the Congo Square Writer's Union in New Orleans and edited the organization's literary journal, *The Black River Journal.* He also contributed to the journal. In 1976 Dent published his first collection of poetry, *Magnolia Street,* and his play, *Ritual Murder,* which became a classic of the Southern black theater, was first staged at the Ethiopian Theater in New Orleans. In the same year he joined with Jerry Ward and Charles Rowell to found the literary journal *Callaloo.* In 1982 he published his second poetry collection, *Blue Lights and River Songs.*

Oral Historian

Although Dent was himself a poet, playwright, and author, he was even more influential as an advocate for civil rights and the black arts, and he spent much of his time between 1978 and 1985 conducting oral histories of Mississippi civil rights workers. He also conducted an oral history of New Orleans musicians. (The tape collections are housed at the Amistad Research Center in New Orleans). He also taught classes at the University of New Orleans from 1979 to 1981 and was a guest lecturer at Tulane University in 1994. Between 1984 and 1986 he collaborated with Andrew Young on Young's autobiography, *An Easy Burden*, and from 1987 to 1990 he served as the executive director of the New Orleans Jazz and Heritage Foundation.

After spending much of 1991 traveling through the South, visiting locations of important civil rights events in North and South Carolina, Florida, Georgia, Alabama, and Mississippi, in 1997 Dent published *Southern Journey: A Return to the Civil Rights Movement*, which documents his findings of how the civil rights movement is remembered and what impact it had on the Southern mindset. Prior to his death Dent was working on a collection of essays addressing the civil rights movement in New Orleans and a collection of personal essays exploring the quest for self-identity and racial identity. He died in Charity Hospital in New Orleans on June 6, 1998, from complications after a heart attack. He was 67 years old.

Selected writings

Nonfiction

(Editor, with Richard Schechner and Gilbert Moses) *The Free Southern Theater, by the Free Southern Theater*, Bobb-Merrill, 1969.
Southern Journey: A Return to the Civil Rights Movement, W. Morrow, 1997.

Plays

Negro Study No. 34A, Free Southern Theater, New Orleans, 1969.
Riot Duty, Free Southern Theater, New Orleans, 1969.
Snapshot, Free Southern Theater, New Orleans, 1970.

Feathers and Stuff, Free Southern Theater, New Orleans, 1970.
Ritual Murder, Ethiopian Theater, New Orleans, 1976.

Poetry

Magnolia Street, privately printed, 1979; reprinted, 1987.
Blue Lights and River Songs: Poems, Lotus Press, 1982.

Sources

Books

Dictionary of Literary Biography, Volume 38: Afro-American Writers After 1955: Dramatists and Prose Writers, Gale Group, 1985.

Periodicals

The Mississippi Quarterly, Spring 1999, p. 213.
Obsidian II, Winter 1989, pp. 100-102.

On-line

"Reporters and Writers: Tom Dent," *Reporting Civil Rights*, www.reportingcivilrights.org/authors/bio.jsp?authorId=12 (January 10, 2005).
"Thomas C. Dent," *Biography Resource Center*, www.galenet.com/servlet/BioRC (February 8, 2005).
"Tom Covington Dent," *Chickenbones: A Journal*, www.nathanielturner.com/tomdentbio.htm (January 10, 2005).
"Tom Dent: A New Orleans Writer," *The Black Collegian Online*, http://www.black-collegian.com/african/dent9.shtml (January 10, 2005).
Ward, Jerry W., Jr., "The Art of Tom Dent: Early Evidence." *Chickenbones: A Journal*, www.nathanielturner.com/artoftomdent.htm (January 10, 2005).

—Kari Bethel

Donald Faison

1974—

Actor

Faison, Donald, photograph. Amanda Edwards/Getty Images.

Though his role as a surgical intern on the NBC hit series *Scrubs* brought him major fame, Donald Faison was no stranger to the limelight. He had acted since he was a child, steadily progressing from school plays to television commercials to major motion pictures. By 2005, in addition to *Scrubs,* he had several films in the works with no rest in sight. The busy schedule suited him fine. "I enjoy working. I don't do it just because it's my job. I do it also because of love," he told *E! Online*.

Born into a Family of Actors

Donald Adeosun Faison was born on June 22, 1974, in New York City and was immersed in acting from the time he was five. His parents, Shirley and Donald, were members of the National Black Theatre in Harlem and one of Faison's earliest memories is of watching his mother direct rehearsals in the empty theater. She went on to influence his career decision. "My biggest hero has always been my mother. She has done a lot for me, and she supported me when I had nothing," he told *E! Online*. Faison attended the Children's School for the Development of Intuitive and God-Conscious Art, a school created by the National Black Theatre. At the

age of six he co-wrote and acted in a play called *When the Lion Roars*. He also made home movies with his two younger brothers Dade and Olamide.

Faison's first taste of professional acting was in a television commercial for Oatmeal Raisin Crisp. He went on to a recurring role on *Sesame Street* and appeared on specials with 1980s celebrities like Marlo Thomas and Bobby McFerrin. Faison studied acting at Manhattan's Professional Children's School and attended La Guardia High School for Music, Art, and the Performing Arts. "I remember I wasn't popular in high school until my junior year, and that's because I got on the yearbook committee and put my face on every page of the yearbook," Faison told *AP Online*. After graduating in 1992 his popularity really started to rise.

Faison made his major film debut in *Juice* opposite rapper Tupac Shakur in 1992. From then on he appeared in a steady stream of films including 1993's *Sugar Hill* with Wesley Snipes and 1995's *Waiting to Exhale* with Angela Bassett. The film that made Faison a famous face, however, was 1995's *Clueless*. The film about rich teens went on to become a cult classic and

At a Glance . . .

Born Donald Adeosun Faison on June 22, 1974, in New York, NY; married Lisa Askey, 2001; children: Sean, Kaya, Dade, Kobe.

Career: Actor, 1992–.

Awards: Audelco Rising Star Award.

Addresses: *Agent*—Gold, Marshak, Liedtke and Associates, 3500 West Olive Ave., Suite 1400, Burbank, CA 91505. *Publicist*—PMK/HBH, 8500 Wilshire Blvd., Suite 700, Beverly Hills, CA, 90211.

inspired a television series of the same name. From 1996 to 1999 Faison reprised his role as Murray in the series.

Found Fame and Family

Faison explained the changes fame brought him in an interview with *AP Online*. "It was kind of weird. One day nobody knew who I was, and I would go out, if I went to a club, I'd ask the girls to dance and they would say 'No.' And then two years later, I'd see the same girls at a different club, and all of a sudden, they're like, 'Hey, remember me?' And it's like, 'Oh yeah, you're the girl that dissed me!'" The success of both the film and the TV show also brought Faison money, but he was too young to know what to do with it. "I spent money on stupid things," he told *People Weekly*. "A motorcycle, a big-screen TV." It did not take long before he was broke.

Fortunately, about that time Faison met nursing student Lisa Askey at a party. "She says she didn't know who I was but I don't believe her and she says she thought I was ugly," Faison told *The News Letter*. Nonetheless, Lisa turned over her phone number and the two soon began to date. Four years later, in 2001, they were married. Faison has often credited Lisa with grounding him. "I was lazy and she straightened me out," he told *People Weekly*. The couple had twin girls, Kaya and Dade, followed by a son, Kobe. Faison had also fathered a son, Sean, with a childhood friend in New York several years earlier. When asked by *In Style* what he considered his biggest success Faison responded, "My four children.... I genuinely love taking care of them."

Faison continued to have success in his acting career as well. From 1996 to 1998 he appeared on the hit television shows *New York Undercover* and *Sabrina, the Teenage Witch*. From 1998 to 1999 he jumped

back to the big screen with roles in several forgettable flicks. Finally in 2000 he landed a major role in the Denzel Washington vehicle, *Remember the Titans*. After having found fame in comedic roles, Faison showed his dramatic skills in this film about integration on a southern football team. It also toughened him up. "My big mouth got me into trouble," he told *Maxim Online*. "I was telling everybody I was doing my own stunts. Then I got hit, real hard. From then on, I wanted to give up all my stunts to my stunt double. But, since I already made [a] point of telling everyone about me doing my own stunts, I still had to do them."

Became a Star in Scrubs

As Faison's film career began to wane—he had small roles in several straight-to-video films, including *Josie and the Pussycats*—his small screen career was taking off. In 2000 he landed a recurring role on the hit series *Felicity*. Then in 2001 Faison became a permanent member of *Scrubs,* a comedy about medical interns. Of the two popular shows, Faison told *E! Online*, "I loved working on both. But in *Scrubs*, I'm part of the cast. In *Felicity*, I was only in little parts, so I didn't feel like a total cast member. Even though I was there two years, I wasn't a regular. On *Scrubs*, I love to come to work every day, because I feel like part of the cast." *Scrubs* became a critical and popular success and made Faison a star. He began to be featured in magazines and on celebrity gossip shows. He was also nominated for a People's Choice Award, an Image Award, and a Teen Choice Award. Faison's character, cocky surgical intern Dr. Chris Turk, became one of the show's most popular characters. "I love playing him, he's a joy to play," Faison told *The News Letter*. "I've never wanted to be a doctor so it's kind of cool to play someone who is one." Fame also brought its downside. "Everyone wants a piece of you," he told *The News Letter*. "They point at you and say, 'I know you. Hey honey look it's that guy from *Scrubs*.' And you might just be sitting in a restaurant when they do that. You can never go anywhere."

In 2002 Faison was back on the big screen playing a struggling actor working as a limo driver in the comedy *Big Fat Liar*. He told the *New York Post* that he enjoyed playing the low guy on the social rung. "I love to portray that side of the coin. I worked at a Hollywood agent's office for a year as an assistant. I had to go get the coffee, pull the files...." He also landed a co-starring role with Brittany Murphy in *Uptown Girls* in 2003. By 2005 he had three more films slated for release, *Vegas Baby*, *Venus & Vegas*, and *All American Game*. He made the films in his time off from *Scrubs*, which shot on a six-month schedule. "I love doing both [TV and film]" Faison told *YM*. "I love the fact that I'm able to do both. I'm very lucky that I have that opportunity."

Faison planned to see *Scrubs* through to the end of its run. "I'm going to be in it until the wheels fall off, it's got the potential to go on and make history," he told

The News Letter. However, he was also looking forward to bigger parts in film, including a leading role. "I've already been offered movies but I'm waiting for the right one," he continued. "I don't want people to say Donald was great in that but the movie sucked. I want to care about the movies I'm in." He also held bigger ambitions. "I want to direct and produce and get behind the camera," he told the *Hollywood Reporter.* "That's where the money is, but not right yet, I still have a lot of acting I want to do."

Selected works

Films

Juice, 1992.
Sugar Hill, 1993.
Clueless, 1995.
Waiting to Exhale, 1995.
Remember the Titans, 2000.
Josie and the Pussycats, 2001.
Big Fat Liar, 2002.
Uptown Girls, 2003.

Television

Clueless, 1996-99.
Felicity, 1999-2001.
Scrubs, 2001–.

Sources

Periodicals

AP Online, June 9, 1999.
Hollywood Reporter, August 11, 2003.
In Style, September 2003.
The News Letter (Belfast, Northern Ireland), June 11, 2003.
New York Post, February 17, 2002.
People Weekly, June 17, 2002.

On-line

"Donald Faison Heads *Uptown*," *YM*, www.ym.com/stars/inthespotlight/aug1203.jsp (December 30, 2004).
"From Clueless to Fearless: *Remember the Titans* Star Donald Faison Talks Football and Movies," *Maxim Online*, www.maximonline.com/sports/articles/article_3691.html (December 30, 2004).
"*Scrubs'* Delicious Docs Open Wide," *E! Online: Watch with Wanda,* www.eonline.com/Gossip/Wanda/Trans/Scrubs/ (December 30, 2004).

—Candace LaBalle

Antonio Fargas

1946(?)—

Actor

The career of actor Antonio Fargas has lasted over 40 years and has encompassed film, television, and live theater. He is most widely recognized, however, for a single role: that of Huggy Bear on the 1970s television series *Starsky and Hutch*. That single role brought Fargas into millions of living rooms around the United States and the world. Decades after the show's run ended in 1979, the image he created was strong enough to make him into a cult hero among artists in the hip-hop genre—which didn't even exist at the time the show aired. Unlike other actors strongly identified with a single role, however, Fargas succeeded in branching out into new endeavors, gaining both steady work and, on occasion, critical acclaim.

Fargas, Antonio, photograph. Dave Hogan/Getty Images.

Antonio Fargas was born in New York City, to a Puerto Rican father and a Trinidadian mother, probably on August 14, 1946 (dates from 1943 to 1947 appear in various sources). He and his ten siblings grew up in a housing project on Manhattan's Lower West Side. Fargas's father was a garbage man who later worked in public relations, and his mother, Fargas told *Boston Herald* reporter Paul Sullivan, "was a great domestic engineer.... There was always bread on the table, not

in abundance, but we always had what we needed."

When Fargas was a sophomore in high school in 1961, he noticed a story in New York's *Amsterdam News* saying that auditions were being held for an independent film called *Cool World*. He got the part. Around the same time, Fargas was a member of a youth group called Harlem Youth Opportunities Limited that offered theater programs to aspiring actors. After receiving instruction from actor Robert Hooks in Hooks's apartment, which wasn't far from that of Fargas's family, he got a part in an off-Broadway stage production called *The Toilet* in 1963.

Early in his career, Fargas was known primarily as a stage actor. He made the first of what would become a lifetime's worth of trips to England in 1965 to appear in the play *The Amen Corner,* and he won positive reviews back in New York two years later when he appeared as Scipio in the original Broadway production of *The Great White Hope,* a play about the life of boxer Jack Johnson. Just 20 years old, Fargas convincingly played the part of a 90-year-old witch doctor. Fargas also made notable appearances in a 1968 New

At a Glance . . .

Born April 14, 1946 (some sources give other dates) in New York, NY; one of 11 children; son of Manuel and Mildred (maiden name Bailey) Fargas; married twice; two children: Matthew and Justin (from second marriage).

Career: Actor, 1960s–. Founder, Granada Entertainment (production company).

Memberships: Langston Hughes Center for the Arts, Rhode Island, board of directors; Mount Vernon Open Case Theatre, chairman of the board; Progressive Symphony's Academy of the Arts, honorary board chair.

Address: *Agent*—J. Cast Productions, 2550 Greenvalley Rd., Los Angeles, CA 90046. *Web*—www.antonio-fargas.net.

York Shakespeare Festival production of *Romeo and Juliet* and in the 1969 play *Ceremonies in Dark Old Men.*

Dividing his time between New York and Los Angeles, Fargas began to break into movies. He had parts in some of the popular black-oriented films of the early 1970s, like *Shaft* (1971), *Cleopatra Jones* (1973), and *Foxy Brown* (1974). In 1974 he also played Quickfellow in *Conrack,* a film made from author Pat Conroy's autobiographical novel about his experiences teaching in an African-American community on one of South Carolina's coastal islands. Fargas also garnered roles in episodes of such hit television series as *The Bill Cosby Show, Police Story, Kojak,* and *Sanford and Son.*

Fargas had appeared in the 1972 film *Across 110th Street,* directed by Barry Shear, and when Shear was signed to direct the pilot episode of the ABC network's *Starsky and Hutch* in 1975, he cast Fargas in the role of Huggy Bear. The role wasn't initially intended to be an ongoing part of the show, but producers noticed the chemistry that quickly evolved among Fargas and stars David Soul and Paul Michael Glaser. Fargas ended up remaining with the cast through the entire run of *Starsky and Hutch,* which left primetime airwaves in 1979 but lived on for years in syndication.

Huggy Bear was a bar owner and streetwise police informant who directed tips to police officers Starsky and Hutch. Dressed to the nines in a leather trench coat that was widely imitated during the run of the series, he was often surrounded by beautiful women; his status as a pimp was suggested but never directly stated. Huggy Bear was charismatic, fashionable, a bit lovable, and unfailingly entertaining. Such traits anticipated the rise of rap music's "gangsta" variant, and thus it was no surprise that Fargas was later cast in films such as the Wayans Brothers' *I'm Gonna Git You Sucka* (1988), even if he took some criticism from activists of the 1970s for perpetuating stereotypes of blacks in the entertainment industry. Fargas was matter-of-fact about his role, telling Mark Grossi of the *Providence Journal* that "I was a character actor and it was a typical role for a black actor at the time. It was good for me because it helped my career." The role of Huggy Bear was played by rapper Snoop Dogg in a 2004 film based on the series.

The end of *Starsky and Hutch* barely slowed Fargas's career. He returned to the stage for a time in the 1980s, explaining to the *Providence Journal* that "I hadn't been on stage for a long time. Your acting muscles atrophy when you don't use them." He had the lead role in a 1985 play called *Toussaint, Angel Warrior of Haiti,* which traced the life of the 19th-century Haitian independence leader Toussaint L'Ouverture. That year he also appeared in a New York Shakespeare Festival production of Shakespeare's *Measure for Measure,* and in 1986 he had a role in a Philadelphia production of *The Amen Corner,* the play that had taken him to England as a teenager.

Fargas continued to act in films, and in the 1990s he kept up a steady schedule of television guest star appearances in such series as *The Fresh Prince of Bel-Air, Martin, Living Single,* and *The Steve Harvey Show.* Married and divorced twice, he moved in with his partner, real estate executive Sandi Reed, in the late 1980s, raising her two children and Fargas's two from a previous marriage. One son, Justin Fargas, became a football star with the Oakland Raiders of the National Football League. The early 1990s offered real challenges for Fargas. He conquered alcohol and tobacco addictions. The 1994 earthquake centered north of Los Angeles trapped he and his wife in different parts of their Northridge, California, home, with each thinking the other had been killed, but Fargas broke down a door and they were reunited.

Traveling to England as often as four times a year, Fargas had the chance to test his survival skills once again in 2002 as a member of the cast of the British reality television show *I'm a Celebrity, Get Me Out of Here!* He also toured in a stage version of the film *The Blues Brothers* that had been rewritten to include a Huggy Bear role, and he teamed with David Soul in a serious play called *The Dead Monkey.* His theatrical career rolled on in the U.S. as well as he starred in 2003 in a St. Louis production of the acclaimed *The Gospel at Colonus,* an African-American adaptation of a drama by ancient Greek author Sophocles. And Huggy Bear remained a household name after three decades.

Selected works

Films

The Cool World, 1963.
Shaft, 1971.
Across 110th Street, 1972.
Cleopatra Jones, 1973.
Foxy Brown, 1974.
Conrack, 1974.
I'm Gonna Git You Sucka, 1988.
The Celluloid Closet (documentary), 1995.

Plays

The Toilet, 1963.
The Amen Corner, 1965.
The Great White Hope, 1967.
Romeo and Juliet, 1968.
Ceremonies in Dark Old Men, 1969.
Measure for Measure, 1985.
Toussaint, Angel Warrior of Haiti, 1985.
The Amen Corner, 1986.
The Dead Monkey, 1998.
The Blues Brothers, 2000-02.
The Gospel at Colonus, 2003.

Television

Starsky and Hutch, 1975-79.
I'm a Celebrity, Get Me Out of Here!, 2004.
Numerous guest television appearances, late 1980s and 1990s.

Sources

Books

Contemporary Theatre, Film and Television, Vol. 33, Gale, 2001.

Periodicals

Boston Herald, July 13, 1998, p. 16.
Chicago Sun-Times, April 4, 2001, p. 62.
Daily Mirror (London, England), December 2, 2004, p. 8.
Houston Chronicle, March 22, 2004, p. 12.
Independent (London, England), September 12, 1998, p. 60.
Providence Journal, October 11, 1985, p. D1.
Seattle Post-Intelligencer, December 30, 2002, p. D12.
St. Louis Post-Dispatch, September 14, 2003, p. F4.
USA Today, November 4, 1997, p. C1.
Voice (London, England), July 2, 1996, p. 29; March 29, 1999, p. 41.

On-line

"Antonio Fargas as Huggy Bear," *Starsky and Hutch,* www.starskyandhutchonline.com/antonio_fargas.htm (January 20, 2005).
Antonio Fargas Online, www.antoniofargas.net (January 20, 2005).

—James M. Manheim

Sylester Flowers

1935—

Pharmacist, entrepreneur

Throughout his career as a pharmacist, scientist, and business entrepreneur, Sylester Flowers has maintained his commitment to his full-service community-based pharmacy and his inner-city clients while taking full advantage of the technological advancements that have revolutionized his profession. As founder and chief executive officer (CEO) of the Ramsell Corporation, Flowers expanded into other pharmacy and healthcare-related businesses, particularly the new specialty of pharmacy benefit management (PBM). Ramsell's Public Health Services Bureau (PHSB) was the first and only PBM business in the country to specialize in prescription information and processing for low-income people infected with HIV.

Mentored by Mother

Born on June 30, 1935, in High Point, North Carolina, Sylester Flowers was the youngest of Carrie Flowers Kelly's four sons. At about age three, Syl (as he was known) and his family moved to Pittsburgh, Pennsylvania, where his mother and stepfather, Isaac Kelly, could take advantage of the unionized jobs that were supplying the war effort in Europe. In Pittsburgh the family lived in a poor minority neighborhood. Isaac Kelly worked in a steel mill and, for the most part, Carrie Kelly was a homemaker who motivated her children toward success.

When Flowers was chosen to appear in Aetna's *2005 African American History Calendar* focusing on pharmacists, he told them: "My mother would not allow my brother or me to use being African American

as an excuse. There is nothing like the opportunity that America provides. I was a kid who grew up in the projects, worked for an education and now has a successful company. Through my mother's mentoring, I learned that anything is possible if you prepare yourself well."

Flowers knew that he wanted to become a professional and improve his economic situation. He told the *Aetna Calendar* that, although he had planned to eventually become a physician, "I thought that the old-fashioned pharmacist was equally appealing to me because of the way I had always seen people in my community respond to and respect the neighborhood pharmacist. The pharmacy had a soda fountain, something that I thought was charming, and it gave me the best chance to become a health care professional."

Studied Pharmacology

With a scholarship to cover his tuition and fees, Flowers spent his freshman year in college taking required courses at Howard University in Washington, D.C. He then entered Howard's four-year School of Pharmacy, graduating with a Bachelor of Science degree as a clinical pharmacist in 1958. However, during Flowers' student years the pharmacy profession began to undergo a major transformation. While Flowers was becoming an expert at compounding individual drugs, antibiotics and other manufactured pharmaceuticals were coming into widespread use.

Following graduation Flowers spent a year as a research assistant in neuro-pharmacology at the Leech

At a Glance . . .

Born on June 30, 1935, in High Point, NC, son of Carrie Flowers Kelly and stepfather Isaac Kelly; married Susan, 1963 (divorced 1990); married Helen, 1993; children (from first marriage): Eric, Gina, Sylvia. *Education:* Howard University, BS in pharmacy, 1958. *Military Service:* U.S. Army ROTC, Howard University, 1953-58; Brooke Army Medical Center, San Antonio, TX, medical supply officer, 1959-61; U.S. Army reserves, 1961-65.

Career: Veterans Administration, Leech Farm Road Hospital, Pittsburgh, research assistant, 1958-59; St. Luke's Hospital, San Francisco, pharmacist, 1961-63; The Apothecary, Oakland, CA, owner-pharmacist, 1964–; Ramsell Corporation, Oakland and Pleasanton, CA, founder and CEO, 1967–; University of California School of Pharmacy, San Francisco, assistant clinical professor of pharmacy, 1970-81; San Francisco County Mental Health Department, pharmacy director for methadone treatment, 1971-82; University of the Pacific, Stockton, CA, adjunct professor of pharmacy, 1975-86.

Memberships: American College of Apothecaries, fellow (F.A.C.A.), 1967–; American Society of Health-System Pharmacists; California Society of Health-System Pharmacists.

Awards: California Pharmacists Association, Academy of Pharmacy Management, Appreciation of Contribution to Pharmacy Management Award, 1980-1985; KQED-PBS California, Hero of the Year, 2004; *Aetna African American History Calendar*, 2005.

Addresses: *Office*—4900 Hopyard Road £282, Pleasanton, CA 94566; 200 Webster Street, Suite 300, Oakland, CA 94607.

Farm Hospital, the psychiatric unit of the Veterans Administration Hospital in Pittsburgh. He had been a member of the Reserve Officers' Training Corps (ROTC) in college. He fulfilled two years of his military requirement as a medical supply officer at the Brooke Army Medical Center in San Antonio, Texas. Since it was a time of relative peace, Flowers was able to exchange his additional two years of required service for four years in the U.S. Army reserves.

In 1961 Flowers went to work as a pharmacist at St. Luke's Hospital in San Francisco, California. Initially he had planned to go on to medical school. However Flowers told *Contemporary Black Biography* that, after becoming a pharmacist, "I never looked back for a minute." He discovered that he loved the profession and that—although he had planned to open his own pharmacy in a middle-class neighborhood—there was a tremendous need for pharmacists in underserved communities.

Founded Ramsell Corporation

On January 8, 1964, Flowers opened his own community-based retail pharmacy—The Apothecary—in Oakland, California. He brought to his pharmacy a deep understanding of the community's values and needs, having grown up in a similar neighborhood. In addition to running his own pharmacy, Flowers held other related positions. Between 1970 and 1981 he was an assistant clinical professor of pharmacy at the University of California's School of Pharmacy in San Francisco. As an adjunct professor of pharmacy at the University of the Pacific—a private school in Stockton, California—Flowers supervised and mentored student interns. He also served as pharmacy director for the San Francisco County Mental Health Department's methadone treatment program from 1971 until 1982. There, in addition to making the methadone solutions, Flowers kept the records and performed laboratory tests. He also developed and managed the first outpatient prescription plan for the department.

In August of 1967, Flowers founded Ramsell—named for the street he lived on in San Francisco—as a sole proprietorship. Later he expanded it into an S-type corporation and served as its CEO. Ramsell Corporation at one time owned six community-based pharmacies. However, in keeping with his belief in individually-owned community pharmacies, Flowers sold them off to his managers, keeping only The Apothecary. As of 2005 Ramsell Corporation was a holding company with 36 employees.

Moved into Information Technology

Flowers was at the forefront of the information technology (IT) transformation of the pharmacy business. In 1981 he was one of the first pharmacists in his area to install a computer for managing patient information. He became an IT professional, devoting both time and money to research in health administration technology.

In 1992 Flowers was asked to develop an outpatient prescription benefit plan for the San Francisco city and county AIDS Drug Assistance Program (ADAP). ADAPs use state and federal funds mandated by the Ryan White CARE legislation to provide most HIV medications, as well as numerous social services, at low or no cost to qualified HIV/AIDS patients. For the next four years Ramsell managed the San Francisco ADAP as a successful pilot program. The company was chosen to manage ADAPs for Santa Barbara County in 1995 and San Mateo County in 1996.

In 1997 Ramsell's nonprofit subsidiary, the Professional Management Development Corporation (PMDC), was awarded a contract by the California Department of Health Services to consolidate all of the county ADAPs under one centralized program. The centralization was completed successfully within 90 days. The contract was renewed for another five years in 2000. In August of 2001, Ramsell/PMDC was awarded a two-year contract to administer the corresponding program—known as the AIDS Prescription Drug Program (APDP)—in the state of Washington. This contract was later extended for an additional two years.

When the requirement for administration by a nonprofit was dropped, Ramsell's PBM company—the Public Health Services Bureau (PHSB)—took over the programs. As of 2005, PHSB was administering 27 to 29 percent of the Ryan funds for California and Washington, serving HIV-positive, low-income clients who did not qualify for Medicaid.

Sought to Improve HIV Drug Programs

PMDC became the copyright holder for the software designed by PHSB. The new software, planned for release in July of 2005, was to be used initially for administration of the California and Washington programs. However, Flowers told the *AETNA 2005 Calendar,* "My driving ambition is to centralize the AIDS assistance programs in the United States so that the level of funding is not based on the policies of individual states but on a centralized federally sponsored program for *every* eligible patient.... We need to be able to provide a level of care to give patients the best chance across the country. For instance, a single black man in the South may not have access to the medication that he needs." Furthermore, a centralized program would ensure "that treatment would be consistent and accessible when [patients] moved to different states." His experiences in California and Washington convinced him that a centralized program would reduce administrative costs, possibly freeing additional funds for treatment.

Flowers continued to support IT professionals investigating ways to make these programs more accessible and centralized. He told the *Aetna Calendar*: "There are no shortcuts to experience. This field is highly specialized, and no other company in the U.S. has our level of experience. Technology gives us the tools to efficiently centralize the program and use our nation's health care resources wisely and efficiently."

In addition to PHSB and The Apothecary, as of 2005 Ramsell operated Alta Tierra, a community investment property, and the Flowers Heritage Foundation, funded by Ramsell profits to support programs at Howard University and other pharmacy schools. The foundation also funded a class on diversity at the University of the Pacific. Flowers told *CBB* that he viewed diversity training as essential for pharmacists with multicultural practices since they are the ones who counsel patients on numerous healthcare and lifestyle issues.

Pharmacy Remained His Avocation

As of 2005 Flowers continued to manage The Apothecary, a 1900-square-foot, state-of-the-art pharmacy, stocking some 3000 drugs and using robotics to fill several hundred prescriptions per hour. Located in Oakland's Wellness Center, The Apothecary remained committed to its ethnically diverse, low-income neighborhood. Flowers told *CBB* that the community he served both fulfilled his needs and provided him with inspiration.

Flowers believes that, in the age of information, the pharmacist's role has become even more critical. With physicians forced to choose among a multitude of available drugs—about which they may not be well-informed—it has become imperative for pharmacists to keep up with the latest scientific information. Computers can provide pharmacists with information about the known allergic reactions, side effects, and interactions of any drug. Flowers told *CBB*: "Do you have a question about a drug? Ask us. We are information managers." Nevertheless, information exchange has remained a barrier to good healthcare and Flowers stressed the necessity of clients staying with a single independent or chain pharmacy to ensure that their records remain intact.

Flowers always has viewed himself as a "client-centric" professional. The *Aetna Calendar* quoted him: "The pharmacist is the most accessible person of the health care team. You don't need an appointment to see a pharmacist. We have the opportunity to take care of the underserved within their environments." Flowers told *CBB*: "No matter how many doctors you see, you always end up seeing me."

Flowers's children from his first marriage include Eric, president of a Ramsell subsidiary, Gina Nightengale, a deputy director of the U. S. Environmental Protection Agency, and Sylvia, a teacher at a Paris business school. His first marriage dissolved in 1990, in part because of his time-consuming career. As of 2005, Flowers lived in Pleasanton, California, devoting as much time as possible to his second wife and two stepchildren.

Sources

On-line

"About Us," *Ramsell Corporation*, www.ramsellcorp. com/about.php (January 5, 2005).
"Sylester Flowers, R.Ph." *Aetna 2005 African American History Calendar*, www.aetna.com/diversity/ aahcalendar/2005/aprprofile.html (January 5, 2005).

Other

Additional information for this profile was obtained through an interview with Sylester Flowers on January 7, 2005.

—Margaret Alic

Christopher Gilbert

1949—

Poet, psychologist

Christopher Gilbert, often known as Chris Gilbert, won the 1983 Walt Whitman Award for his poetry collection *Across the Mutual Landscape*. He was recognized as a major force among the black American poets of the 1970s and 1980s who chanted and sang their poetry for enthusiastic audiences.

Gilbert was born on August 1, 1949, in Birmingham, Alabama, the son of Floyd and Rosie (Walker) Gilbert. He grew up in Lansing, Michigan, and several of his poems describe his experiences growing up in that town, which was dominated by the automobile industry. In "Pushing" he wrote of stopping at a high-priced grocery store on his way to school, and having the owner follow him and his friends about the store, telling them "you better be going your way–// buy something or else you got to leave.' // We'd rattle the pennies we had and go // but coming home buy some nutchews to stay // and try his nerve again, because we didn't steal // but warmed ourselves till Ray would ask why–// till, like big brothers will, one day I guessed, // 'Some things you do because you want to. Some things you do because you can't.'" In the poem "Time with Stevie Wonder in It," Gilbert recalled wintry nights in which his parents and their friends "would group in the long night–// tune frequencies to the Black stations // blasting out of Memphis, Nashville, // still playing what was played down south–// Ray Charles, Charles Brown, Ruth Brown, Muddy and Wolf. //...// This was our rule following–// buy at J.C. Penney and Woolworth's, // work at Diamond Reo, Oldsmobile, Fisher Body."

But Gilbert left Lansing, earning his bachelor's degree from the University of Michigan in 1972, then his master's degree and doctorate in psychology from Clark University in Worcester, Massachusetts, in 1975 and 1986 respectively. During the years in which he earned his education, Gilbert worked as a psychologist and psychotherapist, he did research, and he taught psychology. He worked as a staff psychologist and consultant at the Judge Baker Guidance Center in Boston and as a psychologist at the University of Massachusetts Medical School. He also served as staff psychologist at the Cambridge Family and Children's Services.

At night, on weekends, and sometimes in the early morning, Gilbert wrote poetry. He was quoted in *Contemporary Authors Online* as saying: "Sometimes I wrote between breaths." Before long, Gilbert became a well-known figure in Boston and Cambridge poetry circles. He participated in Etheridge Knight's Free People's Poetry Workshops and wrote for the *Little Apple*, a Worcester journal of arts and literature. Many of his poems first appeared in the *Worcester Review*, published by the Worcester County Poetry Association.

Gilbert's poetry collection, *Across the Mutual Landscape*, was awarded the 1983 Walt Whitman Prize from the Academy of American Poets. Awarded annually to poets who had not published a standard-edition poetry collection, the prize included both cash and publication by an Academy-selected press. The poems in *Across the Mutual Landscape*, or earlier versions, had been published previously in various periodicals including the *American Literary Review*, *Black American Literature Forum*, *Dark Horse*, *Mother Jones*, *Nimrod*, *Obsidian*, *The Runner*, *Small Moon*, *Sunbury*, *Telephone*, *Umbral*, and the *Virginia Quarterly Review*.

Graywolf Press in Port Townsend, Washington, with help from a Washington State Arts Commission grant, published *Across the Mutual Landscape* to good reviews. The poet Denise Levertov wrote for the book jacket: "Chris Gilbert's poems are dense with intellectual content and infused with lyrical imagination; his critique of society, his exploration of its interaction with his own soul or spirit, his elegiac celebrations of Robert Hayden or Muriel Rukeyser or invocations of jazz and

its artists, don't form separate categories but flow in and out of one another."

Like many of his contemporaries Gilbert's poetry was influenced by jazz and made full use of jazz rhythms. *Contemporary Authors* quoted him: "I see the poem itself as a situation. Its formation is thought which must be musically stated. The situation is charged. The situation is sensuous. The situation is moving forward. The situation is music. Jazz pianist and composer Thelonious Monk, placing himself in the exact center of things, finding himself naked in his whole world except for his desire and his skill, could be listened to for a chart of the coming into newness that is the poem's formation."

In poems like "Pitch," Gilbert integrated the personal with a broader world:

"Today it will snow. In the east // a bus is bombed in Herzliya. // In the Atlantic, Canadian sealers // are breaking ice towards an island // and the waiting baby seals. //...I get a call from home // telling how in the Olds parts plant // when the line shuts down for break // my brother pulls his trumpet out–// Orpheus among the abandoned car bodies–// and he blows: //...and, Chris, you know how Gary can be, // don't matter who's around. but one thing // out on the job they listen to him. // seems everyone, no matter who, if he is // who he is he makes us catch our breaths. // and we start questioning, despite whatever troubles, //...we sing through // to declare the future here. and this beats troubles. // for a while."

In 1986 Gilbert took a year off from his career in psychology to write poetry full time at the Robert Frost Center in Franconia, New Hampshire. He was quoted by *Contemporary Authors* at the time: "I feel that my own ability to write poetry wants this; it wants its experience to be grounded in the firsthand world gained through contact with lives and people, with me—as subject—as an empathy, with a reflection toward one's deeper and longer life, with goals, with a concept of use. It is my way of making a living."

In the early 1990s Gilbert became a psychology professor at Bristol Community College in Fall River, Massachusetts. He developed an internet-based general psychology course. He also conducted a study evaluating Bristol's Writing Lab in relation to student retention and academic success and he developed a cross-discipline student writing assessment model.

Chris Gilbert's poems have appeared in numerous anthologies including *City River of Voices*, a 1992 West End Press anthology of poets who lived or worked in Cambridge, and *The Breath of Parted Lips: Voices from the Robert Frost Place*, published by CavanKerry Press in 2004. His elegy to Robert Hayden was reprinted in *Inventions in Farewell*, published by Norton in 2001. Gilbert also contributed two chapters to *The Practice of Poetry*.

Selected writings

Poetry

Across the Mutual Landscape (includes "Pushing," "Muriel Rukeyser as Energy," "Time with Stevie Wonder in It," "Fire Gotten Brighter," and "Pitch"), Graywolf Press, 1984.

Gilbert's poems have appeared magazines and in numerous anthologies, including *Fifty Years of American Poetry: Anniversary Volume for the Academy of American Poets* (1984), *The Morrow Anthology of Younger American Poets* (1985), *The Practice of Poetry: Writing Exercises from Poets Who Teach* (1992), *City River of Voices* (1992), Playing *the*

Changes: From Afro-Modernism to the Jazz Impulse (1994), *Inventions in Farewell* (2001), *The Breath of Parted Lips: Voices from the Robert Frost Place* (2004), and *Approaching Literature in the 21st Century* (2005).

Sources

Periodicals

Worcester Review, 1996, pp. 131-36.

On-line

"Christopher Gilbert," *Contemporary Authors On-line, Biography Resource Center*, www.galenet.com/servlet/BioRC (September 30, 2004).

—Margaret Alic

Henry R(andall) Grooms

1944—

Engineer

Structural engineer Henry R. Grooms has enjoyed a distinguished career of more than thirty years with Rockwell International (now Boeing), where he supervised projects for the Apollo, Skylab, and Space Shuttle programs. He is also noted for his commitment to community programs that promote youth achievement. Described as a "role model for aspiring professionals and students everywhere" by a vice president at his company, Grooms was honored as Engineer of the Year at Rockwell in 1980, and in 2004 received the Black Engineer of the Year Lifetime Achievement Award and the National Society of Black Engineers' Lifetime Achievement Award in Industry.

Had Early Interest in Architecture

Born on February 10, 1944, in Cleveland, Ohio, Grooms grew up in a single-parent family where he learned early to work hard to achieve his goals. Though finances were scarce, his mother encouraged him to pursue a college education. He applied to several schools in Ohio, where he wished to remain during college, but these schools offered him only partial financial aid. A counselor suggested that Grooms apply to Howard University, a historically black school in Washington, D.C., that offered scholarships based on academic ability. Initially reluctant to consider Howard, Grooms scored so well on the school's admission exam that he was offered full financial aid. He enrolled there as an engineering major in 1961.

As a boy, Grooms had dreamed of becoming an architect. But the more he learned about the design of buildings, the more he realized that the profession of architecture required an artistic talent that he felt he did not possess. Since he excelled in math and enjoyed analytical activities, such as solving problems and doing puzzles, he felt that engineering—which shared some characteristics with architecture—would be a profession well-suited to his interests and abilities.

In an interview with *Contemporary Black Biography*, Grooms explained that he was at first leery of attending a traditionally black university. But he soon grew to love Howard, which created an environment that emphasized black pride and achievement. He joined Kappa Alpha Psi, a black fraternity, and was later elected to Tau Beta Pi, an engineering honor society. During his sophomore year at Howard, Grooms married and became a father. With a wife and baby daughter to support, he took on outside work to fulfill his financial responsibilities. Even so, he was able to complete his coursework within four years and graduated with a degree in civil engineering in 1965.

During his senior year at Howard, Grooms decided that he wanted to continue his studies at the graduate level. Seeing an advertisement for graduate engineering at Carnegie Mellon University, he mailed in an attached postcard for more information. Carnegie Mellon responded with an offer of a full scholarship as well as a stipend that would pay living expenses for Grooms and his family. He accepted the offer and enrolled in 1965. Though Grooms initially intended to obtain only a master's degree, two of his professors persuaded him to continue toward a Ph.D. He received his M.S.C.E. from Carnegie-Mellon in 1967 and his Ph.D. in 1969.

At a Glance . . .

Born February 10, 1944, in Cleveland, Ohio; son of Leonard D. Grooms and Lois Pickell Grooms; married Tonie Marie Joseph; children: Catherine, Zayne, Nina, Ivan, Ian, Athesis, Shaneya, Yaphet, Rahsan, Dax, Jevay, Xava. *Education:* Howard University, BSCE, 1965; Carnegie Mellon University, MSCE, 1967, PhD, 1969.

Career: District of Columbia Highway Department, Washington, highway engineer, 1962; Peter F. Loftus Corporation, Pittsburgh, PA, structural engineer, 1966; Blaw-Knox Co, Pittsburgh, structural engineer, 1967-68; Rockwell International (now Boeing Company), Downey, CA, engineer, then engineering manager, 1969—.

Memberships: Tau Beta Pi; Sigma Xi; Kappa Alpha Psi; American Society of Civil Engineers; Watts Friendship Sports League.

Awards: Rockwell International Space Division, Engineer of the Year, 1980; College Recruiter of the Year, 1979-80; Carnegie Mellon University, Alumni Merit Award, 1985; Western Reserve Historical Society, Cleveland, OH, Black History Archives Project honoree, 1989; Institute of Advancement in Engineering, Outstanding Engineering Volunteer Award, 1999; African Scientific Institute, Fellow, 2002; National Society of Black Engineers, Black Engineer of the Year Lifetime Achievement Award and Lifetime Achievement in Industry Award, 2004.

Addresses: *Office*—Engineering Manager, HO13-C326, Boeing, 5301 Bolsa Ave., Huntington Beach, CA 92647.

This achievement placed Grooms in an elite group. In the 1960s, perhaps only 4 or 5 percent of engineering graduates obtained doctorates; today the figure is not much higher, perhaps 7 to 8 percent. The majority of engineering Ph.D.s teach on college campuses. Grooms, however, chose a career in industry.

Ironically, Grooms had encountered some resistance from his family when he decided to major in engineering. His mother did not support his choice, fearing that an African-American engineer would not be able to find a job. But, he told *Contemporary Black Biography*, he was stubborn and independent, and followed his own path despite his mother's objections. Grooms excelled in school, and worked part-time and during summers first as a highway engineer for the Washington, D.C., highway department, and then in Pittsburgh as a structural engineer at the Peter F. Loftus Corporation and at the Blaw-Knox Company. After completing his Ph.D. he landed a job with North American Rockwell, a company that designed and manufactured aircraft, defense systems, and spacecraft. The company became Rockwell International in 1973, and in 1996 its space and defense divisions merged with Boeing, the world's leading aerospace company.

Worked on Space Systems Programs

At Rockwell, Grooms joined the technical staff as a structural engineer. This position, he explained, entails the analysis of structures to determine whether they are strong enough to perform the task for which they are designed. Over the course of his career he has worked on a wide variety of projects and supervised several technical teams; he has also authored or coauthored more than 20 technical papers. He is now senior manager of Strength, Structural Analysis, and Design for the Engineering organization at Boeing's operations in Huntington Beach, California.

Grooms has received particular recognition for work on technical, structural, and stress analysis of materials for various space systems programs. These include the Delta launch vehicle, which was developed to launch satellites and which has become the world's leading commercial launcher; Skylab, the country's first experimental space system, which was launched in 1973; and the Apollo program, which included the first vehicle to orbit the earth, the first vehicle to orbit the moon, and the lunar landing modules. Grooms' team has also worked on the Space Shuttle, for which Boeing has provided engineering support since 1981. Grooms has published several technical articles on space shuttle operation, including "Structural Analysis of the Space Shuttle Orbiter" and "What Is an Optimal Spacecraft Structure?"

Among his team's most recent projects is the X-37 Reusable Space Plane, which is designed as an air-launched vehicle that can remain in orbit for 21 days and then land on a conventional runway. The X-37 program will allow engineers to observe how reusable launch vehicle technologies actually work in space, and could lead to improvements in materials that protect spacecraft from intense heat during reentry. The project, according to a NASA fact sheet, is part of NASA's "new innovative business strategy to dramatically reduce the cost of space transportation."

In 1980, Rockwell International honored Grooms with its Engineer of the Year Award. He has also been a fellow of the Institute of Advancement in Engineering, and received an Outstanding Engineering Volunteer

Award in 1999. In 2002 he was elected a fellow of the African Scientific Institute. In recognition of his contributions to the Apollo, Skylab, and Space Shuttle programs, Grooms received both the Black Engineer of the Year Lifetime Achievement Award and the National Society of Black Engineers' Lifetime Achievement Award in Industry in 2004.

Co-founded Project REACH

Grooms, the father of twelve children, has also earned recognition for his longstanding involvement in community programs. He has served as a Boy Scout scoutmaster, youth basketball and youth soccer coach, and tutor. In particular, he has been honored for his work promoting education and achievement for at-risk youth. In 1993 he co-founded Project REACH, a nonprofit organization that provides financial, academic, and support services to help minority students prepare for success in college. The need for such a program, he told *Contemporary Black Biography*, became apparent to him when he coached his children's soccer and basketball teams and got to know students who had the potential to succeed but needed help. "Too often," he said, "organizations just throw money at the problem" without providing other kinds of assistance. With his wife, who worked with the Housing Authority of the City of Los Angeles, and two coworkers—Dwayne Orange at the Housing Authority and Faye Belson-Hardin at Boeing—Grooms started REACH to provide guidance, mentoring, study skills, and scholarships to students planning to enroll in college.

REACH began with 20 students, and conducted about 15 workshops the first year. The program has since grown to accommodate between 20 and 40 students each year. REACH provides many workshops and activities, including college visits, study sessions, and guest speakers from various fields. It is important, Grooms explained, for students to be able to identify with "real live people" of color who hold jobs in professions to which the students themselves aspire. REACH tracks students through college and helps them to deal with issues that might pressure them to consider dropping out. The aim, Grooms said, is to encourage students to stay in school and graduate. Just watching Project REACH succeed, Grooms said—which can mean keeping students "on a good path"

even if they do not necessarily graduate—"is a great reward." The program now boasts about 20 students who have earned their B.S. degrees or higher and have come back to participate in the program as mentors.

Grooms continues to serve as executive director of Project REACH. He has written about the importance of education for minority students in "Why Are There So Few Black Students in Engineering?," "Reaching Out to 'At-Risk' High School Students," and "Trying to Influence 'At-Risk' High School Students."

In addition to his awards for professional achievement, Grooms received the Alumni Merit Award from Carnegie-Mellon University in 1985, and was an honoree of the Case Western Reserve Society Black History Archives Project in 1989. He is a member of Tau Beta Pi, Sigma Xi, Kappa Alpha Psi, and the American Society of Civil Engineers.

Sources

Periodicals

Howard University Matrix, Fall, 2004, pp. 8-9.

On-line

"Four Boeing Engineers Receive National Black Engineer Awards," *Boeing,* www.boeing.com/news/releases/2004/q1/nr_040218s.html (February 18, 2005).

"National Society of Black Engineers 2004 Golden Torch Awards," *National Society of Black Engineers,* www.nsbe.org/publicrelations/winner_bios.php (January 6, 2005).

"Space Shuttle," *Boeing,* www.boeing.com/defense-space/space/hsfe_shuttle/flash.html (January 6, 2005).

"X-37 Demonstrator to Test Future Launch Technologies in Orbit and Reentry Environments," *NASA,* www.nasa.gov/centers/marshall/news/background/facts/x37facts2.html (May, 2003).

Other

Additional information for this profile was obtained through a telephone interview with Dr. Henry R. Grooms on January 10, 2005.

—E. M. Shostak

Darryl Hazel

1949—

Automotive executive

Hazel, Darryl B., photograph. Bill Pugliano/Getty Images.

President of the Lincoln Mercury Division of the Ford Motor Company Darryl Hazel knows how to make the most out of his opportunities. Growing up as the only child of parents who had been young adults during the Great Depression of the 1930s, Darryl Hazel learned early the importance of hard work and personal responsibility. Beginning with his first job as a restaurant dishwasher, he set a pattern of working his way up to positions of increasing responsibility. Hazel met with success not only because of his willingness to do whatever work needed to be done, but also because he has a lively intellectual curiosity that enables him to turn any job into an opportunity to learn about the business world and the people around him. His efforts have earned him one of the top positions in an American giant of a company.

Learned Importance of Education Early

Darryl Barton Hazel was born on June 10, 1948, in the Manhattan borough of New York City. His father Osborne worked as a civilian clerk for the Department of the Navy, while his mother Olive taught various grades in the New York City schools. Olive Hazel had earned two master's degrees and her husband had attended college but had not graduated. Almost forty when their only son was born, the Hazels passed on to young Darryl their expectations that he would get a higher education, find a productive career, and make a contribution to society. Though they had certainly experienced racism and prejudice during their lives, they had little patience for those who blamed others for their problems. They taught their son that each person is responsible for making the most of his life. Darryl respected his parents and took their words to heart.

When Darryl was eight, the Hazels moved from the inner city neighborhood of Harlem to the liberal suburb of Teaneck, New Jersey. Though they were one of the first black families to move into the neighborhood, Hazel was far more surprised by the darkness of the suburban streets and the nighttime racket of crickets and cicadas than by the race of his neighbors. He soon settled in to his new life.

As his 16th birthday approached, Hazel's father mentioned that it might be time for him to think about

At a Glance . . .

Born Darryl Barton Hazel on June 10, 1948, in New York City; married Sheila McEntee, 1978; children: Osborne and Margaret. *Education:* Wesleyan University, Middletown, CT, BA, economics, 1970; Northwestern University, Evanston, IL, MA, economics, 1973.

Career: Ford Motor Company, various management positions, 1972-95, Ford Motor Company Lincoln Mercury Division, general sales manager, 1995-97; Ford Division, general marketing manager, 1997-99; Ford Customer Service Division, vice president, 2002, Lincoln Mercury Division, president, 2002–.

Selected memberships: Police Athletic League, City of Detroit, chairman of the board; Congressional Black Caucus Foundation, board member; Oakland Family Services, board member.

Selected awards: On Wheels, Inc., Edward Davis African American Executive of the Year, 2003; Power-Networking Training Conference, Business Excellence Award, 2004.

Addresses: *Office*—Lincoln Mercury Division, Ford Motor Company, 16800 Executive Plaza Drive, Dearborn MI 48216-4261.

getting an after-school job. The next day Darryl Hazel had secured his first job, as dishwasher and bus boy at a local restaurant called Friendly's. He found many things to appreciate about his new job. First, he discovered that he liked earning his own money. Moreover, he was enthralled with the dynamics of the business itself. As he learned about the business, he also began to learn about the people involved, his coworkers, supervisors, and customers. He learned that if he worked hard, he could be promoted to positions of greater responsibility and that those positions offered even more chances to learn.

Hazel worked at Friendly's for the next several years. Once his supervisors learned that he was a hard worker, they promoted him to shift supervisor, then to night manager. There he learned more about the day-to-day aspects of the business, such as how to predict which flavors of ice cream would sell the fastest, so that the restaurant would order the right supplies. He also learned how to evaluate the performance of his co-workers, a skill he would put to use later in his management career at Ford.

In 1966 Hazel graduated from Teaneck High School and enrolled at Wesleyan University, a respected college in nearby Middletown, Connecticut. One of his professors suggested that he major in economics, the study of how the world's resources and manufactured goods are produced, distributed, and used. Hazel graduated with a bachelor's degree in economics in 1970.

Committed to His Studies

World events guided his next choice. During the 1960s and the first half of the 1970s, the United States was involved in an undeclared war in the Southeast Asian nation of Vietnam. A military draft was in place, which required all young men to serve in the military. Many of the young men drafted during these years were sent to fight in Vietnam. Though sometimes college students were allowed to delay the draft until their studies were completed, this was not always true. One of Hazel's friends had been drafted while attending law school. He had gone to Vietnam, where he had been killed.

Hazel had no desire to enter the military or to go to war. Neither he nor his parents supported the U.S. involvement in the far-away conflict, and he did not want to lose his life fighting a war he considered irresponsible. He applied for and received a university fellowship, or scholarship, to study economics at Chicago's Northwestern University. Fellowship students were unlikely to be drafted, which would allow Hazel to complete his education.

Hazel earned his master's degree in 1973. But by that time, Hazel had begun to question whether the academic world of economic study was right for him. He began to feel the need of more "real-world" experience, and looked for other opportunities. He accepted an invitation by the Ford Company to travel to an interview in New York City in December 1972.

Began Work at Ford

Though Hazel had first considered the interview mainly as an opportunity for a free trip home to visit his parents, he soon found himself working in the New York sales office of Ford's Lincoln Mercury Division. As he had when working as a dishwasher at Friendly's, Hazel immediately began to work hard and learn about the business. He began to learn that the principles of economics functioned quite differently in the real world than they had in the classroom. Just as at Friendly's, he quickly earned promotions, as his supervisors grew to appreciate his dedication and lively interest in his work.

While at the New York sales office, Hazel earned promotions to marketing manager, business management manager and field manager. He was also given managerial positions in Washington, D.C., Philadelphia, Cleveland, and Boston. These promotions encouraged him to place even more priority on his work and career, and this, in turn led to even more promotions. Moving to Ford's national offices, he held several staff positions, including marketing programs and strategy manager, education and training manager, and marketing research director. He also worked in product development, serving as business planning manager for North American Car Product Development.

In July 1995 Hazel was given the job of general sales manager for Ford's Lincoln Mercury Division. In April 1997, he was appointed general marketing manager for Ford Division, and in 2002 he became vice president of the Ford Customer Service Division. In August of the same year he was promoted to president of the Lincoln Mercury Division of the Ford Motor Company.

At the helm of Lincoln Mercury, Hazel dug in immediately to reinvigorate the Lincoln and Mercury brands. He told the *Detroit Free Press* that "We need to re-establish ourselves in the car market." Within five months, Hazel had rolled out a plan to do so, including advertising, concentration on four key vehicles, and new promotions. Speaking with *Automotive News,* Hazel explained that "One of the traps we fell into is that we did not put as much attention and emphasis on our traditional business. Now we have to work at getting back what historically has been ours." By 2005, Hazel's efforts were beginning to pay off. The brand had new products that reached younger audiences and sales were beginning to pick up. "We had a while where

we were anchored in yesterday, but I think we are moving forward," he told *Automotive News.*

Hazel continues to place a high value on education and has become a promoter of a Ford-sponsored academic program to focus on black business education. Though frequently working 60-hour weeks, he has also placed great importance on his own family and considers his children to be his greatest accomplishment. Like his own parents, he has tried to raise them to be self-sufficient hard workers who will make their own contribution to society.

Sources

Periodicals

Automotive News, January 13, 2003, p. 26; February 14. 2005.
Black Enterprise, November 2002, p. 72.
Detroit Free Press, February 11, 2003.

On-line

"Ford Motor Company Names Hazel To Head Lincoln Mercury," *Automotive Intelligence News,*www.au tointell-news.com/News-2002/July-2002/July-20 02-4/July-24-02-p8.htm (March 11, 2005).

Other

Information for this profile was obtained through an interview with Darryl Hazel on January 28, 2005.

—Tina Gianoulis

Beverly Wade Hogan

1951—

College president

Hogan, Beverly Wade, photograph. AP/Wide World Photos. Reproduced by permission.

When Mississippi's Tougaloo College was looking for a president in 2002, it did not have to look far. Lifelong Mississippian and Tougaloo alumna Beverly Wade Hogan had served six years on the school's board of trustees and five in its administrative ranks. She also had 25 years of leadership in government and non-profit agencies. However, Hogan's most important credential may well have been one not quantifiable in a résumé. "I've always felt very strongly about civic engagement and social responsibility," Hogan told *The Planet Weekly*. "It has a lot to do with my upbringing and my college years. I was involved in voter registration, with protests against things I felt were unjust or unfair. I was encouraged by my family to speak out against those kinds of things." After taking over the top spot at Tougaloo, Hogan not only sought higher academic standards, but she also impressed her belief in civic responsibility on the student body. Considering that her life has been defined by the work she has done to better society—she has founded programs to help the mentally impaired, battered women, welfare recipients, and the homeless—students needed look no farther than the president's office to find a role model for both academic and civic inspiration.

Encouraged to Better Society as a Child

Beverly Wade was born on July 5, 1951, in Crystal Springs, Mississippi, and raised in nearby Mount Wade. "[It] was a real community," Hogan told *The Planet Weekly*. "I was surrounded by relatives and close friends." Her father, Willie Dell Wade, was a farmer, and her mother, Mae Ether Easley Wade, stayed at home taking care of Hogan and her four older siblings. "I grew up watching my parents and friends work in the community, work in the church, and share with each other," she told *The Planet Weekly*. "I was encouraged along those lines. So, as I grew up, I naturally took on the role of wanting to make a difference in my community." She was also encouraged to do something outside of her community. "We were always encouraged as children to be somebody and it was always a spoken expectation," she told *Contemporary Black Biography (CBB)*. "'The Wade children are smart, they are going to be something one day, just watch.' We heard this all the time."

Hogan excelled in school. "I was very active in the student government association, class president,

At a Glance . . .

Born on July 5, 1951, in Crystal Springs, MS; married Marvin Hogan, 1971; children: Maurice, Marcellus. *Education*: Tougaloo College, BA, psychology, 1973; Jackson State University, MA, public policy and administration, 1990; doctoral studies, Fielding Graduate University.

Career: Friends of Children of Mississippi, health services coordinator, 1970-71; Jackson Mental Health Center, mental health therapist, 1973-74; Mental Health Association, Hinds County, executive director, 1974-80; Mental Health Association, Mississippi, executive director, 1980-83; Governor's Office of Federal State Programs, Mississippi, executive director, 1984-87; Workers' Compensation Commission, Mississippi, commissioner, 1987-97; Owens Health and Wellness Center, Tougaloo College, executive assistant to the president/director, 1997-2000; Tougaloo College, Office of Institutional Advancement, vice president, 2000-02; Tougaloo College, president, 2002–.

Selected memberships: White House Conference on Families, Mississippi chairperson and national delegate, 1980; National Coalition of 100 Black Women, Central Mississippi Chapter, president, 1994-98; Tougaloo College, board of trustees, 1991-97; Foundation for the Mid-South, board member, 1999–; Entergy Mississippi, board member, 1999–.

Selected awards: American Society of Public Administrators, Mississippi Chapter, administrator of the year, 1986; Council of State Governments, Toll Fellow, 1987; State of Mississippi, Now Award of Distinction, 1987; United Negro College Fund, Distinguished Leadership Award, 1988; Mississippi Majesty Awards, honoree, 2003.

Addresses: *Office*—President, Tougaloo College, Tougaloo, MS, 39174.

American and Mississippi history," she told *The Planet Weekly*.

Upon graduation, Hogan headed to Tougaloo University, a historically black college located near Jackson, Mississippi. Tougaloo was founded in 1869 with the intent of providing African Americans with the same standard of education found in universities whose doors were closed to African Americans. As such it was a school with a long history of social awareness and activism—a good match for Hogan. "I felt the responsibility to go to school, get an education, and use that education to try to serve humanity," she told *The Planet Weekly*. "Whatever I did, I wanted to be involved with something I really cared about, that I had a passion for doing, and that I really felt was worthwhile and would make a difference in the lives of others."

Turned Talents to Politics

Hogan began a life of public service even before she finished college. As an undergraduate she worked as health services coordinator at the non-profit Friends of Children of Mississippi. There she met Marvin Hogan, the executive director of the organization. They married in 1971 and had two sons, Maurice and Marcellus. Meanwhile Hogan graduated with a bachelor's degree in psychology in 1973. She worked briefly as a mental health therapist before becoming executive director of the Mental Health Association in Hinds County, a post she held for eight years. During that time Hogan helped open Jackson's first rape crisis center and battered women's shelter and established Mississippi's first psychiatric halfway house. In 1983 she moved up to executive director for Mississippi's Mental Health Association. Hogan also pursued causes outside of her job. She organized the Mississippi Advocates for Minority Adoption and the Mississippi Professional Voluntary Leadership Association. Her commitment was recognized by President Jimmy Carter when he made Hogan a delegate to the 1980 White House Conference on Families.

Hogan left mental health to work on the 1983 Mississippi governor's campaign for democrat Bill Allain. After Allain won the election he appointed Hogan CEO of the Governor's Office of Federal State Programs. Hogan oversaw the administration of all federally funded programs. She commanded a staff of 250 and a budget of more than 150 million dollars. Highlights of her tenure included the Rental Rehabilitation Program and Low Income Tax Credit Program of 1986, designed to increase housing for low-income Mississippians, and the Self Employment Demonstration Project of 1987, aimed at reducing welfare dependency. In 1987 Hogan left the governor's office to become a commissioner with Mississippi's Workers' Compensation Commission, a position she held for nearly a decade.

homecoming queen, and high honor roll student," she told *CBB*. Yet, even as she focused on her studies, the world was erupting around her. "I grew up in the age of integration, the civil rights movement, the Vietnam War, all of those profound social-change events in

Led Active Civic, Volunteer, and Academic Life

During 14 years in the government, Hogan honed her skills as a leader. "I learned a lot about leadership, in ways that books couldn't teach me," she told *The Planet Weekly*. "I learned a lot about process, about compromise, not so much compromising your principles, but working with people and the art of negotiation and how to establish relationships...." She also became an expert at managing her own time. In addition to her work duties, Hogan volunteered with a slew of civic groups. Locally she was a board member of the United Way and president of the central Mississippi chapter of the National Coalition of 100 Black Women. At the state level she was chairperson for the Campaign for the United Negro College Fund, president of the American Society of Public Administration, and founder of the Martin Luther King Holiday Commission. Nationally, Hogan was the chairperson of the National Child Support Enforcement Implementation Project. She also held positions with the Council of State Governments and the National Governors' Association. With the latter Hogan worked on a task force to develop the National Welfare Reform Policy of 1986.

Despite her full calendar, Hogan earned a master's degree in public policy and administration from Jackson State University in 1990. She also served as chairperson for the school's Business Advisory Council and taught leadership courses to graduate students. After leaving the Workers' Compensation Commission in 1997, Hogan became more involved in higher education. She had served on the board of trustees for Tougaloo College from 1991 to 1997 and, after a brief post at Hinds Community College, she joined the staff of Tougaloo full-time. Her first position with her alma mater was as executive assistant to the president in matters related to daily administration of the school. Concurrently she served as founding director of the school's Owens Health and Wellness Center.

In 2000 Hogan became Tougaloo's vice president of the office of institutional advancement. Her main focus was fundraising. It was a good fit for Hogan, as she explained to *CBB*, because "[Tougaloo] has always been my charity of choice." For two years she oversaw all activities relating to securing resources for the school, including development, public relations, and alumni relations. True to form, Hogan did not limit her focus, nor her intellect, and while working at Tougaloo she also began to pursue doctoral studies in human and organizational management at the Fielding Graduate Institute. She also became a scholar at the Kettering Foundation where her research on higher education and civic responsibility was published in 2000.

Became First Female President of Tougaloo

In May of 2002 Tougaloo's board of trustees appointed Hogan president of the school. She was the first woman to hold that distinction. She told *CBB* that her goals were "to provide the leadership to move Tougaloo College to the forefront of higher education in the nation with academic excellence, social commitment, and fiscal responsibility as our trademarks." According to a 2004 article in *Ebony*, she was succeeding. "Under Dr. Hogan's dynamic and visionary leadership, the College boasts a student retention rate of 88 percent, well above the national average, and ranks as one of the top five historically black colleges and universities whose graduates earn their PhDs in the sciences."

Hogan's personal measure of success was Tougaloo's students. "Graduating exceptionally prepared and committed students who will make a difference in society is our profit margin," she told *Mississippi Business Journal*. Contributing to society has long been one of Hogan's most dearly held beliefs. "With becoming an educated citizen comes responsibility, the responsibility to use one's education in ways that will effect change, to make a difference," she told *The Planet Weekly*. To achieve that Hogan has directed Tougaloo staff and faculty to offer opportunities for students to make a difference outside the campus, whether through community service, political debate, or social action. Hogan summed up her goals in an interview with *The Clarion-Ledger*, "If we can introduce [the students] to those concepts so they can begin to think about that before they leave, that's as important a part of education as what they get in the classroom."

Sources

Periodicals

Ebony, September, 2004.
Mississippi Business Journal, March 1, 2004.

On-line

"Biographical Profile for President Hogan," *Tougaloo College*, www.tougaloo.edu/matriarch/OnePieceP age.asp?PageID=297&PageName=presbio (December 28, 2004).
"Effecting Change Through Education," *The Planet Weekly*, www.planetweekly.com/mt/archives/0004 63.html (December 28, 2004).
"Tougaloo Student Learns True Role of College President," *The Clarion-Ledger*, www.clarionledger.com /news/0310/15/m09.html (December 28, 2004).

Other

Additional information for this profile was obtained through an interview with Beverly Wade Hogan on January 7, 2005.

—Candace LaBalle

Lenon Hoyte

1905-1999

Museum founder and curator, teacher

After 40 years as an art and special education teacher in New York City public schools, Lenon Hoyte—commonly known as Aunt Len—founded Aunt Len's Doll and Toy Museum in her Harlem home. It was one of the nation's largest private collections of dolls and related toys and became one of New York City's most popular specialty museums during its years of operation between 1970 and 1994.

Became a Teacher

Hoyte was born Lenon Holder in New York City on July 4, 1905. She was the oldest of five children of Rose Pari (Best) and Moses Emanuel Holder. After attending the New York Teachers Training School, she began teaching in New York City public schools in 1930, where she remained until her retirement in 1970.She earned her Bachelor of Science degree in education from the City College of New York (CCNY) in 1937. In 1938, she married a pharmacist named Lewis P. Hoyte.

Lenon Hoyte remained a student as well as a teacher for much of her career. She earned her teaching certificate in special education from Columbia University in 1940. Over the following years she studied art at CCNY and Columbia, and with private teachers. In 1959 Hoyte earned her PhD equivalent from CCNY.

Between 1940 and 1950 Hoyte taught mentally disabled children. Between 1950 and 1970 she taught art, crafts, and puppetry. She was a lecturer at the Museum of Natural History and the workshop coordi-

nator for the Workshop Center for Open Education at CCNY. After 41 years in her profession, Hoyte retired from teaching art at Junior High School 149 in the Bronx. Her decision to retire was explained in her obituary. The *New York Times* obituary by William H. Honan quoted Hoyte as saying: "When they started killing teachers, I got out."

Founded Her Doll Museum

In 1962 Hoyte was asked to organize a doll show as a fundraiser for Harlem Hospital. Following her husband's death, Hoyte's new-found passion occupied her retirement years. She traveled throughout the United States, Europe, and the Caribbean, visiting doll shows and collecting dolls and accessories from flea markets, garage sales, and antique stores. Hoyte referred to all of her dolls as her "babies," from the rarest antiques to well-used dolls with broken arms.

The year that they married, the Hoytes had bought a three-story brownstone at 6 Hamilton Terrace between Convent and St. Nicholas Avenues in Harlem. In the 1960s they turned over a part of their home to Aunt Len's Doll and Toy Museum. The public spaces consisted of narrow passageways winding through the ground floor and basement of the building. From 1970 until 1994, Lenon Hoyte served as the museum's full-time executive director, president, curator, and tour guide.

Aunt Len's Doll and Toy Museum officially opened in 1974, with irregular hours several times per week.

Admission fees never exceeded two dollars for adults and 50 cents for children. At one time the museum held between 5,000 and 6,000 dolls. Eventually it outgrew its space and Hoyte began to store her most valuable dolls in a rental across the street.

Attracted Collectors from Around the World

In general Hoyte's collection was organized historically. However sometimes exhibits occupied glass cabinets with particular themes. The dolls ranged in size from one or two inches up to two-three feet. There were fine nineteenth-century French dolls made of bisque, an unglazed ceramic. There were rare, antique porcelain dolls and United States presidents and first ladies. There were numerous versions of Shirley Temple dolls,

Barbie dolls, Betsy Wetsy dolls, and Cabbage Patch dolls.

Hoyte's collection included extremely rare black dolls from the nineteenth century. Among them were rag dolls made by slaves from scraps of fabric, muslin, and feed bags. A pair of papier-mâch´ dolls named Lillian and Leo had been made by Leo Moss, a nineteenth-century black handyman from Atlanta. Lillian and Leo had tears running down their cheeks. Legend claimed that after separating from his wife and children, Moss only made sad dolls. According to Hoyte's obituary in the *Los Angeles Times*, she once told reporters that these black dolls represented "the beginning of our heritage."

Hoyte had dolls from Africa, France, Germany, Russia, and the Philippines. One of her favorites was a baby doll with wide eyes and long eyelashes, carved out of mahogany in 1977 by a California artist named Patty Hale. The museum also included doll houses, doll clothing and costumes, stuffed animals, and tin toys. Harlem children, as well as collectors from around the world, delighted in Aunt Len's museum.

Hoyte also continued to design her own original dolls, for which she was awarded numerous blue ribbons. In 1983 her dolls were exhibited at several special art showings. Hoyte wrote a column, "Our Museum," for *Doll News* and continued to teach doll-making and produce doll shows. Proceeds from her doll shows were donated to St. Philip's Episcopal Church, of which she was a lifelong member.

In addition to her church and doll clubs, Hoyte was a member of Beta Epsilon and served as secretary and president of the Hamilton Terrace Block Association. She received numerous awards throughout her career, including a 1980 Self Help Neighborhood Award, a service award from the United Federation of Doll Clubs, Inc.; a Building Brick Award from the New York Urban League in 1985; an Educator of the Year Award in 1988 from the City University of New York; and the Mayoral Award of Honor for Art and Culture New York City Mayor Edward I. Koch in 1990.

Sold Off Her Collection

In 1990 Hoyte's home and museum were broken into and at least nine dolls—including a priceless two-foot-tall English king—were stolen. Hoyte was broken-hearted. According to her *New York Times* obituary, she said at the time: "People any more don't let you live. You struggle to keep something up for joy and beauty, and you find yourself having to watch for thieves. It's not right." Soon after the break-in, four of the dolls—replicas of Benjamin Franklin, George and Martha Washington, and Abraham Lincoln—were returned to Hoyte's front room, broken but repairable. According to her obituary, she responded: "I don't ask questions about how. I'm just happy to have them back."

As Hoyte aged she was no longer able to care for the museum. She closed its doors in the early 1990s and began to dismantle her collection. Thousands of Hoyte's dolls were sold to dealers and private collectors around the world. In 1994 700 of her finest antique dolls were auctioned at Sotheby's. Prices ranged from $200 for a pair of German all-bisque dolls to "a black Bru pressed-bisque-head bebe doll," valued at $18,000. Hoyte died at the age of 94, on August 1, 1999, in a New York hospital.

In 2002 Alva Rogers' *The Doll Plays* premiered at the Actor's Express in Atlanta, Georgia. A tribute to Lenon Hoyte, the play depicted Hoyte on her deathbed, with dolls acting out her life, as well as presenting their own histories as toys and collectibles. A fancy French doll described her feelings as a discarded toy and a Grace Kelly doll recalled her transition from Hollywood glamour girl to Princess Grace of Monaco.

Sources

Periodicals

Atlanta Journal and Constitution, January 11, 2002.
Los Angeles Times, September 11, 1999, p. A18.
New York Times, January 2, 1989, p. A16; September 9, 1999, p. C22.
Newsday (Long Island, NY), May 28, 1991, p. 25.

On-line

"Toys in the Attic," *Creative Loafing Atlanta*, http://atlanta.creativeloafing.com/2002-01-23/arts_theater.html (December 21, 2004).

—Margaret Alic

Chaka Khan

1953—

Singer

Chaka Khan has enjoyed a long and fruitful recording career that spans over two decades, but her soaring voice has failed to put her in the same superstar strata as other African American divas of her generation like Patti LaBelle or Tina Turner. Khan's career came of age as disco dawned in the early 1970s, and with her first hit as a member of Rufus the singer became a dynamic presence on the scene. "She was funkier, more contemporary than Aretha Franklin, as she could be just as diverse. Within a mere six years, she would have her own cult of singers who would try to emulate her sound," wrote Curtis Bagley in *Essence*. An even more successful solo career followed, as well as more Grammy Awards, but her presence on the pop/R&B scene by the mid-1990s had become a lightweight one. The London-based singer was remedying that by 1996, however, with her contributions to the soundtracks of several successful films and plans for a new record as well as a tell-all autobiography.

Khan was born Yvette Marie Stevens, the oldest of four children, on the South Side of Chicago. Both parents worked for the University of Chicago, one as a photographer, the other as a research supervisor. Unlike other future R&B stars who cut their musical teeth in church gospel choirs, Khan was raised Roman Catholic—but was exposed to jazz. The singer recalled for Essence writer Isabel Wilkerson that she was first exposed to Billie Holiday through her grandmother's record collection. "She's one of my mentors," Khan said of Holiday. "She's one of the first jazz players I ever heard.... The naivete, the suffering, the pain and all the things that come along with the suffering and the

pain. She was victimized, and that led to excesses I can relate to and understand. She's a Black woman who went through a lot."

Khan formed her first ensemble with a group of her preteen friends who called themselves the Crystalettes. Their name came from her observation of how the street lights sparkled against the new snow below their Hyde Park high-rise. Big fans of Gladys Knight, Khan and the Crystalettes sang in talent shows where local fans dubbed her "Little Aretha." The official name change to "Chaka" came when she was thirteen and joined an African music group called Shades of Black; it was the onset of the Black Power movement in the mid-1960s and its leader rechristened her Chaka Adunne Aduffe Hodarhi Karifi. Her teen years were spent singing in a number of bands, but Khan also pushed her luck in more potentially self-destructive ways. She told *Essence* that she used to carry a gun, and even practiced with it once a week: "When I did think about killing people with it, I developed ulcers, and I just threw the gun in the lake."

After dropping out of high school, Chaka moved out of her parents' house when she entered into a common-law marriage with Assan Khan, a bass player from East India. Both wore matching bleached blond coifs, and she was now singing in a group called Lock and Chain. Khan then jumped ship to an act called Lyfe before joining up with another ensemble called Rufus, which had attracted a large Chicago-area following. Working as a file clerk by day, she began hanging around Rufus by night and befriended their frontperson, a woman named Paulette McWilliams. At the time, Rufus was

At a Glance . . .

Born Yvette Marie Stevens, March 23, 1953, in Chicago, IL; daughter of a photographer and a research supervisor; married Assan Khan 1970 (divorced 1971); married Richard Holland 1974 (divorced 1980); married Doug Rasheed 2001; children: Milini, Damien.

Career: Singer. The Crystalettes musical group, co-founder, 1964(?); Afro-Arts Theater, member, 1960s(?); Lyfe musical group member, late 1960s; The Babysitters, musical group member, late 1960s; Rufus musical group member, 1972-78; solo career, 1978–; Earth Song record label, co-founder, 1996–; Raeven Productions, co-founder, 1996–

Selected awards: National Academy of Recording Arts and Sciences, eight Grammy Awards, 1983 (2), 1984, 1993, 1996 (with Bruce Hornsby) 1997, 2003 (with the Funk Brothers), 2004 (with Kenny G); American Society of Composers, Authors and Publishers, Rhythm & Soul Heritage Award (first honoree), 1998; Granville White Lifetime Achievement Award, 2000; World Music Awards, Legend Award, 2003; Berklee College of Music, honorary doctorate, 2004.

Addresses: *Home*—London, England. *Office*—c/o Chaka Khan Foundation, 9100 Wilshire Boulevard, Suite 515 East Tower, Beverly Hills, CA 90212; *Web*—www.chakakhan.com.

doing dance songs and Sly and the Family Stone covers; when McWilliams quit in 1972, Khan took her place. She was eighteen.

Rufus won a record deal with ABC-Dunhill, and Khan followed them out to California. Their debut LP, *Rufus*, was released in 1973 to scant notice and little commercial success. During the recording of a second release, recent Grammy Award-winner Stevie Wonder showed up one day at the Torrance studio, much to the astonishment of the band. The visit would spark Rufus's first hit, the Grammy-winning "Tell Me Something Good." Khan recalled the event in a 1974 interview with Jay Grossman of *Rolling Stone*. "He sat down at the clavinet, y'know, and just wrote the song," she related about Wonder. "The first tune that he laid down, y'know, the first rhythm track, I said, 'I don't like that one so much.' And it seemed as though he was a little upset over that, and I thought, 'Well, a lot of people

must not say that to him!' So he said, 'What's your birth sign?' I said 'Aries-Pisces,' and he said, 'Oh, well here's a song for you.'"

After members of Rufus wrote lyrics for the track, Khan began to sing the "Tell Me Something Good" in her own style, but Wonder, still at the studio, interrupted. "NO NO NO!" Khan recalled him protesting in the interview with Grossman. "'Sing it like this!' And it turned out for the better," she said in the *Rolling Stone* interview with Grossman. "I don't know what would have happened if I'd done it myself, but just him being there—I'd been loving this guy for like 10 years." Khan was nine months pregnant when she recorded the LP; they exited the studio on December 17, 1973, and she gave birth to daughter Milini four days later.

"Tell Me Something Good" catapulted Khan and Rufus to instant stardom, complete with gold records on their living-room walls, a Grammy, sold-out tours—and the accompanying heady lifestyle. Khan soon gained a reputation as a wild child of the 1970s. To *Essence*'s Wilkerson, Khan described those drug-fueled days of her life as a "runaway carriage, the reins flying." Much of it she only knows through others' accounts of her behavior. Discussing the possibility of an autobiography, the singer told Wilkerson that "I need to get a hypnotist, okay? I'm trying to write my life story, and it's like we're going to have to call in a professional at some point and put me in a trance because it's deep."

Despite the substance abuse problems, Khan still went on to record several hit albums with Rufus during the 1970s, such as *Rufus Featuring Chaka Khan*. Her career was her saving grace, she told Bagley in *Essence*. "Throughout all my whimsical flights, I have never let anything get completely away from me," Khan said. "Music has always been a grounding factor for me. It has been my one reality check. Even when my head was in the clouds, I always had at least one foot on the ground. That's why I'm alive today."

In 1978 Khan made a successful transition to a solo recording career when she signed with Warner Brothers. Her solo debut came later that year with *Chaka Khan*, an overwhelming hit buoyed by its first single, "I'm Every Woman." She continued to record several solo efforts, achieving a minor hit in 1981 with *What Cha' Gonna Do for Me?* However, Khan preferred to make scat and jazz-influenced records instead of straightforward, commercial R&B, until Warner Brothers insisted on a more mainstream sound in 1984 when it came time for her to record her sixth solo effort. Khan remembered a song called "I Feel for You" by Prince that appeared on his second album in 1979. Her producer modernized it a bit for her, bringing in Stevie Wonder to blow harp and Grandmaster Melle Mel, then one of the biggest names in the breaking rap scene, to add his own distinctive voice to the mix.

"I Feel For You" was an overwhelming success upon release, charting in the Top Five, and perhaps best remembered for Melle Mel's distinctive triple-fast "Cha-ka Khan" rap. Khan recalled the moment she first heard it in an interview with *Rolling Stone*'s Debby Bull. After laying down her own vocals, Khan went into the studio the next day and listened to the new version. "I thought 'Oh, God.' It was great, yes, except for how am I going to live this down? Every time a guy walks up to me on the street, I think he's going to break into that rap. And most of them do." The album, also entitled *I Feel For You*, won Khan her third Grammy and was her biggest success to date.

By this time Khan was living in New York City with Milini and son Damien, born in 1979. She was married a second time briefly in the 1970s but during the mid-1980s was romantically involved with a Harlem schoolteacher who had originally tutored her daughter: "His salary is nowhere near mine, but he still brings his money in. He didn't give up his job like my other two husbands did—immediately stop work and groove and say, 'My work is now you,'" Khan told Bull in *Rolling Stone*. "No woman wants to hear that. A woman wants to wake up in the morning to the smell of aftershave lotion and not see anybody there."

Still single, Khan relocated her family to London at the onset of the 1990s after stopping briefly there on a tour and falling in love with the city. She also thought it would be a better environment in which to bring up her teenage son. "Right now in America there's a bounty on young Black boys," Khan told Wilkerson in *Essence*. "And I want him to get some kind of quality education, to speak other languages and live until he's 20 at least." Other members of her family stay for extended periods, including Milini with Khan's grand-daughter Raeven, Khan's father from Chicago and sister Yvonne, who followed her older sister into the music business in the 1970s as Taka Boom.

Khan continues to record, and has done a number of works for the soundtracks of popular movies. For the Wesley Snipes/Patrick Swayze film *To Wong Foo: Thanks for Everything, Julie Newmar*, Khan contributed "Free Yourself." She also sang "Love Me Still," the theme song for the 1995 Spike Lee film *Clockers*. Throughout the 1990s, Khan collaborated with such an eclectic mix of musicians as Prince, The Funk Brothers, George Benson, and Freddie Hubbard.

She also dabbled in acting, performing in a number of television sitcoms from the late 1980s. In early 1995 Khan did a stint on the London stage as Sister Carrie in the gospel musical *Mama, I Want to Sing*, and had performed in a handful of movies, including *The Messiah XXI* (2000) and *Roof Sex* (2003). She hobnobs in aristocratic circles and enjoys a cult-like following in Europe, where she moved in 1991 and tours occasionally to great success.

By the 2000s Khan had cemented her stature as a rhythm and blues legend; many of her early music had become staples in the R&B and jazz formats of radio programming. The eight-time Grammy winner released her *ClassiKhan* album in 2004, and it was hailed as "ambitious" and "elegant," according to *PRNewswire*. Chuck Arnold of *People Weekly* praised the album as proof that Chaka Khan is "one of the greatest song stylists of her time." The album helped to bolster the AgU Music Group record label, which formed in 2003 to serve listeners between their mid-twenties to their mid-fifties.

Khan also used her fame to start a charity in the late 1990s; the Chaka Khan Foundation provides help and education for such things as domestic violence, substance abuse, and autism. The service of the foundation is near to Khan's heart as witnessed in her memoir *Chaka!: Through the Fire*, which traces her troubled teenage years, struggles with drugs, and rise to fame. Her story was produced as a touring musical in 2005 and the proceeds were slated to benefit the Chaka Khan Foundation. Khan had a firm grasp on her desires for her future, as she said in her chairman's message on the Chaka Khan Foundation Web site: "I realize that I can't change the world, but I can do my part in contributing to society. If I leave this world knowing that I've helped one woman break the cycle of addiction and abuse; that one child has believed enough to get the education he/she deserves, then I can rest in peace."

Selected works

Books

Chaka!: Through the Fire, Rodale, 2003.

Recordings

(With Rufus) *Rufus*, 1973.
(With Rufus) *From Rags to Rufus*, 1973.
(With Rufus) *Rufus Featuring Chaka Khan*, mid-1970s.
Chaka Khan, 1979.
What Cha' Gonna Do for Me?, 1981.
I Feel for You, mid-1980s.
Destiny, 1986.
C.K., 1988.
The Woman I Am, 1992.
Dare You to Love Me, 1995.
Come 2 My House, 1998.
ClassiKhan, 2004.

Sources

Periodicals

Essence, January 1986, p. 69; October 1995, p. 84; March 2003, p. 130.
Interview, November 1998, p. 70.
Jet, January 10, 2005, p. 24; January 19, 1999, p. 56.
People Weekly, November 29, 2004, p. 48.

Rolling Stone, October 24, 1974, p. 17; February 14, 1985, p. 11.

On-line

"Alternatives: Chaka Khan: Still Every Woman," *All Hip-Hip,* www.allhiphop.com/alternatives/?ID=1 10 (March 9, 2005).
Chaka Khan, www.chakakhan.com (March 9, 2005).
Chaka Khan Foundation, www.chakakhanfounda tion.org (March 9, 2005).

—Carol Brennan and Sara Pendergast

Angelique Kidjo

1960—

Vocalist, songwriter

A powerful singer and tireless performer, Angelique Kidjo has been one of the most successful performers to emerge on world music stages in the 1990s and 2000s. Her music not only draws from African traditions but also interprets the ways those traditions developed after Africans were seized and taken to the New World. Thus elements of American soul, funk, rap, and jazz, Brazilian samba, Jamaican reggae, and Cuban and Puerto Rican salsa all show up on her recordings, along with various African styles. Early in her career she told *Guardian* reporter Jonathan Romney that "my records sound like dance music because that's the only way for Europeans to approach something they don't know," and as she evolved into one of the international music scene's most popular concert attractions, she accumulated a large fan base that happily came on stage and danced with her.

Kidjo is a native of Benin, on Africa's Atlantic coast adjacent to Nigeria; the first of her eight languages was Fon. She was born in the coastal city of Ouidah on July 14, 1960, to government postal official Franck Kidjo (an enthusiastic photographer and banjo player on the side) and his choreographer wife Yvonne. Kidjo was

Kidjo, Angelique, photograph. AP/Wide world Photos, Reproduced by permission.

lucky enough to have parents who backed her performing ambitions—female popular vocalists are rare in many African countries, and, she told the *Guardian,* "It's very, very rare in Africa to find parents who aren't there mainly to stop you doing what you want."

Among her eight siblings were several brothers who started a band when she was young, inspired by James Brown and other American stars who flooded Benin's airwaves. Kidjo was musically eclectic from the start, listening avidly to juju sounds from neighboring Nigeria, to pop music from other African countries, to Cuban salsa music. But, asked by the *Boston Globe* to list her musical influences, she first named "the traditional music which I grew up with, [which taught] me the importance of music as a communication tool."

Raised in the Catholic Church, Kidjo found that its tenets were compatible with traditional African religious beliefs. "In Catholicism," she explained to Ira Band of the *Toronto Star,* "we're taught not to kill, to preserve human life. In voodoo-ism, we have a different God—you live with the wind, the sea, the sun, you live with nature. It's a God of nature. Voodoo is seen as

At a Glance . . .

Born July 14, 1960, in Ouidah, Benin; daughter of Franck (a government official) and Yvonne (a choreographer) Kidjo; moved to France, early 1980s; married Jean Hebrail (a composer and bassist); children: Naima. *Education:* Attended law school, Paris, France. *Religion:* Roman Catholic and traditional African voodoo.

Career: Recording artist, 1970s–; Pili Pili, African jazz band member, early 1980s; Mango label artist, 1991-2001; Columbia label artist, 2001–.

Addresses: *Label*—Columbia Records, 550 Madison Ave., New York, NY 10022. *Web*—www.angeliquekidjo.com.

something negative, but it's not. It's based on anima and on respect for a human being's life."

Left Benin for Political Reasons

Kidjo made her stage debut at age six with her mother's dance troupe, and in the late 1970s she formed a band of her own and recorded an album that featured a cover version of a song by another of Kidjo's idols, South African singer Miriam Makeba. In 1980, however, Kidjo found her musical activities restricted by a new leftist regime that took power in Benin and tried to force her to record political anthems. Kidjo fled to Paris in 1983 with the intent of studying law there and becoming a human rights lawyer. But she realized that she was not cut out for political life. "I decided I would try to touch poor people with my music," she told the *Globe.*

Her partner in this enterprise was French bassist and composer Jean Hebrail, whom Kidjo married and with whom she has written much of her music; the pair has a daughter, Naima Laura, born in 1993. For several years Kidjo played in a French African jazz band called Pili Pili, led by pianist Jasper van t'Hof, but in 1989 she struck out on her own, forming a band and releasing the album *Parakou.* That debut had its intended effect: it attracted the attention of the biggest name in world music at the time, Chris Blackwell of Britain's Island Records. He signed Kidjo to the label's Mango subdivision, and her second album, *Logozo,* was released in 1991.

That album gained Kidjo a faithful core of fans who could be counted on to attend her highly participatory live shows. Her unusual image contributed to her

success; in place of the expansive look of other African female vocalists, Kidjo sported a lean dancer's body clad in denim pants, and she cut her hair very close to her head. "On stage, I move too much to wear skirts," she explained to the *Guardian.* "I don't want to show off my ass—my music isn't about sex." The music on *Logozo* skillfully mixed traditional African beats with hip-hop and electronic styles.

Recorded Traditional Musicians

The year 1994 saw Kidjo create a bona fide international hit; her *Aye* album received strong reviews and generated "Agolo," a dance-floor favorite throughout Africa and Europe. She followed that album up with *Fifa,* which grew from a set of tape recordings Kidjo and her husband made of traditional instrumentalists during a tour of small towns in Benin. The resulting disc mixed such sounds as cow horns, traditional flutes, and bamboo percussion with modern African pop, American gospel, and rap. The album, an ambitious effort that used roughly 200 musicians, featured a guest guitar solo from one of Kidjo's many admirers in the U.S. music industry, Carlos Santana.

Fifa included several songs in English, but Kidjo scoffed at the idea that she was singing in English for commercial reasons. "I do what pleases me," she told the *Toronto Star.* "I do the music I like. I don't know if it's going to be English or French or some African dialect. Music is music; it's all about communication." She believed that the sentiments in a piece of music could be understood even if the hearer were unfamiliar with the language of the text, and later in her career she encouraged the efforts of pop stars Sting and Celine Dion to sing in Spanish rather than English. One modern form of communication Kidjo adopted was the Internet; she established a website in 1996, well in advance of many Western pop stars. Backing up her claim that she was not affected by commercial considerations was her cancellation of an African tour that year when she discovered that it was to be sponsored by tobacco companies.

Kidjo's next three albums formed parts of a trilogy exploring African-derived music styles of the Western Hemisphere. *Oremi,* released in 1998 on the Island label itself after Mango's demise, was the U.S. chapter in the trilogy, mixing traditional music from Benin with black American styles and featuring a Kidjo cover of Jimi Hendrix's "Voodoo Child." The album won Kidjo a spot on the all-female Lilith Fair tour in the U.S. A hiatus in Kidjo's recording career followed, during which she was signed to the Columbia label and began dividing her time between Paris and Brooklyn, New York.

Part of the reason for the move involved Kidjo's desire to work with American musicians like Roots drummer Ahmir Thompson and rock singer and bandleader Dave Matthews, with whom Kidjo toured in the summer of 2001. The following summer saw her on the road with Santana in the wake of his smash collaborative success *Supernatural*. Santana recorded "Adouma," a Kidjo song from the *Aye* album, on his 2002 release *Shaman*.

Followed Slave Routes Musically

In 2002 Kidjo returned to her African diaspora trilogy with *Black Ivory Soul,* an album that focused on the rhythms of the Brazilian state of Bahia, musically linked to Benin by centuries of the slave trade. "I've been following the route of the slaves," she told the *Boston Herald* in reference to the entire trilogy project. Kidjo recorded with contemporary Brazilian musicians Carlinhos Brown and Vinicius Cantuaria and included a cover of Gilberto Gil's classic song about Brazil's hillside slums, "Refavela." The All Music Guide opined that *Black Ivory Soul* "might just be her most consistent and satisfying effort to date."

Kidjo toured with a constantly changing complement of top-notch international musicians as she released new music. From 1994 onward, she was rarely off the road, and she was saddened that she rarely had time to visit her parents in Benin. Her shows, noted Beth Pearson of the Glasgow, Scotland *Herald,* "require a broad dancing repertoire from the audience," for Kidjo often invited audience members to come up on stage and join the dancers who were part of her show.

The final installment of her trilogy, 2004's *Oyaya!,* featured music from Cuba, Haiti, Jamaica, and other parts of the Caribbean basin. The album included a duet with the octogenarian Guyanese-born French crooner Henri Salvador, and Kidjo also updated rumbas, salsa pieces, and other Caribbean dance music with a variety of African instruments and sounds that closed the transatlantic circle. Another force affecting the album was Kidjo's work as a goodwill ambassador for the United Nations Children's Fund (UNICEF); in "Mutoto Kwanza," she set to Jamaican ska music a song she had learned in Tanzania from a group of HIV-infected orphans.

"To me, you don't think of her just in terms of world beat or African music. You have to think of Tina Turner or something, her whole dynamic energy up there," said New Orleans Jazz and Heritage Festival director Quint Davis (as quoted in the *Boston Globe*) after Kidjo

appeared at the festival in 2003. In a way, Kidjo had become a musical bridge-builder between Africa and the West. "I want to show you the links back to Africa," she told a Boston audience of children (as reported by the *Boston Globe*) as she instructed her percussionist to break down the rhythms behind one highly danceable tune. "That's important for you to know."

Selected discography

Parakou, Island, 1989.
Logozo, Mango, 1991.
Aye, Mango, 1994.
Fifa, Mango, 1996.
Oremi, Island, 1998.
Keep On Moving: The Best of Angelique Kidjo, Sony, 2001.
Black Ivory Soul, Columbia, 2002.
Oyaya!, Columbia, 2004.

Sources

Books

Contemporary Musicians, volume 39, Gale, 2002.

Periodicals

Australian, September 11, 1996, p. Local-7.
Boston Globe, July 22, 1993, p. Calendar-13; June 15, 2001, p. C14.; July 1, 2002, p. B10; June 22, 2003, p. N7.
Boston Herald, July 1, 2002.
Essence, June 2002, p. 82.
Gazette (Montreal, Quebec, Canada), October 2, 1992, p. C5.
Guardian (London, England), October 8, 1991; May 9, 1996, p. T15.
Herald (Glasgow, Scotland), October 29, 2004, p. 23.
Toronto Star, August 1, 1996, p. G10; June 17, 2004, p. G4.
Toronto Sun, April 4, 2002, p. 74.
Washington Post, August 16, 2003, p. C9.

On-line

"Angelique Kidjo," *All Music Guide,* www.allmusic.com (January 18, 2005).

—James M. Manheim

B. Waine Kong

1943—

Chief executive officer, Association of Black Cardiologists

Throughout his life, B. Waine Kong has retained the good-natured sociability that he learned growing up in a small agricultural community in Jamaica. However, beneath his relaxed and likable personality, Kong has proved himself to be a dedicated and tireless worker. Whether earning a graduate degree by attending classes at night while working a full-time day job, or changing the face of health care by organizing blood pressure clinics in dozens of Maryland churches, Kong has quietly devoted his life to learning ways to improve the health of the African-American community. As chief executive officer of the Association of Black Cardiologists, Kong continues to work to increase the lifespan of black Americans, so that the multigenerational black community will include more and more grandparents and great-grandparents.

Basil Waine Kong was born in the tiny community of Woodlands, in St. Elizabeth Parish, or county, in southwestern Jamaica. His father, Chan Kong, had been one of many Chinese refugees who fled China after a Japanese invasion in the early 1940s. Chan Kong had experienced starvation, so he determined to make sure he would always have access to food. When he settled in Jamaica, he supported himself by opening a restaurant. He soon developed a relationship with a young woman named Violet McKenzie who worked as a cashier in his restaurant. The couple had two children, Basil Waine and his brother, Earl DeCarlton Kong.

Though they were teased a bit because they were the only half Chinese children in Woodlands, the Kong children suffered little real discrimination. Jamaica had been a British colony for many years. Not only British colonists, but slaves, traders, sailors, and other immigrants from all over the world had come to Jamaica, forcibly or voluntarily, giving the island population a rich racial mix.

Poverty Taught Creativity

Life in the little farming town of Woodlands was simple. The community of 500 people had no electricity, running water, newspaper, library, or even a radio. Even so, Kong's childhood was peaceful and happy. With little money or access to stores, the children of Woodlands made their own toys, using whatever scraps they could find to create marbles, slingshots, toy trucks, even bicycles made of wood. As a child, Kong played cricket and soccer, climbed trees, jumped rope, ran to the market, and ran to school. However, his walk to church with his grandmother was slow and dignified.

When Kong was four years old, his father abandoned the family. In order to support her children, Violet Kong left to seek work in the United States. For the next years, she worked as a domestic, taking care of other people's children to earn money to send back to her own family in Jamaica. While in the United States, she married Author Johnson and had two sons. The American dollars his mother sent to his grandmother allowed Kong's family a few luxuries beyond the modest community standard. Kong wore a wristwatch, shoes, and even had a "store-bought" bicycle, which was a source of great pride.

The general poverty of Woodlands extended to the community school, which could afford few books. Only the teacher had a book, and the class had to memorize the math problems, poetry, and history of England that she read to them. Learning was extremely hard under these circumstances, and, even as a teenager, Kong had difficulty reading, writing, and spelling.

The summer of his 14th year, Kong was sent to live with his uncle Cleve Allen, a veterinarian in Kingston, Jamaica's capitol city. Though there were many new sights and experiences in Kingston, the sight that amazed Kong the most was the library. Having grown up in a home where the only books were the Bible and a book of hymns, Kong was dazzled to see an entire room filled with books. He took down the first book that caught his eye, a science book about invertebrates, and read it. When he began to tell his uncle about all that he had learned from his reading, his uncle became very excited.

Began a New Life in the United States

Because Kong had had so little access to learning, no one had ever considered him intelligent. His family had supposed that he was best suited to become a farmer in Woodlands. However, when his uncle saw that he could not only read and understand, but that he had an interest and desire for learning, he contacted Kong's mother. Dr. Allen encouraged his sister-in-law to bring Kong to live with her and her new family in the United States. She agreed, and at age 15, Kong began a new life in Morristown, New Jersey.

When he arrived in the United States, Kong experienced yet another kind of culture shock. Americans could not understand his speech. Like most Jamaicans, he did not speak English, but the rhythmic *patois* of the island. *Patois*, sometimes called "pidgin" or "Creole" is a combination of English and French with various African and Native languages to form a unique language, particular to the place where the *patois* has evolved. Though some English speakers in the past have simply considered Jamaican *patios* to be incorrect English, many Jamaicans take pride in their language and see it as an important part of their Caribbean culture.

Determined to help her son enter his new society, Kong's mother immersed him in lessons. Every evening after school he studied language, reading, grammar, and piano. He even took swimming lessons, since, though he had grown up on a tropical island, living only 20 miles from the sea, he had rarely visited the beach and never learned to swim. Perhaps more than any of these lessons, however, Kong's skill at sports helped him to fit in at his new school. During his first year of high school, he earned seven varsity letters in cross-country running, wrestling, and track. He even set a track record for the school in the 400-meter race. Along with gaining him friendship and respect in high school, this athletic skill would also ensure him a higher education.

As graduation approached, Kong's high school counselor began to urge him to consider a carpentry job, since woodshop seemed to be his best subject. However, a recruiter from Simpson College in Iowa came to Morristown with scholarship money for good athletes. Simpson offered Kong $500 per semester, and, in

1963, Waine Kong, who everyone had thought would be a farmer all his life, went to college in the Midwest.

Continued His Education

Even with the scholarship money, Kong had to work his way through college. He worked as a dishwasher, a janitor, and a photographer for the school newspaper. As his college career progressed, he began to do more academic jobs, working as a student lecturer, a lab assistant in the biology department, and a research assistant in the sociology department. His cheerful, helpful attitude won him friends wherever he worked.

At the end of his first semester, he almost lost his scholarship money when his grade average fell below the required 2.0. However, while working as a custodian cleaning buildings, he had become friendly with the dean's secretary. Because she liked Kong, she told him that she would not show his grades to the dean, giving him a chance to bring his average up. He took her warning to heart, and by the time he graduated in 1967, he had earned A's in his last five courses. During his senior year, he had also married and started a family.

Kong majored in psychology and sociology. He put these social sciences to work, taking a job as a probation officer for the state of Maryland. While working full time supervising juvenile offenders, he attended graduate school classes in school guidance counseling in the evenings. After earning his masters degree from American University in 1970, he took a job as assistant professor at the University of the District of Columbia, teaching classes in such subjects as human growth and development, juvenile delinquency, and criminology.

However, Kong had neither finished his education nor found his life's work yet. He soon developed an interest in hypertension, especially among African Americans. Two of his relatives had recently died from strokes, a common and very dangerous effect of high blood pressure. As a psychologist, Kong began to wonder how an individual's state of mind and personality type contributed to high blood pressure. He began his studies at the University of Maryland, and had completed all the course work for his doctoral degree, but the university did not have doctors to supervise a thesis about hypertension. Kong's interest in the subject led him to Walden University, where physicians supervised his thesis work. Among them was Dr. Elijah Saunders, an African-American cardiologist and head of research at Baltimore's Providence Hospital.

Developed Hypertension Clinics

Though Kong's research work did not prove that personality type and psychological state were important factors in hypertension, he developed an interest in the heart health of black Americans that would guide

the rest of his career. After earning his PhD, he returned to work at University of the District of Columbia for two years. In 1978 he took a sabbatical, or leave from work, to join Elijah Saunders in researching ways to combat high blood pressure among African Americans. It was during this time that Kong made a major contribution to public health, one that he would consider his major accomplishment.

In 1978 only trained doctors and nurses were permitted to take a patient's blood pressure, because such tests were considered medical procedures. During his work with Saunders, Kong got the idea that if volunteers could be trained to set up hypertension clinics in churches, they could not only check the blood pressure levels of church members but also educate them about the importance of continuing check-ups. Kong believed that trained community volunteers would prove to be far more effective at providing this personal attention than occasional visits from a visiting doctor.

During the next three years, Kong and Saunders got grants to set up clinics in 100 Maryland churches, training and certifying over 500 people as "Blood Pressure Measurement Specialists." These trainees learned to check the blood pressure of fellow church members, refer them to a doctor if necessary, and monitor their health. Most importantly, the Blood Pressure Measurement Specialists offered the support and encouragement needed for blood pressure control.

When Kong and Saunders realized that these church clinics did not reach many black men, they began training barbers to operate hypertension clinics in their barbershops. These church and barbershop blood pressure clinics marked a major change in the practice of medicine, with community members helping each other take responsibility for their own health care.

With the help of grant money from the American Heart Association, they also began a media campaign to educate African Americans about the warning signs of heart attack. They set up classes in public libraries to teach cardio-pulmonary resuscitation (CPR), a method for reviving people who have had a heart attack. Almost 10,000 people were certified in CPR through the program that Kong helped initiate.

Kong never returned to his teaching job. Instead, he had become committed to working in the field of public health, first through grants from pharmaceutical companies, the National Institutes of Health and the American Heart Association, then through Providence Hospital and the Urban Cardiology Research Center. In 1986, he was offered the job of chief executive office of the Association of Black Cardiologists (ABC). The ABC had been formed in 1974, by 17 black physicians who wanted to work on improving the heart health of the African-American community. Heart diseases were responsible for 50 percent of the deaths among American blacks. The ABC intended to follow the model of modern dentistry, which had eliminated many dental problems with a three-fold program of public health, regular professional care, and personal health awareness. ABC developed and publicized a program of seven steps to good health, which it hoped would have a similar effect on the heart problems of many American blacks.

Pursued a Law Degree

The goals of the ABC fit perfectly with Kong's personal career goals, and he was happy in his new job. However, the easy-going man who had never considered himself a good student was not yet finished with his education. In 1986, he had married again. His wife Stephanie, a physician and managed care expert, encouraged Kong to follow yet another dream and enter law school. Sure that he was "too old" to get into law school, Kong took the entrance examinations and applied. To his own surprise, he was accepted at Dickinson School of Law in Pennsylvania. The next four years were a whirlwind of intensive study in law school, hard work as the new head of a national health organization, and moving several times as the family followed Stephanie Kong's career from Pennsylvania to California, Florida, and Georgia. Finally, Kong graduated from law school in 1990 and passed the

Georgia bar exam. His eldest daughter, Jillian, attended law school at the same time.

Kong has continued to work as CEO of the ABC, managing a staff of 24, overseeing the creation of a new $10 million headquarters and conference center, and initiating research and community programs to further the organization's mission—to ensure that as many black children as possible get to know their grandparents.

Sources

On-line

Association of Black Cardiologists, www.abcardio. org (January 8, 2005)

Other

Information for this profile was obtained through an interview with B. Waine Kong on January 3, 2005.

—Tina Gianoulis

Jawanza Kunjufu

1953—

Writer, educator, publisher

Jawanza Kunjufu has dedicated his career to addressing the ills afflicting black culture in the United States, working primarily as an educational consultant and author but more recently expanding into video and film production. All aspects of the African American experience occupy Kunjufu's attention, but the main thrust of his work has been directed toward improving the education and socialization of black youths. He is the founder and president of African American Images, a Chicago-based publishing company that sponsors dozens of workshops intended to help educators and parents develop practical solutions to the problems of child-rearing in what he perceives to be a racist society. Kunjufu holds advanced degrees in business and economics that have enabled him to place the problems of black society in the larger context of national and international economic models.

Born on June 15, 1953, in Chicago, Kunjufu—who adopted a Swahili name in 1973—credits his parents, Eddie and Mary Brown, with affording him the encouragement, discipline, and stability that would later become the core of his program for the renewal of black society. As a young man, Kunjufu was urged by his father to volunteer his time at a number of different jobs, working without pay in exchange for learning firsthand how businesses and skilled craftsmen went about their work. Kunjufu attended Illinois State University at Normal and received a bachelor of science degree in economics in 1974. Ten years later he finished a doctorate in business administration at Union Graduate School.

Despite his formal training in business, Kunjufu was early on fascinated—and appalled—by the educational system for black students in America, and from 1974 onward he began delivering lectures and workshops treating the problems facing black educators. His presentations were well received, and Kunjufu eventually decided to make educational consulting his career; in 1980 he founded a publishing and consulting company in Chicago called African American Images. The birth of Kunjufu's two sons, Shikamana and Walker, further focused his energies on the contradictions inherent in black education and especially in the education of young black males. The fruit of these observations was the 1982 publication of *Countering the Conspiracy to Destroy Black Boys* —probably Kunjufu's best-known book—in which he analyzes and offers alternatives to the frequent failure of black males in school and in the marketplace.

In Kunjufu's view, the "conspiracy" against black males is fundamentally rooted in the need of a white minority to control the world's far greater population of people of color; but in addition to overt racism, Kunjufu includes in his indictment all teachers, parents, and especially adult black males who fail to provide the support and discipline needed to keep black boys off the streets and in the classroom. Kunjufu sees black males as caught in a self-perpetuating cycle of failure, in which the absence of stable, successful adult role models ensures that young blacks will do poorly in school, turn to street life, and father yet another generation of boys without adequate male role models. The net result is the prevention of black males from attaining positions of social and economic power—thus continuing what Kunjufu perceives as the effective servitude of the black race in spite of America's claims to democracy and freedom.

Kunjufu has developed counter-strategies to this "conspiracy" in a number of his other books. In 1986's *Motivating Black Youth to Work*, he suggests that black Americans shift the basis of their value system from money to the encouragement of each individual's natural talents, a shift Kunjufu characterizes as a difference between European and African value systems. The author casts doubt on the usefulness of jobs programs in and of themselves; in a culture saturated with images of luxury and the power of money, minimum-wage jobs can hold little attraction for today's young black men and women. Kunjufu instead urges that each black child be helped to identify and cultivate his or her talents; from these discoveries, the child must build a means of livelihood, preferably, according to Kunjufu, by starting his or her own businesses. But in order to do this, children need the support and discipline of strong, loving, and concerned parents.

In another of his books, 1984's *Developing Positive Self-Images and Discipline for Black Children*, Kunjufu cites a University of Chicago study of 70,000 schools across the United States; the study concluded that the most important factor in pupil performance was the expectations of his or her parents and teachers. This conclusion supports Kunjufu's belief in the

utmost importance of parental interest and support for schoolwork, along with the stimulation and challenge of a talented teacher. In this, as in all of his books and workshops, Kunjufu finds in the family the only effective defense against what he views as an inherently racist society; he particularly stresses the critical role of black men as role models and providers of discipline.

In conjunction with his writings, Kunjufu's African American Images organizes workshops for schools, community groups, and parents concerned with issues of education and economic independence. Kunjufu travels constantly in his role as moderator of these workshops and frequently lectures as well, addressing schools from the elementary grades on up to the college level. In addition, he has appeared on a number of well-known television programs, including *The Oprah Winfrey Show* and *Tony Brown's Journal*.

In the late 1980s, Kunjufu entered a new sphere of activity as the executive producer of a full-length motion picture, *Up Against the Wall*. Inspired by the success of independent black filmmakers such as Spike Lee and Robert Townsend, Kunjufu set out to make a film about black urban culture that would address the problems facing young black males without indulging in scenes of violence, sex, and drug abuse. Kunjufu told Frank James of the *Chicago Tribune*, "I wanted a movie that could take a black boy through positive and negative peer pressure and see if he could survive…and be a responsible young man."

Kunjufu persuaded actors Marla Gibbs (of "The Jeffersons") and Ron O'Neal (star of the 1972 megahit "Super Fly") to appear in the film without advance payment; O'Neal also agreed to serve as the film's director. Despite severe financial difficulties, *Up Against the Wall* was completed in two years at a cost of approximately $2 million and was released in January of 1991 to a limited number of theaters, primarily in the South. Kunjufu was unable to interest major film distributors in his project, which they thought too tame for today's audience, but the film did well enough at the box office to encourage Kunjufu to plan a second production.

Kunjufu's best claim to authority in the black community may well be the example of his own life. As he has recommended in book after book, Kunjufu managed to use the American educational process to develop his talents, create a successful business, and with his wife, Rita, raise two sons in a stable household. His success as a businessman and a father lends considerable weight to Kunjufu's ideas, which have been enthusiastically received by much of the black community. In 1992, Kunjufu opened a retail bookstore for African American Images which has since grown to be one of the largest black-owned bookstores in the country, with over 10,000 square feet of space and over 4,000 titles. Kunjufu has continued to compile studies and write books offering advice to black Americans about gaining a better education and creating a nurturing community in which to thrive.

Nearly twenty years after his first publication, Kunjufu offered another groundbreaking study about the state of life for African American males. The picture looked grim, with a rising number of black men in prison and alarming numbers of black boys relegated to special education classes in schools. In *State of Emergency: We Must Save African American Males,* Kunjufu offers statistics to show the magnitude of the social problem, but more importantly he lays out detailed advice for how to improve the situation he calls a "state of emergency." Noting that the nation's schools, economic system, pharmaceutical companies, and the prison system have institutionalized prejudices against blacks, Kunjufu also points to the preponderance of fatherlessness in black families for the difficulties facing black males. As with his other books, Kunjufu offers a series of best practices and approaches for parents, teachers and community activists to help address the problems he identifies.

Where some black leaders have been criticized for blaming the problems facing African Americans on racism alone, and others have occasionally stressed self-reliance while glossing over difficult discussions of racism, Kunjufu has found an important middle ground; by helping African Americans chart a course through racist waters and, at the same time, indicating the importance of black role models, strong families, and economic self-sufficiency, this learned author and educator has established himself as a leading voice of black empowerment.

Selected writings

Books

Children Are the Reward of Life, African American Images, 1978.
Countering the Conspiracy to Destroy Black Boys, African American Images, volume one, 1982, volume two, 1986, volume three, 1990.
Developing Positive Self-Images and Discipline for Black Children, African American Images, 1984.
Motivating Black Youth to Work, African American Images, 1986.
Lessons From History: A Celebration in Blackness, African American Images, 1987.
Critical Issues in Educating African American Youth, African American Images, 1989.
To Be Popular or Smart: The Black Peer Group, African American Images, 1989.
Black Economics: Solutions for Economic and Community Empowerment, African American Images, 1991.
Black Students' Survival Guide, African American Images, 1998.
State of Emergency: We Must Save African American Males, African American Images, 2001.
(With Carter G. Woodson) *The Mis-Education of the Negro,* African American Images, 2002.

Sources

Periodicals

Black Issues in Higher Education, February 19, 1998, p. 36; January 17, 2002, p. 33.
Chicago Tribune, February 18, 1991.
Essence, November 1988; December 1996, p. 60.
Herald and Review (Decatur, IL), January 17, 2005.
Publisher's Weekly, August 4, 1997, p. 38.

On-line

African American Images, www.africanamericanimages.com (March 10, 2005).

—Jonathan Martin and Sara Pendergast

Jennifer Lawson

1946—

Television executive

As executive vice president of national programming for the Public Broadcasting System (PBS) until 1996, Jennifer Lawson is, according to Jeremy Gerard in the *New York Times*, "the most powerful programming executive in public television." Lawson is responsible for overseeing the creation, promotion, and scheduling of national programming for the 330-station public television system. Prior to PBS, Lawson was a senior programming executive at the Corporation for Public Broadcasting and also had several years' experience working as a funding liaison with filmmakers. According to PBS president Bruce Christensen in the *New York Times*, Lawson's "strong ties to the independent filmmaking community" made her especially well-qualified to oversee PBS's programming needs.

The naming of Lawson was a landmark appointment for PBS, which, for the first time, centralized national program decision-making in one executive. Among Lawson's primary responsibilities are to expand public television programming and broaden its audience. Lawson's priorities in doing so, as Gerard reports, are "to offer more cultural diversity in public television, to improve and expand programming for children and to increase the audience through better promotion." Already in her first year, Lawson recorded two notable achievements for PBS. *The Civil War*, a five-night series, drew over 50 million viewers and became the most-watched show in PBS history. Also under Lawson, PBS began promoting its programming on commercial networks for the first time.

Lawson has stated that her parents were the biggest influence in her life. "From my early childhood, they taught me a whole range of skills, from carpentry to painting," she told Darlene Gavron Stevens in the *Chicago Tribune*. "…. My father always insisted I learn how to work on cars. His notion was that if I could do a transmission job, I could make my living anywhere in the world." Lawson grew up in the deep South, and in the 1960s the Civil Rights Movement emphasized for her the importance of helping people.

Although Lawson won a scholarship and was in pre-med studies at Tuskegee Institute, she interrupted her career plans and joined black voter registration efforts in the South. She was quoted in *Jet*: "The Civil Rights Movement became the turning point for me because I began to see that there was a larger ill. To me, it required more courage to try to address that ill than it did to deal with the individual sick person. I felt the time was ripe for us to change this society and eradicate institutionalized racism."

From 1970 to 1972, Lawson worked in Tanzania on an African publishing project, and it was then that she became aware of the power of visual media. She realized, as she told Stevens, "how ironic it was that we were working in print in a society that for the most part did not read. I began to feel that film and TV would be the educational media of the future." Lawson returned to the United States and completed a master's degree in film at Columbia University, after which she worked as a film editor and taught film classes. In 1980, she joined the Corporation for Public Broadcasting as coordinator of their television program fund, and worked as a liaison with independent filmmakers. By

At a Glance . . .

Born Jennifer Karen Lawson in 1946; grew up in Fairfield, AL; daughter of William (owner of a repair shop) and Velma (a schoolteacher) Lawson; married Anthony Gittens, 1982; children: two sons. *Education*: Attended Tuskegee Institute; received undergraduate and masters degrees from Columbia University.

Career: Student Nonviolent Coordinating Committee (SNCC), staff member, c. 1964-67; worked with National Council of Negro Women, 1968-69; Whitman County, MS, director of adult education program, c. 1969; Drum and Spear (publisher), Washington, DC, art director, c. 1970, lived in Tanzania, 1970-72, and worked on joint government publishing project; William Green Productions (film company), editor; Brooklyn College, Brooklyn, NY, film instructor; The Film Fund, executive director; Corporation for Public Broadcasting, Washington, DC, 1980-89, began as program fund coordinator, became senior programming executive; Public Broadcasting Service, Washington, DC, executive vice president of programming, 1989-95; Magic Box Mediaworks, Inc., founder and president, 1995–; WHUT, Howard University, general manager, 2004–.

Memberships: Women in Film & Video (WIFV), board of directors; PBS, board of directors.

Awards: Named one of "101 Most Influential People in Entertainment Today," *Entertainment Weekly*, 1990; Power 50 list, *Hollywood Reporter*, 1994; International Film and Video Festival, Gold Camera Award, for three episodes of *Africa* series, 2002; Women in Film & Video, Washington, DC, Woman of Vision Award, 2004.

Addresses: *Home*—Washington, DC; *Office*—Magic Box Mediaworks, 1838 Ontario Place NW, Washington, DC 20009; Howard University Television WHUT, 2222 Fourth Street, NW, Washington, DC 20059.

the time Lawson left in 1989, she was associate director of drama and arts programming, and was responsible for a $42 million budget.

In her position at PBS, Lawson was able to further the ideals of her work in the civil rights movement. "In a way," she told Stevens, "I'm still continuing my mission of helping people, but using a different and powerful medium: television." Lawson believed that being the highest-ranking black woman ever to serve in public television sent a positive message to viewers. She told Gerard: "I think it speaks to public television's recognition and tradition of serving the entire country, and in presenting the cultural realities of America in a way not necessarily presented in the rest of television." She added: "When you say public television is an alternative, you should be able to see that clearly."

During her tenure as PBS's first chief programming director, Lawson brought such award-winning programs as Ken Burns' *Civil War* and *Baseball* and such children's programs as *Barney and Friends* and *Where in the World Is Carmen Sandiego.*

Lawson resigned from her top PBS post in 1995 after the company reorganized. She explained her move to *Jet* as "my choice," adding that she was considering new ways to make meaningful contributions to television programming. Although offered other high-profile jobs, Lawson started up her own production company, Magic Box Mediaworks, in the Washington, D.C. area. "I thought it would be fascinating to take the risk to be out on my own," Lawson told *USA Today*. Lawson began working as a consultant from such clients as Maryland Public Television, but within a short time, Lawson had devised an ambitious plan for herself: to produce a multi-part documentary series on Africa. She explained in an interview on the *All Africa* Web site that "I was thinking I want to present the Africa that I feel I have seen. And I want to present the Africa that is not overwhelmingly disease, famine, warfare, brutality, mutilations—oddities, but is real people going about their lives and doing so in a way that despite incredible poverty I somehow feel inspired and enriched by their presence. So I wanted to try and capture that and share that with viewers." The eight-part *Africa* series was aired on PBS in 2001. Lawson won kudos for presenting a previously unseen view of the continent and the culture of those who live there. Lawson also served as the executive producer of a Web site called *African American World* for PBS; the site provides browsers with comprehensive insights into African American experiences and history.

While continuing to develop projects through Magic Box Mediaworks, Lawson took the position of general manager at Howard University Television, WHUT, in 2004.

Selected works

Africa (eight-part documentary television series), PBS, 2001.

Sources

Periodicals

Broadcasting and Cable, July 1, 1996.
Chicago Tribune, June 3, 1990.
Ebony June 1991.
Entertainment Weekly, November 2, 1990.
Essence, April 1991.
Jet, December 18, 1989; March 6, 1995.
New York Times, October 20, 1989; June 21, 1990.
Time, December 10, 1990.
USA Today, October 20, 2003.

On-line

"African American World," *PBS,* www.pbs.org/wnet/
   aaworld/ (March 9, 2005).
"Africa: The Series," *PBS,* www.pbs.org/wnet/africa/
   index.html (March 9, 2005).
"Jennifer Lawson, Executive Producer, on the 'Africa'
   Series," http://allafrica.com/stories/2001091004
   27.html (March 9, 2005).

—Michael E. Mueller and Sara Pendergast

Laura Love

1960—

Singer, songwriter, bassist

The music of Seattle-based artist Laura Love has been labeled as Afro-Celtic or folk-funk; it merges the rhythms of urban styles with the stringed-instrument sounds of folk and acoustic music, using the whole fusion to support an impressive set of original songs. After the 1997 release of her major-label debut, *Octoroon,* Love became one of the folk scene's brightest stars. But few of her fans knew the difficult personal background from which her music grew. She told of that background in her 2004 memoir, *You Ain't Got No Easter Clothes.*

Of black, white, and Native American background, Love was born Laura Jones in Lincoln, Nebraska, in 1960. Her father Preston Love was a jazz saxophonist in nearby Omaha, but Love met him for the first time only when she was 16 and sneaked into a club to hear him play. For most of her childhood, she believed that he had died. Love was raised by her mother, Winifred Jones, a former jazz singer (who used the name Wini Winston) who was studying at Nebraska Wesleyan University during her intermittent lucid periods.

Survived Group Suicide Planned by Mother

Most of the time, however, Love's mother was in the grip of mental illness. Love's earliest memory was of her mother being taken to a mental hospital by police when she was three. Love and her sister were dragged through a nightmare of shelters, social service bureaucracies, substandard housing, and foster homes for

years, first in Lincoln and then in Omaha. Love's memoir, *You Ain't Got No Easter Clothes,* is a matter-of-fact litany of these woes, the culmination of which was an episode in which Love's mother instructed her and her sister Lisa to hang the family Siamese cat in a noose, after which the three would hang themselves together and look forward to the afterlife to come. The plan was fortunately scotched when the cat struggled out of its noose.

In addition to dealing with painful situations created by her mother, Love faced racial prejudices from both white and black schoolmates. After moving to a new predominantly black school in Omaha, Love wrote in *You Ain't Got No Easter Clothes,* "The only real difference was that here I became 'that high-yellow bitch that acts like a honky and think she so cute' instead of 'the only nigger at our school.'" A bright spot for Love came when she sang "Anticipation" at a junior high school assembly, accompanying herself on the guitar; she brought the house down. "There in the Everett Junior High School auditorium, soaking up all that positive energy, I understood that I would never do anything else for the rest of my life but sing," Love wrote.

Love left home at age 16, and this added hardship made it difficult to follow through with her teenage wish of singing for a living. However, Love did manage to sing whenever she could. She sang for inmates at the Nebraska State Penitentiary, and she performed on one occasion with her father's band, although he showed little interest in being part of her life. Moving first to Portland, Oregon, and then to Seattle, she enrolled at the University of Washington and graduated with an honors degree in psychology in 1989. By that time, however, she had already begun to immerse herself in the vital music scene of her new hometown. Starting out as a bassist with enthusiasm but few skills, she soon took on lead vocal duties with a proto-grunge band called Boom Boom G.I.

Formed Own Label after Negative Review

Her first band "was loud and bad," Love told the *Omaha World Herald.* "The first review we got said that we were annoyingly pointless." She took the review to heart and joined another band, an all-female outfit called Venus Envy. In 1989 she struck out independently, forming a label of her own called Octoroon Biography and releasing her debut album, *Menstrual Hut.* She developed her distinctive mixture of urban and Americana sounds over the course of four albums, aided by the crack instrumental sounds of performers such as fiddler Barbara Lamb.

Sales of Love's albums mounted, and 1994's *Helvetica Bold* got the attention of a New York City clothing-store-chain owner who set out to organize a Carnegie Hall concert featuring music he felt was underexposed. Love was offered the chance to perform one song, to be chosen by the concert organizer. She bowled the audience over to such a degree that she landed on *Billboard* magazine's 1995 list of the country's ten best unsigned acts, attracted notice from the *New York Times,* and gained an opening-act slot at one of the city's legendary clubs, the Bottom Line. The world music-oriented Putumayo label released her album *The Laura Love Collection.*

Signed to the major Mercury label, Love released *Octoroon* (the word denotes a person who is one-eighth black) in 1997. The album included a nod to Love's Seattle background in the form of a cover of Nirvana's "Come As You Are," but also featured the traditional pieces "Blind Bartimus" and "Amazing Grace." Love followed that album up in 1998 with *Shum Ticky,* which featured a guest appearance from rapper Sir Mix-a-Lot on a new version of "The Clapping Song."

Used Liner Notes to Locate Mother

Love's 2000 album *Fourteen Days* was more political in nature than her other work, having taken shape during Seattle's anti-globalization demonstrations in which Love participated. That year, she also began making notes about her childhood, at first without any intention of having them published. Having moved in with her life partner, Pam, Love became a foster mother to a seven-month-old girl named Khristy. She also cared for large numbers of homeless cats. For many years she lost touch with her mother, but she was able to locate her in 1998 after including a plea for help in the liner notes of *Octoroon.*

Love released *Welcome to Pagan Place* in 2003 and followed it up the next year with *You Ain't Got No Easter Clothes,* conceived as a companion to her memoir. She decided to publish the book, she told the *Seattle Times,* because "I wanted to put a name and a face to what [some politicians] call welfare queens, the dregs of society, the drain on our economy." Hard as her childhood had been, Love argued that without the support of social welfare programs, it could have been much worse. "Society made an investment in me," she told the *Times,* "and it has been spared a very angry person who would have cost much, much more."

Selected works

Books

You Ain't Got No Easter Clothes, Hyperion Books, 2004.

Recordings

Menstrual Hut, Octoroon Biography, 1989.
Z Therapy, Octoroon Biography, 1990.
Pangaea, Octoroon Biography, 1992.
Helvetica Bold, Octoroon Biography, 1994.
The Laura Love Collection, Putumayo, 1996.
Octoroon, Mercury, 1997.
Shum Ticky, Mercury, 1998.
Fourteen Days, Zoe, 2000.
Welcome to Pagan Place, Koch, 2003.
You Ain't Got No Easter Clothes, Koch, 2004.

Sources

Books

Love, Laura, *You Ain't Got No Easter Clothes,* Hyperion, 2004.

Periodicals

Boston Globe, April 27, 1995, p. 57.
Columbus Dispatch, January 7, 1999, p. 5.
Omaha World Herald, June 18, 1995, p. 22; November 21, 1995, p. 36; September 3, 1998, p. 50.

Seattle Times, January 20, 2005, p. H9; August 8, 2004, p. K1.
Tampa Tribune, November 17, 2000, p. 16.
Washington Post, August 18, 2004, p. C3.

On-line

"Laura Love," *All Music Guide,* www.allmusic.com (January 13, 2005).
Laura Love, www.lauralove.net (February 8, 2005).

—James M. Manheim

William Lucy

1933—

Labor union leader

For over three decades William (Bill) Lucy was at the forefront of the labor movement. As Secretary-Treasurer of the American Federation of State County and Municipal Employees (AFSCME) for 30-plus years, Lucy helped the group grow from 200,000 to over 1.4 million members in 3,500 unions nationwide. He also helped define the role of African Americans in the labor unions when he founded the Coalition of Black Trade Unionists (CBTU) in 1972. Along the way he has stood alongside the Rev. Dr. Martin Luther King Jr. in civil rights struggles and Nelson Mandela in opposition to apartheid. Though his name is not as well known as these famous men, Lucy has carved out a legacy based on living wages, health care benefits, and job safety. And like Mandela and King's, Lucy's legacy lives on through the lives of hundreds of thousands of working families around the world every day.

Lucy, William, photograph. AP/Wide World Photos. Reproduced by permission.

Launched Labor Career amid Social Strife

Born on November 26, 1933, in Memphis, Tennessee,

William Lucy was raised in Richmond, California, after moving there as a boy with his parents Susie and Joseph Lucy. After studying civil engineering at the University of California at Berkeley in the 1950s, he landed a job as an assistant materials and research engineer for Contra Costa County, California. Though he held that position for 13 years, Lucy's true career calling lay in unions. In 1956 he had joined the AFSCME Local 1675 union of Contra Costa employees and in 1965 he was elected its president. The following year, he left engineering to work full-time for the AFSCME international organization as the associate director of the legislation and community affairs departments.

At the time Lucy began his career in labor leadership, American society was experiencing great changes. The civil rights movement was steadily overturning years of racism and segregation to claim equal rights for African Americans. The news of the day was filled with both violent and inspiring images from such events as the Montgomery bus boycott, federal troops enforcing school segregation, and the 1963 March on Washington, where Martin Luther King gave his famous "I Have

At a Glance . . .

Born on November 26, 1933, in Memphis, TN; married Dorotheria Lucy; children: Benita, Phyllis. *Education:* University of California, Berkeley, studied civil engineering.

Career: Contra Costa County, California, assistant materials and research engineer, early 1950s-66; American Federation of State County and Municipal Employees (AFSCME), Washington, DC, associate director of the legislation and community affairs departments, 1966-72; AFSCME, Washington DC, secretary-treasurer, 1972–; Coalition of Black Trade Unionists (CBTU), president, 1972–; Public Services International, president, 1994–.

Selected memberships: Free South Africa Movement, founder, 1984; American Federation of Labor and Congress of Industrial Organizations (AFL-CIO), executive council member, 1995–; AFL-CIO African American Labor Center, board member; African America Institute, board member; Americans for Democratic Action, board member; Center for Policy Alternatives, board member.

Selected awards: Bowie State College, honorary doctorate of humane letters; *Ebony*, named one of "The 100 Most Influential Black Americans."

Addresses: *Office*—CBTU, 1900 L Street NW, Suite 405, Washington, DC 20036. *Office*—AFSCME, 1625 L Street NW, Washington, DC, 20036.

a Dream" speech. Meanwhile the Vietnam War was claiming the lives of tens of thousands young Americans and sparking nationwide anti-war demonstrations.

The labor movement was not immune to the tumultuous times. As it struggled to secure collective bargaining rights—the right for employees to negotiate with employers on everything from wages to job safety—for its members, AFSCME chapters country-wide launched marches and strikes. Sadly consistent with the times, those actions were often met with violent police reaction. The history of AFSCME is riddled with stories of members being beaten, tear-gassed, and jailed. Lucy received his own fair share of beatings and jailing over the years.

Worked with King on Memphis Strike

By 1968, the civil rights movement had led to laws banning segregation in publicly funded programs from health care to housing. However, working conditions for African Americans still lagged far behind those for white laborers. It became clear that the goals of civil rights and labor rights movement were intertwined. One of the most potent cases to prove this connection was the 1968 sanitation worker's strike in Memphis. Black sanitation workers had no rights, no sick pay, no health care, and no job security. Pay was so low that many of them qualified for welfare. They also suffered racism and disrespect. "There were two battles being fought in the Memphis march. One of racial oppression and the other oppression of jobs," Lucy told *The Philadelphia Tribune.* "Those 1,300 sanitation workers in 1968 were a classic picture of the working rural poor, looking for a better life."

The sanitation workers had formed AFSCME Local 1733 in 1964, but the Memphis city government refused to acknowledge the union. In 1968 the workers decided to strike. Lucy traveled to Memphis to lend his support. Pickets and marches were met with police batons and beatings. Replacement workers were brought in. Strikers were arrested. It was chaos. "We didn't have job descriptions," Lucy told *The Philadelphia Tribune.* "We did whatever had to be done."

The strike's logo was "I am a Man," a sentiment that struck a deep chord within Memphis's African-American community, which supported the strikers by providing meals and raising funds. After two months, the sanitation department still would not budge. Striker morale began to wane. Finally, AFSCME convinced Martin Luther King Jr. to become involved. The *Labor Net* Web site noted that Lucy said he "saw King bring tears to the eyes of strikers and their families just by walking into a meeting." King assured the strikers that the right to unionize was a civil right. It was also the only way to escape the racism they suffered on the job. On the morning of April 4th, 1968, King was preparing to lead a striker's march when an assassin's bullet took his life. International outcry over King's death brought an intense spotlight on Memphis and the city had no choice but to settle the strike. Lucy was part of the negotiations that led to the recognition of the sanitation workers' union.

Founded the Coalition of Black Trade Unionists

In 1972 Lucy became the highest ranking African American in the labor movement when he was elected secretary-treasurer of AFSCME, the organization's second highest post. His main job was auditing and budgets, but he remained active in labor issues from negotiations with government and corporations to strikes and marches, both for workers and for oppressed communities in general.

In September of 1972 Lucy led a conference of 1,200 black union members, representing 37 different unions. A key topic was the 1972 presidential elections. The American Federation of Labor and Congress of Industrial Organizations (AFL-CIO) had taken a neutral stance on the elections. The black unionists believed this attitude would help re-elect Richard Nixon. Notes from the conference reprinted on the *CBTU* Web site stated, "We are concerned that the re-election of Richard Nixon will almost certainly result in four more years of favored treatment for the rich and powerful; continued unemployment; frozen wages; high prices; appointment of additional members of the U.S. Supreme Court who are conservative and insensitive to the rights of workers, minorities, and the poor; more repression and restriction of civil liberties; and the reversal or total neglect of civil rights." However, more infuriating to the black unionists was that their viewpoint had been ignored by AFL-CIO leadership.

The group decided to found the Coalition of Black Trade Unionists (CBTU) to ensure African Americans a voice in labor. "We are in nobody's pocket, do not intend to get in anybody's pocket, and we are going to assume a position of full partners," the *CBTU* Web site quoted Lucy as saying at the organization's founding. Forming CBTU was potentially tricky. The *St. Louis Post-Dispatch* noted, "[CBTU was] indicating that a labor movement founded on unity and solidarity lacked both when it came to racial matters. Many observers predicted divisiveness and an early demise." Those observers underestimated Lucy and his colleagues. Lucy became the first president of CBTU—a post he held into 2005—and helped grow the group into a 13,000 member strong force in labor. "We've managed to evolve to a situation where we're no longer pounding on the door but are participating in the development of policy," Lucy told the *St. Louis Post-Dispatch*.

Fought to Overturn Apartheid in South Africa

Lucy's work was not limited to the United States. In 1974 CBTU called for an economic boycott of the apartheid regime of South Africa. Apartheid was a political and social policy that deemed blacks second-class citizens and institutionalized segregation. Lucy later founded the Free South Africa Movement, a grassroots campaign that sparked widespread opposition to apartheid across the United States. After the release of Nelson Mandela—the South African leader who had been imprisoned by the apartheid government for 27 years—Lucy led a fundraising effort to bring Mandela on a United States tour. Four years later, when South Africa had its first post-apartheid elections,

Lucy went as part of an AFL-CIO monitoring delegation. After twenty years of fighting apartheid, Lucy was present when Mandela was elected the first black president of South Africa.

Throughout the 1990s Lucy continued to move through the upper ranks of international labor. In November of 1994 he was elected president of Public Services International (PSI), the world's largest union federation. The first African American to hold this position, Lucy oversaw 10 million members from over 100 nations.

In 1995 the AFL-CIO appointed Lucy to its executive council, the federation's highest decision-making body. He also served as vice president for several of AFL-CIO's departments including the Industrial Union, Maritime Trades, and Professional Employees. In addition Lucy served on the boards of directors of civic groups such as the African America Institute, Americans for Democratic Action, and the Center for Policy Alternatives.

Remained Loyal to Labor after 30 Years

Lucy had been re-elected secretary-treasurer by AFSCME members every four years since 1972 and by 2004 he was ready to retire. He announced his retirement at AFSCME's 2004 International Convention. However, the conventioneers refused to accept his resignation. After several days of negotiations, Lucy agreed to accept another nomination to the post and was promptly re-elected to another four-year term.

The labor movement, and CBTU, still had much work to do. In 2003 reports had revealed that the loss of manufacturing jobs resulted in the unemployment rate among blacks rising at twice the rate as that among whites. "The number of jobs and the types of jobs that have been lost has severely diminished the standing of many blacks in the middle class," Lucy told the *International Herald Tribune*. Additionally, education continued to be a problem. "Our kids are coming out of school with an education for a past era," Lucy told *The Philadelphia Tribune*. "With the minimum wage at $5 an hour, they have already been relegated to the status of working poor." In reaction AFSCME offered scholarship and educational programs. However, Lucy revealed in an interview with the *People's Weekly World Newspaper* that the biggest challenge unions faced was membership. "For many years the dominant view within the AFL-CIO was that you really did not need to organize the maximum number of workers or your maximum potential, but simply organize enough to control a particular industry." He concluded, "The numbers tell the tale. Today unions only represent about 12-13 percent of eligible workers and considerably fewer in private employment."

With over 30 years in labor union organizing, management, and administration, Lucy is one of the few people with the skills and experience to tackle the myriad problems that affect the labor movement. In 2003 and 2004 he led demonstrations against the Iraq War, grassroots movements to defeat George W. Bush's presidential reelection, and a campaign to end political unrest in Zimbabwe. It is no wonder AFSCME members refused to let him retire. Not only did they need him, but so did laborers and their families worldwide.

Sources

Periodicals

International Herald Tribune, July 14, 2003.
Philadelphia Tribune, June 30, 2000.
St. Louis Post-Dispatch, May 17, 1996.

On-line

"Martin Luther King: A Champion of Labor," *Labor Net,* www.labornet.org/viewpoints/meister/mlk.htm (December 28, 2004).
"Memphis 1968: We Remember," *People's Weekly World Newspaper,* www.pww.org/article/view/3213/1/155/ (December 28, 2004).
"Memphis: We Remember," *Public Employee,* www.afscme.org/about/memphis7.htm (December 28, 2004).
"President William Lucy," *CBTU,* www.cbtu.org/cbtu president.html (December 28, 2004).

—Candace LaBalle

Miriam Makeba

1932—

Singer, writer, activist

South African singer and political activist Miriam Makeba is a preeminent chronicler of the black South African experience. In a career spanning more than three decades, she has established herself as a powerful voice in the fight against apartheid—the practice of political, economic, and social oppression along racial lines. Often referred to as "Mother Africa" and "The Empress of African Song," Makeba is credited with bringing the rhythmic and spiritual sounds of Africa to the West. Her music is a soulful mix of jazz, blues, and traditional African folk songs shaded with potent political overtones. Using music as a primary forum for her social concerns, the singer became a lasting symbol in the fight for racial equality and a strong voice for the struggle against AIDS.

Restricted by Her Government

Makeba's first encounter with the severity of government rule in her native land came when she was just two-and-one-half weeks old: following her mother's arrest for the illegal sale of home-brewed beer, young Makeba served a six-month jail term with her. Makeba's formative years were equally difficult. As a teenager she performed backbreaking domestic work for white families and endured physical abuse from her first husband. She found solace and a sense of community, though, in music and religion. Singing first in a choir, Makeba soon showcased her talents with local bands, achieving success on the regional club circuit.

Makeba first captured international attention with her role in the pseudodocumentary *Come Back, Africa*, a controversial anti-apartheid film released in 1959. Following the film's showing at the Venice Film Festival, Makeba traveled to London, where she met respected American entertainer and activist Harry Belafonte. Impressed with her unique and profound renderings of native folksongs, he served as her mentor and promoter in the United States, arranging gigs for her in New York City clubs and a guest spot on *The Steve Allen Show*. The exposure brought her worldwide acclaim and launched a cross-cultural musical career of epic proportions.

The 1960s proved to be an especially tumultuous decade for Makeba. Her outspoken opposition to the repressive political climate in South Africa set the stage for harsh government retaliation. Makeba's call for an end to apartheid became increasingly powerful, and her recordings were subsequently banned in South Africa. More than three decades of exile began for the singer in 1960, when, seeking to return to her native land for her mother's funeral, her passport was invalidated by the government of Pretoria. Around the same time, Makeba endured additional turmoil in her personal life. Between 1959 and 1966, for instance, she experienced two failed marriages, one to singer Sonny Pilay, which lasted for only three months, and another to trumpeter Hugh Masekela. And in the early 1960s, she faced threats to her health, battling cervical cancer through radical surgery.

Perhaps the biggest blow to Makeba's career came with her 1968 marriage to American black activist Stokely

At a Glance . . .

Born Zensi Miriam Makeba on March 4, 1932, in Prospect, near Johannesburg, South Africa; immigrated to United States, 1959; daughter of a Xhosa teacher and a Swazi domestic worker; married Sonny Pilay (a singer), 1959 (divorced, 1959); married Hugh Masekela (a musician), 1964 (divorced, 1966); married Stokely Carmichael (a civil rights leader), 1968 (divorced, 1978); married fifth husband, Bageot Bah (an airline executive); children: (first marriage) Bongi (daughter; deceased). *Education:* Attended Kimerton Training Institute in Pretoria, South Africa.

Career: Domestic worker in Johannesburg, South Africa; vocalist touring in South Africa, Rhodesia (now Zimbabwe), and the Belgian Congo (now Zaire) with the Black Mountain Brothers, 1954-57; singer in Africa, the United States, England, France, Denmark, and Italy, 1957–; United Nations delegate from Guinea, West Africa, 1963; Goodwill Ambassador for South Africa to the United Nations, 2000s(?).

Memberships: American Society of Composers, Authors, and Publishers.

Awards: Grammy Award for best folk recording, 1965, for *An Evening With Belafonte/Makeba*; Dag Hammerskjoeld Peace Prize, 1986; Swedish Polar Music Prize, 2002; French government.

Addresses: *Home*—South Africa.

Carmichael. A self-avowed revolutionary, Carmichael took a militant "Black Power" stance that was often perceived as divisive and threatening to the existing fabric of American society. Having long used song as a vehicle to raise social and political awareness, Makeba was stunned by the devastating effects of her marriage on her musical career. Her affiliation with Carmichael effectively eliminated her arena for social expression in the West. In her autobiography *Makeba: My Story*, she recalled the curtailment of her success in the United States: "My concerts are being canceled left and right. I learn that people are afraid that my shows will finance radical activities. I can only shake my head. What does Stokely have to do with my singing?" When her record label, Reprise, refused to honor her contract in the States, Makeba moved with Carmichael to Guinea.

Sang for Freedom

Although Makeba's marriage to Carmichael ended in 1978, she remained in Guinea for several years. She continued performing in Europe and parts of Africa, promoting freedom, unity, and social change. During the singer's time in Guinea, though, heartbreaking misfortune again touched her life. Her youngest grandson became fatally ill, and her only daughter, Bongi, died after delivering a stillborn child. Yet, through all of her trials, Makeba has derived consolation from her music and her undying faith in God.

In the spring of 1987, Makeba joined American folk-rock legend Paul Simon's phenomenal *Graceland* tour in newly independent, antiseparatist Zimbabwe. An unprecedented display of racial unity and multicultural sounds, the concert focused attention on the injustice of imperial racist policies in South Africa and showcased the talents of generations of South African musicians. Following the success and exposure afforded her by the *Graceland* tour, Makeba recorded her first American release in two decades, a tribal collection titled *Sangoma*, which means diviner-healer. Featuring African chants that the singer learned in her youth from her mother, the solo album casts a new light on the soulful, spiritual sounds of her native land. Makeba's follow-up album—the 1989 PolyGram debut *Welela*—blends traditional songs with newer pop pieces.

In a *Chicago Tribune* interview with Leigh Behrens, Makeba summarized her thoughts on her life in exile since 1959: "I have love, but I also have suffering. I am a South African. I left part of me there. I belong there." In June of 1990, Makeba finally reentered Johannesburg for the first time in 31 years, on the invitation of Nelson Mandela. The following year PolyGram released *Eyes on Tomorrow*, an upbeat protest album recorded in a Johannesburg studio. Featuring pioneering jazz trumpeter Dizzy Gillespie, rhythm and blues singer Nina Simone, and Masekela, *Eyes on Tomorrow* is generally considered a more commercial mix of pop, blues, and jazz than the singer's previous efforts.

Turned Her Attention to AIDS

Makeba continued her musical career as well as her activist efforts around the world. As Robert Farris Thompson put it in the *New York Times*, "She is a symbol of the emergence of Afro-Atlantic art and a voice for her people. Her life in multiple cultural and political settings—and her rich musical career, drawing on traditional and contemporary sources—have resonance for us all." During her nearly 30 years in exile, Makeba took her message around the world, performing for some of the most powerful leaders, including John F. Kennedy, former French president Francois Mitterrand, and Cuban dictator Fidel Castro. But with the end of apartheid in 1994, Makeba found new reasons to sing, continuing her activism by turning her attention to the AIDS epidemic in Africa. "In our society, we have always passed messages and expressed ourselves through song. This is why the former government was so scared of musicians," she told the *UNESCO Courier.* "I'm trying to see how I can fit in [to the fight against AIDS]. I have asked all those who write songs for me to compose a short song or poem to broadcast to try to broaden the whole thing. I feel this thing very personally. I have lost many friends to AIDS," she explained to *Newsweek*:

Even as Makeba aged critics reveled in her charisma and talent. *Variety* remarked at 68-year-old Makeba's "majestic dominance," calling her a "natural wonder." She released her album *Homeland* in 2000 and it was nominated for a Grammy Award in 2001. *Time* called *Homeland* a "musical love letter" to Africa. Marking the tenth year anniversary of the end of apartheid in South Africa, Makeba released *Reflections* in 2004. The album is a collection of some of her most well-known songs over the past 50 years, including of "Pata Pata," and "Click Song." *Billboard* called the album "wondrous," and Makeba remarked to the magazine that "These are some of the songs most associated with me from different times in my life, and it was a joy to sing and record them again."

In 2005 mentions of Makeba's impending retirement stirred through the media. She announced her intentions while on tour in Zambia in late 2004. But reviewers were quick to note that she certainly had not lost any of her appeal: "Every bit as delightful as her singing was her natural warm rapport with the audience. More than once she playfully lamented the travails of growing old—none of which she exhibits. Instead, she imbued her big joyful international hit 'Pata Pata' with the same impish charm as she did 40 years ago. In contrasting style, the stunning a-cappella encore involving the whole band was the model of integrity and sincerity, sealing the impression that Miriam Makeba is not just a wonderful singer, but an extraordinary human being," reported *The Scotsman.* Although she has continued to perform in occasional concerts, Makeba has refocused her efforts as a "spokeswoman" for African culture, politics and social responsibility. She spent a great deal of time with the Makeba Rehabilitation Centre for Girls in Midrand, South Africa, which she founded in 1997 to help abused children. She also worked as the Goodwill Ambassador for South Africa to the United Nations

Selected works

Singles

"Pata Pata," 1967.

Albums

Miriam Makeba Sings, RCA, 1960.
The World of Miriam Makeba, RCA, 1963.
Back of the Moon, Kapp.
An Evening With Belafonte/Makeba, RCA, 1965.
Sangoma, Warner Bros., 1988.
Welela, PolyGram, 1989.
Eyes on Tomorrow, PolyGram, 1991.
Homeland, Putumayo, 2000.
Reflections, Heads Up International, 2004.

Books

The World of African Song, edited by Jonas Gwangwa and E. John Miller, Jr., Time Books, 1971.
(With James Hall) *Makeba: My Story* (autobiography), New American Library, 1987.

Films

Come Back, Africa, 1959.

Sources

Books

Makeba, Miriam, and James Hall, *Makeba: My Story*, New American Library, 1987.

Periodicals

Africa Report, January 1977.
Billboard, May 22, 1993; April 15, 2000; June 12, 2004; July 3, 2004.
Chicago Tribune, March 20, 1988.
Down Beat, April 2001.
Ebony, April 1963; July 1968.
Interview, May 2001.
Jet, April 18, 1994.
Ms., May 1988.
Nation, March 12, 1988.
Newsweek, July 17, 2000.
New York Times, February 28, 1960; February 15, 1987; January 27, 1988; January 31, 1988; March 8, 1988; March 13, 1988; June 11, 1990.
Playboy, October 1991.
Rolling Stone, July 2, 1987.
Scotsman (Edinburgh, Scotland), October 25, 2004.
Time, February 1, 1960; May 1, 2000.
Times Literary Supplement, March 11, 1988.
Tribune Books (Chicago), January 24, 1988.
UNESCO Courier, July 2000.
Variety, July 24, 2000.
Washington Post, April 19, 1988.

—Barbara Carlisle Bigelow and Sara Pendergast

Sam Morrison

1936—

Library administrator

On October 23, 1999, Sam Morrison, then director of the Broward County (Florida) Library System, watched the ground break for the African-American Research Library and Cultural Center. The center was the realization of his wish to build a facility for the exchange of information and ideas relating to African culture and the black experience that would attract visitors, researchers, historians, and filmmakers from around the globe. Opening to the public on October 26, 2002, the center became the third of its kind in the United States, joining the Schomburg Center for Research in New York and the Auburn Research Library in Atlanta. This 60,000-square-foot research center was built by the largest African-American architectural and engineering firm in the United States. Decorated by an award-winning African-American design team, the library boasts 5,000 square feet of gallery space and houses over 75,000 books, manuscripts, historical documents, and artifacts.

Morrison's vision turned the county's proposal to build a small traditional library in Broward County into a plan to build a facility that honors black culture. Seeking to promote black history and an appreciation for black achievement, the center houses a collection that is a treasure trove of both well known and little known gems. For African Americans, especially, the center provides the resources for a substantial exploration of the black experience in America, an experience filled with pain, hope, and achievement. The center's many collections—including FBI files from the civil rights era and slave narratives—provide ample evidence of a past both troubling and profoundly encouraging.

Discovered Life Among the Bookshelves

Sam Morrison was born in Flagstaff, Arizona, on December 19, 1936, and spent most of his youth in Phoenix. Morrison lived in a tight-knit community of family and friends. He attributes his success in life to these influences, his church, and especially his maternal grandfather, James W. Swain, a man Morrison remembers as being loved and respected in the community. "I never heard anyone say anything bad about him," Morrison said in an interview with *Contemporary Black Biography (CBB)*. "I knew if I grew up to be like him I would be fine."

When Morrison was 15 his father, Travis, passed away, and his mother, Ruth, was left to run the family restaurants alone while raising Sam and his sister. Ruth later sold the business and moved the family to Los Angeles. Morrison had been a top student back in Phoenix, but when he was forced to work to help the family his studies suffered. Morrison persevered and upon graduating high school he entered community college. A year-and-a-half later, in 1955, Morrison dropped out of college and joined the Air Force, planning to take advantage of the military's tuition assistance program. From his base in Marrakech, Morocco, Morrison traveled often to countries in Europe. He also used this time to complete junior college.

After his tour in the military, Morrison spent the next decade working as a manager for Lucky supermarkets in Los Angeles and completing a bachelor of arts in

Born Samuel F. Morrison on December 19, 1936, in Flagstaff, AZ; married Judith Moore, 1964 (divorced). *Education:* California State University at Los Angeles, BA, English, 1971; University of Illinois at Champaign, MS, library science, 1972; attended Harvard University, Kennedy School of Government, 1989. *Military service:* United States Air Force, Marrakech, Morocco, 1955-1959.

Career: Frostproof Living Learning Library, Frostproof, FL, director, 1972-74; Broward County Library System, Fort Lauderdale, FL, assistant to director and deputy director, 1974-87; Chicago Public Library, Chicago, IL, deputy commissioner and chief librarian, 1987-90; Broward County Library System, Fort Lauderdale, director, 1990-2003; Southeastern Consulting Group, Boca Raton, FL, associate, 2003–.

Selected memberships: NAACP; Broward Public Library Foundation, board of directors; Southeast Florida Library Information Network; Bonnet House; Boys and Girls Clubs of Broward County; Gold Coast Jazz Society.

Selected awards: *Sun Sentinel* Publisher's Award, 1997; Urban League, Diversity Champion Award, 1998; NAACP President's Award, 1998; University of Illinois Graduate School of Library and Information Science, Distinguished Alumnus Award, 1999; Cato and Margaret Roach Award for Exemplary Human Relations, 2003; City of Fort Lauderdale, Citizen Recognition Award, 2003.

Addresses: *Office*—Southeastern Consulting Group, LLC, 21218 St. Andrews Blvd., No. 307, Boca Raton, Florida 33433.

English at the California State University at Los Angeles. Pondering his future, Morrison thought perhaps his life-long love of reading should guide him towards work at the library. "It wasn't that I knew a lot about salaries or what the work was really like as a librarian," Morrison said. "I was wrapped up in the romance of being in a place with a lot of books." There had always been books around his home as a child and he had found enjoyment among the bookshelves as he worked at local libraries during high school and college. Real-

izing a passion had developed, Morrison enrolled at the University of Illinois at Champaign to pursue a master's degree in library science. Later he completed his studies in a local government program for elected and appointed officials at Harvard University's Kennedy School of Government.

Morrison's career advanced through the years, and he was invited to sit on numerous boards, heading up several of them, and earning a long list of awards and honors for his extensive civic work around Fort Lauderdale, Floridia. In 1972 he was appointed director of the Frostproof Living Learning Library and in 1974 he became assistant to the director of the Broward County Library System. Morrison was promoted to deputy director of the county system in 1976. From 1987 until 1990 Morrison served as deputy commissioner and chief librarian of the Chicago Public Library, and he was responsible for the planning, design, and construction of the Harold Washington Library, the largest municipal library in the United States. The library was named in honor of the late Harold Washington, the much-loved African-American mayor of Chicago. Morrison returned to Broward County when he was appointed director of the county library system. At this time he began to develop his vision for the African-American Research Library and Cultural Center.

Idea for Library Started Small

At first, library administrators planned to build a small traditional library funded through a bond issue that Morrison worked on back in 1974. The county had grown considerably in recent years and was badly in need of new libraries. Just a handful of small libraries existed in the county and there was only a single large facility, located in Fort Lauderdale. Morrison saw an opportunity to fill the void in an important way. "Being black myself, I had mixed feelings about the job I had done as an African American," Morrison told CBB. Realizing the needs of the underserved minority community, Morrison felt compelled to push the idea of building a crowning piece to the library system that would serve and represent black culture.

"Also, I wanted to make sure that local tax dollars were spent in predominately minority communities. I felt they should and could build something better than the small library they were planning in the bond issue," Morrison told CBB. "It would be the first library in northwest Fort Lauderdale, a predominately black area, and would be a permanent library to replace a historical facility, the Von D. Mizell library, named after a prominent local African-American physician. Besides being a traditional library I felt it should have a research component to collect, preserve, and promote the history of the black experience, particularly in the Southeast. Additionally I wanted a cultural component with an auditorium and meeting rooms, because nothing of that kind existed in the community." The completed structure holds a full stage for entertainment, dance, theater, and lectures, making it attractive to tour groups as well as local performers, and provides a full range of library services.

It took Morrison two-and-a-half years to sell county officials on his vision. "My job was to find the money," he said. "My efforts to find additional funding were successful because people responded to my intensity and they knew the library services were really needed in the community."

Created Valuable Resource for Scholarship

The African-American Research Library and Cultural Center has a full spectrum of offerings: electronic material, oral histories, special collections, office space, computer labs, and a small business resource center. Visitors have many services available to enhance their experience, including literacy programs, genealogical research training, internet access, computer skills development, and technology assistance.

Morrison oversaw the purchase of the impressive collection of Dorothy Porter Wesley, a noted librarian from Howard University in Washington, D.C. The collection includes artwork and historical documents relating to women's studies, reference and bibliographical material, and many other important materials relating to blacks from North America, Africa, South America, and the Caribbean. The library is host to manuscripts and other documents from noted author Alex Haley; the Charles Mills Phonograph Album Collection of blues and jazz albums; the 5,000-volume collection of Daniel M. Johnson, which contains the works of African-American doctors, authors, musicians, artists, and educators; personal interviews and first-hand accounts of slavery from the Fisk University Collection; the 96-volume collection of Jack Abramowitz on slavery and reconstruction; the Hewitt Haitian Art Collection; the Kitty Oliver Oral Histories Collec-

tion; and the Library of the Spoken Word, with 5,000 recordings of interviews, dramas, and lectures on many aspects of Caribbean life and history.

The center has an extensive collection of works on microfilm and microfiche which includes the Bethune-Cookman College Collection; the Black Abolitionist Papers; the Langston Hughes Collection; the Conrad/Harriet Tubman Collection; the FBI files and personal papers of W.E.B. Du Bois; and the Paul Robeson Collection. A collection of bronze and wood sculptures are on display from Benin Kingdom, Nigeria, and slides of the local African-American community of Sistrunk in Broward County document its early history.

A visit to the center will touch many, not unlike a visit to Goree Island off the coast of Senegal, where many Africans last saw their homeland as they boarded slave vessels. To visit this center in Broward County is to walk away with a notion of having been spoken to by ancestors, black and white, urging us to heed what history tells as we learn how to go forward. With the building of the Von D. Mizell African-American Research Library and Cultural Center, Morrison has done us all a great favor.

Sources

On-line

"From the Former Broward County Library Director," *African-American Research Library and Cultural Center,* www.broward.org/library/aarlcc.htm (December 19, 2004).

Other

Additional information for this profile was obtained through an interview with Sam Morrison on December 28, 2004.

—Sharon Melson Fletcherx

Ving Rhames

1959—

Actor

Forging his reputation by playing tough and often frightening characters, Ving Rhames has built a career as a stage, film, and television actor that has had few lulls since he landed his first role in the early 1980s. Many of the characters he has played have been prototypes of real-life thugs and criminals who were commonplace in the gritty urban environment where he grew up. On the Cinemania Web site on the Internet, Rhames is defined as a "character player of stage and screen who has embodied complex and credible heavies, and flawed men of authority."

Grew up with Gangsters

"I grew up in the same neighborhood with drug kings and gangsters," admitted Rhames on the *People* magazine Web site. Raised on 126th Street in the Harlem area of New York City, he credits his mother with helping him stay on the straight path toward adulthood. "She has been such a strong influence in my life," noted the actor about his mother in press materials from Rogers & Cowan, a public relations firm serving the entertainment industry. "That, in large part, is the reason why I didn't allow myself to fall into the peer pressure of my neighborhood. I just always aimed to be a good son to my mother, who I felt deserved more and far better."

Rhames cited a ninth grade teacher, Miss Goodblatt, as an important catalyst for his future acting career. "When we would do reading in class, Miss Goodblatt would call on me to read," Rhames recalled in *People*. "She said I had a talent." He auditioned for the prestigious High School of Performing Arts in New York City, and became the only student from his junior high school to be accepted. Rhames's talent blossomed during his years at the High School of Performing Arts, allowing him to earn a drama scholarship to the Juilliard School.

Upon graduation from Juilliard in 1983, Rhames quickly found work. "I graduated on a Friday," he said in *People*. "By Monday, I was doing Shakespeare in the Park." Rhames's training in the classics landed him numerous roles in plays by Ibsen, Moliere, and others on the regional theater circuit. He also appeared in Off-Broadway productions of *Map of the World*, *Short Eyes*, *Richard III*, and *Ascension Day*. John Simon remarked in his *New York* magazine review of *Short Eyes* that "the only totally successful acting comes from the black contingent, Ving Rhames, Reggie Montgomery, and especially Larry Fishburne." In 1984, Rhames broke into television with roles in daytime soap operas such as *Another World* and *The Guiding Light*. He also made his film debut as author James Baldwin's young father in Baldwin's autobiographical *Go Tell It on the Mountain*, which aired on PBS. "He delivered a vigorous performance as a young Baptist preacher attempting to escape the strictures of the 1920s South," noted the Cinemania website of Rhames's performance in the film.

On Stage and Screen

Throughout the 1980s, Rhames made frequent appearances on television, in the movies, and on Broad-

At a Glance . . .

Born Irving Rhames on May 12, 1959, in New York, NY; son of Ernest (retired auto mechanic) and Rather (homemaker) Rhames; married Valerie Scott 1994 (divorced 1999); married Deborah Reed 2000; children: Rainbow (daughter), Freedom (son), Tiffany (stepdaughter). *Education*: Attended State University of New York, Purchase; Juilliard School of Drama, BFA, 1983.

Career: Actor, 1983–.

Awards: Golden Globe Award for best actor in a miniseries, 1998 (handed over his award to Jack Lemmon).

Addresses: *Home*—Los Angeles, CA.

way. He was cast as a soldier in Vietnam in the Broadway production of *The Boys of Winter* in 1984, as a guest star on the television war drama *Tour of Duty*, in Brian DePalma's *Casualties of War* in 1989, and in *Jacob's Ladder* in 1990. Also, he appeared in the films *Native Son* in 1986 and *Patty Hearst* in 1988. In 1990, Rhames played Whoopi Goldberg's sensitive husband in *The Long Walk Home*, a film dealing with the early struggle for civil rights. This role offered Rhames an opportunity to expand his range beyond tough, bitter characters. In 1993, Rhames revealed a flair for comedy as well, playing an uptight Secret Service man in *Dave*.

In 1993, during the filming of *The Saint of Fort Washington* in New York City, Rhames was unexpectedly reunited with his brother, Junior, a troubled, homeless Vietnam veteran who'd been estranged from the Rhames family for years. Several scenes of the film were shot at a homeless shelter, with Rhames playing a street tough who took advantage of the homeless men. One day, Rhames recognized one of the men at the shelter as his long-lost brother. He brought his brother back to his apartment and helped him find a job. "I realized then, more than ever, that I am my brother's keeper and we as human beings are all our brothers' keepers," Rhames remarked in a Rogers & Cowan publicity release. "We have to take some responsibility in helping those less fortunate."

Rhames enjoyed a great deal of professional success in 1994. Partly due to his friendship with Eriq La Salle, a fellow classmate at Juilliard, he was selected to play La Salle's auto-mechanic brother-in-law on the top-rated television series *ER*. Acting opportunities for Rhames increased dramatically after his role as an ominous

gangster baron in Quentin Tarantino's widely acclaimed film *Pulp Fiction*. According to Cinemania's review of his performance, Rhames "brought a distinct blend of suaveness and menace to his portrayal of crime boss Marsellus Wallace...." In 1995, Rhames was cast opposite Nicholas Cage and David Caruso (of N.Y.P.D. Blue) in *Kiss of Death*. He also landed roles in 1996 as a nightclub bouncer in *Striptease* with Demi Moore and a hard-edged computer genius in the blockbuster film *Mission: Impossible* with Tom Cruise. Janet Maslin of the *New York Times* offered special praise for Rhames's performance in *Striptease*, saying that his "surly, deadpan delivery (as when he complains furiously because a video store is out of 'Free Willy') is the film's biggest treat."

In 1997, Rhames continued his hot streak by landing a role in *Dangerous Ground*, a film about a search for a missing person in the underworld of Johannesburg, South Africa. He also appeared in John Singleton's *Rosewood*, a film about a racially motivated massacre in a primarily black town in Florida during the early 1920s. "In all of his other movies he was a bad, kick-ass guy," said Singleton in a *People* magazine interview. "In *Rosewood* he gets to work with kids, gets to dance and sing and be a bad dude. He got so happy about doing this sensitive role."

Won Kudos for Generosity

Although nominated for several awards over the years, Rhames made headlines when he won a Golden Globe Award in 1998. Honored for his portrayal of Don King—a man Rhames called "the American Dream personified," according to the *Guardian*—in HBO's miniseries *Don King: Only in America*, Rhames stunned the audience by asking nominee Jack Lemmon onto the stage in order to turn over the award to him. Lemmon remembered it as "one of the sweetest things" ever to happen to him, according to *Jet*.

Over the next few years, Rhames continued to work steadily in films and on television. Offering solid performances in *Bringing Out the Dead* (1999), *Mission: Impossible II* (2000), *Baby Boy* (2001), as the voice for the character of Cobra Bubbles in *Lilo & Stitch* (2002), and in *Dawn of the Dead* (2004). However, in 2005 news of Rhames breathing new life into the 1970s iconic character Kojak made famous by Telly Savalas seemed promising. Rhames never watched the original *Kojak*, but television executive Jeff Wachtel told *Daily Variety* that "Ving's a world-class actor who has reinvented Kojak as a prince of his city—a man who will do whatever it takes to make his world a better place."

As Rhames' star continues to rise, he remains grounded in his strong moral principles. "I was never a struggling actor, for which I feel very blessed," Rhames admitted to *People*. He also credits his strong religious faith as a key to his success. As Rhames stated in a

Rogers & Cowan publicity release, "Since God is the foundation of my life, anything that streams from that can only be positive."

Selected works

Films

Go Tell It on the Mountain, 1985.
Casualties of War, 1989.
Jacob's Ladder, 1990.
The Long Walk Home, 1990.
Dave, 1993.
The Saint of Fort Washington, 1993.
Pulp Fiction, 1994.
Kiss of Death, 1995.
Mission: Impossible, 1996.
Striptease, 1996.
Dangerous Ground, 1997.
Rosewood, 1997.
Bringing Out the Dead, 1999.
Mission Impossible II, 2000.
Baby Boy, 2001.
Lilo & Stitch, 2002.
Undisputed, 2002.
Dawn of the Dead, 2004.

Plays

The Boys of Winter, Broadway, 1985.

Television

Another World, 1984.
The Guiding Light, 1984.
ER, 1994-96.
Don King: Only in America (miniseries), 1997.
The District, 2002.
Kojak, 2005–.

Sources

Periodicals

Daily Variety, October 28, 2004, p. 12.
Guardian (London), March 19, 1999.
Jet, January 27, 2003, p. 66; February 9, 1998, p. 36.
New York, December 10, 1984, p. 80.
New York Times, November 29, 2002, p.B28.
People, June 24, 1996, pp. 77-78.
USA Weekend, October , 1995, p. 14.

On-line

"Ving Rhames," Internet Movie Database, www.imdb.com/cache/person-exact/a114963 (March 10, 2005).
"Ving Rhames," Microsoft Cinemania, updated November 1, 1996, http://Cinemania.msn.com/Cinemania/Artists/Biographies/VingRhames.htm (January 1997).

Other

Additional information for this profile was obtained from publicity materials of Rogers & Cowan, 1888 Century Park East, Los Angeles, California.

—Ed Decker and Sara Pendergast

Rochelle Riley

1959(?)—

Journalist

One of the top young African-American journalists in the United States, Rochelle Riley received several awards for her nationally syndicated columns in the late 1990s and early 2000s. Originating at the *Detroit Free Press* and, prior to that, the *Courier-Journal* in Louisville, Kentucky, those columns found audiences beyond those cities because of Riley's down-to-earth observations about parenting, friendship, and family history. She also wrote about political and social issues, however, and did not hesitate to ruffle reader feathers by taking controversial stands.

Rochelle Riley was born around 1959 in Tarboro, North Carolina, a community she sketched in detail in her columns and returned to often as an adult. Her childhood home was destroyed by Hurricane Floyd in 1999. She was unsentimental about growing up black in a Southern town that had changed slowly and begrudgingly during the civil rights movement. "No one understands what it's like to grow up in the South, unless you grew up in the South," Riley wrote in a *Detroit Free Press* column defending the long silence of South Carolina Senator Strom Thurmond's half-black daughter. "I did, in a post-civil-rights-era North Carolina town where white men still called black men boy, and black women carried the burden of healing those wounds."

Found Life Unimaginable without Books

Her life also served as a case study in how to overcome the barriers that come with that kind of background,

however. Her schooling began at home at age three, when her mother gave grammar lessons to her and her three-year-old friends in the family living room. "I can't imagine my life without books, such has been their impact," Riley wrote in the *Courier-Journal*. Riley attended St. Paul's African Methodist Episcopal (AME) church and played in her high school band. She was raised at least partly by a grandfather who drove a cab and cleaned a lawyer's office after hours, and his wife, Riley's grandmother Moant.

At the University of North Carolina, Riley liked to tell friends that she majored in journalism and white people. "One was an educational tool, the other a social tool; greater veterans than I have written about the toil of keeping a foot in each world," she wrote in the *Detroit Free Press*. Her first jobs in journalism were reporter posts at the *Washington Post* and *Dallas Times-Herald*. She moved on to the *Dallas Morning News*, where she rose to the positions of senior writer and metropolitan editor.

Riley became deputy managing editor of the *Courier-Journal* in Louisville in September of 1992, turning down the chance to work for one of her mentors, Detroit newspaper executive Robert McGruder, in order to become the Louisville paper's first African-American news executive. The following year, she produced a videotape dealing with the attitudes of black managers in the journalism business toward their black employees. It was the first step in a long involvement with issues pertaining to young journalists. McGruder

At a Glance . . .

Born in 1959(?) in Tarboro, NC; mother's name Marva; raised partly by grandparents; one daughter. *Education:* University of North Carolina, Chapel Hill, BA, journalism. *Religion:* African Methodist Episcopal.

Career: *Washington Post* and *Dallas Times Herald,* reporter; *Dallas Morning News,* senior writer and metropolitan editor; *Courier-Journal* (Louisville, KY), deputy managing editor, 1992-96, associate editor and columnist, 1996-2000; *Detroit Free Press,* columnist, 2000–.

Awards: National Journalism Award for Distinguished Service to Literacy, Scripps Howard Foundation, 2003.

Addresses: *Office—Detroit Free Press,* P.O. Box 828, Detroit, MI 48231.

(writing in the *Detroit Free Press*) later called her a "surrogate mom to hundreds of high school and college students, particularly future journalists, around the country."

Led Teen Discussion

In 1996 Riley was promoted to the position of associate editor and columnist at the *Courier-Journal.* She continued her mentoring role as the organizer of a weekly roundtable discussion with Louisville-area teens, which provided material for a teen page Riley edited and for a teen-oriented column, one of three columns Riley wrote each week. Among the most moving of Riley's columns was a personal account of her return to hurricane-devastated Tarboro after her grandfather's death. Her columns were picked up for distribution by the Gannett syndicate, and some of them were collected into a book, *From the Heart.*

Riley also worked on more extended feature articles at the *Courier-Journal,* the best-known of which was a three-part portrait of former heavyweight boxing champion Muhammad Ali, a Louisville native, that appeared in December of 1996. Riley's writings about Ali were credited with stimulating an $80 million fundraising effort aimed at building a Louisville museum devoted to the boxer's career. Often, Riley's columns made a direct difference in the community; one portrait of a struggling community center serving a pair of poor neighborhoods inspired donations of a new computer lab and a thousand books for its library.

In October of 2000, Riley joined the *Detroit Free Press* as a three-day-a-week columnist. She continued to find a national audience, now syndicated by the Knight-Ridder newspaper chain. Riley, a single mother of one, now found her daughter old enough to provide a constant source of column material as she began, for example, to hang back a few steps from her mother during a mall shopping trip. Parenting formed a common theme in Riley's Detroit columns, including those published in *Life Lessons,* her second book. A section of that book also dealt with the aftermath of the terrorist attacks of September 11, 2001.

Backed Cosby

Some of Riley's parenting columns sounded a theme also argued by comedian Bill Cosby, who took black parents to task in a series of speeches for what he saw as a lack of involvement in the education and moral upbringing of their children. Riley emerged as a strong defender of Cosby's often controversial positions. "Like Cosby, I'm sick of people not holding up their ends," she wrote in the *Detroit Free Press.* "Am I my brother's keeper? Of course I am, unless my brother is selling drugs or doing drive-bys. Then I want my brother in jail. Am I my sister's keeper? Not when she continues to have babies she can't financially or emotionally afford to raise."

Riley couldn't be classified as a conservative, however. She was frequently critical of President George W. Bush during the 2004 election campaign, and she rejected the anti-affirmative action initiatives spearheaded in Michigan and elsewhere by African-American California businessman Ward Connerly. "I wish the America he sees was the America that exists," wrote Riley in her column. "But that is not our America, the glorious, messy, free, convoluted, racist, tolerant, intolerant America that evolves every day. In our America, past discrimination created our present, and present discrimination hurts our future."

As of late 2004, Riley's future in journalism looked bright. She was a frequent guest on National Public Radio, and she had won several professional awards, including a National Journalism Award for Distinguished Service to Literacy from the Scripps Howard Foundation, honoring her adult literacy campaign Metro Detroit Reads. That effort led to the recruitment of more than 1,000 literacy tutors and to $35,000 in contributions. Scripps Howard judges, according to a press release that appeared on *PRNewswire,* said that Riley "stirred people up and got them moving." That seemed to be a recurring motif in her distinguished career.

Selected writings

From the Heart, 1998.
Life Lessons, 2004.

Sources

Periodicals

Courier-Journal (Louisville, KY), November 25, 1999,
    p. C1; February 3, 2000, p. C1; April 11, 2000, p.
    D1.
Detroit Free Press, October 7, 2000, p. 1; April 15,
    2002; October 9, 2002; April 5, 2004; June 1,
    2004; January 16, 2005.
Editor & Publisher, August 28, 1993, p. 28; December 18, 1999, p. 33.
Houston Chronicle, November 8, 2002, p. 2.
Knight Ridder/Tribune News Service, December 29,
    2003, p. K2685.
PRNewswire, March 12, 2004.

On-line

"Coming Home: Muhammad Ali," *Courier-Journal*
    (Louisville),   www.courier-journal.com/ali/coming_
    home_story1.html (January 27, 2005).

—James M. Manheim

Aminah Robinson

1940—

Artist

"For me, art is not a job or a career," Columbus, Ohio, artist Aminah Robinson told the Cleveland *Plain Dealer*. "It's a way of life. Always has been." Many artists live by a similar credo, but few have immersed themselves in art as intensely as Robinson, who is reported to rise at 4 a.m. to begin work and to continue working until midnight or beyond. Robinson works in her Columbus home and a small backyard structure she calls the Doll House. It would be inaccurate to say that Robinson has a studio, for her home is a studio and sometimes a medium—she makes art from scraps of material that she finds or that people bring to her, from doors, walls, porch components, and even floors. Her kitchen floor is a complex mosaic of materials that includes the baby teeth of her son, who committed suicide at age 27.

Yet Robinson's art has not focused primarily upon her own life. Rather, she is creatively rooted in a specific place, to a degree matched by few other artists. "My work and life are about Columbus, Ohio…the community, ancestors, and spirits," Robinson told the *Cincinnati Enquirer*. Her thousands of works are made from an astonishing assortment of materials including fabric, needlepoint, paint, ink, charcoal, plastic, metal, glass, clay, a huge miscellany of found objects, animal skins obtained from a Columbus slaughterhouse, and a concoction called hogmawg that her father taught her to make from mud, pig grease, red clay, crushed brick, sticks, and glue. Many of them show scenes of Columbus life past and present, often focusing on Robinson's east-side neighborhood of Poindexter Village. Considered a community treasure by Columbus art lovers,

Robinson was gradually discovered by the wider art world. She was awarded a $500,000 MacArthur Foundation "genius" grant in the year 2004.

Aminah Robinson was born on February 18, 1940, in Columbus. The name Aminah, meaning faithful or trustworthy in Arabic, was given to her by an Egyptian religious leader she met on an African trip in 1979; Brenda Lynn Robinson was her given name. The year she was born, her family moved to Poindexter Village, a new housing project that replaced what had been a semi-rural African-American community known as Blackberry Patch. Her family told her stories about the old neighborhood, including colorful local characters like the Chickenfoot Woman and the Crowman, who carried a pet crow on his head. Robinson later wove these figures into her artistic world. Another storyteller in Robinson's childhood was her great-aunt Cordelia (or "Big Annie"). Born into slavery in Georgia, Big Annie recounted the grim history of the Middle Passage and of the life of African Americans under slavery. Robinson wrote down her aunt's words and expanded on them in works that depicted the history of African peoples in the New World.

Robinson's parents inspired her creativity; her father, a school custodian, was adept at finding artistic uses for everyday materials like wood and leather, and her mother was a skilled seamstress. Despite being raised in a Catholic family, Robinson followed the beat of her own drum, and would defy her parents by sneaking out of her house by climbing out a bathroom window to take drawing lessons at a local community center. "It didn't matter how many spankings or Hail Marys I got,"

At a Glance . . .

Born Brenda Lynn Robinson on February 18, 1940, in Columbus, OH; daughter of Leroy Edward William Robinson, a custodian, and Helen Elizabeth Zimmerman Robinson; given name Aminah by an Egyptian religious leader, 1979; married Charles Robinson, an Air Force serviceman, 1964 (divorced, 1971); children: Sydney (died, 1994). *Education:* Attended Columbus School of Art (later Columbus College of Art and Design, 1956-60; attended Ohio State University, 1960-61; Franklin University, 1962-62; Bliss College, 1963.

Career: Illustrator in Idaho and Mississippi, late 1960s; Columbus Recreation and Parks Department, art instructor, 1972-90; full-time artist, 1990–.

Selected awards: Forum for International Study, Travel-Study Fellowship, 1979; Governor's Award for the Visual Arts, Ohio, 1984; MacArthur Foundation, Fellow, 2004.

Addresses: *Agent*—c/o Susan Saxbe, 2226 Bryden Rd., Columbus, OH 43209-1611.

she told the *Cincinnati Enquirer.* She never went anywhere without a sketch pad, and she gave herself a basic education in figure drawing by sketching bodies at a nearby funeral parlor. "She'd draw whatever she'd think of," Robinson's sister Sandra Sue told the *Plain Dealer.* "I remember one time she did a self-image with a rabbit coming out of her head." By the time she was eight, Robinson was ready for her debut solo exhibition: a series of pictures hung on a clothesline during a church revival.

Mentored by Barber

Sometimes wrongly characterized as a folk artist because of her strong attachment to a specific community, Robinson actually had various kinds of training. She attended the Columbus Art School (now the Columbus College of Art and Design) from 1956 to 1960, later taking classes at Ohio State University, Franklin University, and Bliss College. She also had as a mentor a Columbus barber named Elijah Pierce, who displayed his woodcarvings in his shop and, Robinson told the *Plain Dealer,* taught her to take in the world through "four ears"—the heart, soul, "illuminations," and ancestors.

In 1958 Robinson got a job at the Columbus Public Library, where she did illustration work and also took the chance to read about the history of the city's African-American neighborhoods, enriching her fund of stories. She married an Air Force serviceman, Charles Robinson, in 1964 and followed him to several bases around the country, finding illustration jobs with a telephone company in Idaho and a television station in Mississippi. The couple had a son, Sydney, who inherited his mother's creativity but went into engineering instead after witnessing his mother's dire financial conditions. Not fulfilling his creative impulses, "he became very depressed," Robinson told the *Enquirer.*

Robinson's marriage ended in 1971. Back in Columbus, she got a job with the Columbus Recreation and Parks Department, teaching art at the same community center—the Beatty Recreation Center—she had sneaked out of the house to study at as a child. She worked there until 1990, making very little money and at one point going on welfare after she was hospitalized with a back injury—she had no disability benefits. Through a clerical error, Robinson was overpaid. She returned the extra payment to the state in installments of ten dollars a month, spread over ten years.

Used Animal Skin for Chair Seat

All through the years of her marriage, Robinson had kept on making art, but she began a new period of development when she returned to Columbus and moved into a house there in 1974. She began by building herself an incredibly ornate chair with a home-tanned skin for a seat, and eventually the house became so packed with materials awaiting use and half-finished artworks that only narrow corridors were left for her to move around in. Robinson's reputation spread out from her Columbus neighborhood in widening circles, beginning with an Ohio Arts Council grant she received in 1979. That year, she embarked on a tour of Africa, visiting the sites from which slaves began their deadly journeys to the Americas.

Although Robinson was reluctant to part with her works, which she never considered really finished but sometimes conceded were sufficiently "resolved" to display, she began to agree to museum exhibitions in the early 1980s. A one-woman show at Chicago's Esther Saks Gallery in 1984 was followed by others at the Akron Art Museum (1987 and 1988), the Columbus Museum of Art (1990), the National Museum for Women in the Arts in Washington, D.C. (also 1990), and various colleges and university art galleries. As her fame grew, she sold some works if she approved of the buyer; they commanded prices of up to $20,000 apiece.

Many of Robinson's works were large in scale, and some were enormous narrative scrolls that she might work on for years or even decades, incorporating the full range of materials she used. She called these scrolls

Button Beaded Music Box RagGonNon Pop-Up Books, or RagGonNon for short. The RagGonNons (the term, she told the *Columbus Dispatch,* means "it's made of rag, and it's gone–into the future") could be 200 feet or more in length and were embellished at intervals with music boxes. Not quite that long were the 40-foot panels she was commissioned to create for the Columbus Metropolitan Library in 1990, depicting historic African-American neighborhoods in the city. Robinson considered that commission a breakthrough, for it enabled her to begin to make art full-time.

Robinson's depictions of Columbus became more and more intricate. Her 1992 painting "Life in Sellsville 1871-1900" led her to research city directories and maps of the time in search of such details as exact house numbers and residents' names. Robinson illustrated several children's books in the 1990s, and in 1998 she undertook a second major voyage. Accompanied by her agent, Susan Saxbe, and by Ohio Arts Council director Wayne Lawson, she visited Israel in 1998. She wandered into a neighborhood populated by Hasidic Jews, stirring up interest with her incredibly slender frame (she eats very little, mostly fruit) and multiple body piercings. "When they got to know her, they gave her ties and used material to include in her work," Lawson told the *Cincinnati Enquirer.*

Created Tapestry

Along with other chapters of her life, Robinson included her Israeli experiences in an ongoing tapestry called "Journeys" that she had begun in 1968. Various panels depicted the Rev. Martin Luther King Jr., the Ohio General Assembly, and the victims of the terrorist attacks of September 11, 2001. "It's very medieval," curator Annegreth Nill told the *Columbus Dispatch.* "It encompasses all of the effort and changes that Aminah's gone through." The work became the centerpiece of a retrospective exhibition of Robinson's work called *Symphonic Poem: The Art of Aminah Robinson.* Organized by the Columbus Museum of Art in 2003, the exhibition was slated to travel to other museums in the East, Midwest, and South in the mid-2000s. Her 1974 chair was removed from her house for the show, a process that involved knocking down a wall; Robinson agreed to let it happen if the museum would install a fresh wooden door that she could carve into a new artwork.

The year 2004 saw Robinson preparing to install two giant cloth works that had been commissioned for the National Underground Railroad Freedom Center in Cincinnati, to show her children's books at the Art Institute of Chicago, and to travel to Santiago, Chile for an artist-in-residence program and a museum showing of her works at the Museo Nacional de Bellas Artes. All the attention "gives me something to do in my old age," Robinson quipped to *Columbus Dispatch* reporter Bill Mayr. In the fall of that year, Robinson was surprised to learn that she had been named a MacArthur Fellow and was slated to receive its unrestricted $500,000 stipend—a prize intended not to reward past accomplishments but to stimulate new creative activity. The MacArthur Foundation, according to its Web site, called her works "Homeric in content, quantity, and scale."

Robinson's works astound those who have never encountered them, and they have been something of a mystery even to her. "I don't know what I do," she told the *Plain Dealer.* "The process is a divine mystery because I'm usually in a trance when I work." The small room in which she sleeps is stacked floor-to-ceiling with books on African-American history and literature, but she has also acknowledged a more distant influence—Italy's Leonardo da Vinci, the painter of the "Mona Lisa." "I love him," Robinson told the *Plain Dealer.* "His work talks to my soul. Always has."

Sources

Periodicals

Associated Press, March 24, 2003, BC cycle.
Cincinnati Enquirer, August 1, 2003.
Columbus Dispatch, April 24, 2002, p. F8; December 8, 2002, p. E1; August 5, 2003, p. E6; December 28, 2003, p. H1; August 22, 2004, p. D1; September 5, 2004, p. D5; September 28, 2004, p. A1.
Jet, October 18, 2004, p. 36.
Plain Dealer (Cleveland, OH), October 31, 2004, Sunday Magazine, p. 10.
Publishers Weekly, September 7, 1992, p. 62; October 10, 1994, p. 70; March 23, 1998, p. 99.

On-line

"Aminah Robinson: Folk Artist," *MacArthur Foundation,* www.macfdn.org/programs/fel/fellows/robin son_aminah.htm (January 20, 2005).

—James M. Manheim

Philippa Schuyler

1931-1967

Classical pianist, writer

One of the most unusual and perhaps most tragic figures in American cultural history, Philippa Schuyler gained national acclaim as a child prodigy on the piano. Her picture graced the covers of weekly news magazines, and she was hailed as a young American Mozart. Schuyler's life during adulthood, however, was a difficult one. She struggled with racial discrimination and with issues related to her mixed-race background, traveling the world in an attempt to find not only musical success but also an identity and a place in the world. She turned to writing in the early 1960s, visiting war zones as a newspaper correspondent, and she was killed in a helicopter crash in Vietnam in 1967. After her death she was mostly forgotten for several decades, but her life story was told in a 1995 biography, and in 2004 American R&B vocalist Alicia Keys, a classically trained pianist of mixed-race background herself, announced plans to star in a film about Schuyler's life.

Philippa Duke Schuyler was born on August 2, 1931, in New York and brought up in Harlem at the height of the area's cultural flowering. The complexities of her life began with her background, for she had two singular parents. Her father George Schuyler was a journalist who wrote for one of the leading black newspapers of the day, the *Pittsburgh Courier,* and he was well acquainted with numerous writers in both black and white journalistic circles. He was not a civil rights crusader like many of his Harlem contemporaries, but rather a conservative satirist who rejected the idea of a distinctive black culture and later in life joined the ultra-right-wing John Birch Society. Philippa Schuyler's mother, Josephine Cogdell Schuyler, was a

white Southern belle from a Texas ranch who had married George Schuyler after coming to New York to escape a wealthy family of unreconstructed racists. They all refused to attend concerts Philippa Schuyler gave in Texas at the height of her fame.

Schuyler's parents were in the grip of several novel theories and fads, some of which they devised themselves. They fed Philippa raw vegetables, brains, and liver, ·believing that cooking leached vital nutrients out of food. And, in contrast to the now-discredited but at the time widely held belief in eugenics, which formed the basis for Nazi ideas of racial purity, they claimed that racial mixing could produce a superior "hybrid" sort of human. That notion had strong effects on Philippa Schuyler's life, for the Schuylers planned to make their daughter into Exhibit A for the gains that could be realized from black-white intermarriage.

Tests Revealed Genius-Level IQ

And, indeed, the plan seemed to work. Schuyler walked before she was a year old, was said to be reading the *Rubaiyat* poems of Omar Khayyam at two and a half, and playing the piano and writing stories at three. When she was five, Schuyler underwent an IQ test at Columbia University; it yielded the genius-level figure of 185. She made rapid progress on the piano, and due to Mr. Schuyler's connections it wasn't long before stories about Philippa began to appear in New York newspapers.

Schuyler's mother, described by the *New York Times* as "the stage mother from hell, blending a frustrated artist's ambition with an activist's self-righteousness," started to enter her in musical competitions. Schuyler did spectacularly well and was a regular concert attraction by the time she was eight. Just short of her ninth birthday, New York mayor Fiorello LaGuardia named a day after her at the New York World's Fair. But her childhood was an isolated one; she was taught mostly by private tutors and had no friends her own age. Her mother, who fired her piano teachers whenever she began to get close to one emotionally, beat her regularly.

For a period of time during World War II, Schuyler was a national child star. She wrote a symphony at age 13, and leading composer and critic Virgil Thomson pronounced it the equal of works that Mozart had written at that age after the New York Philharmonic performed it in 1945. A concert Schuyler performed with the Philharmonic soon after that was attended by a crowd of 12,000, and profiles of the attractive teen appeared in *Time, Look,* and *The New Yorker.* Schuyler was promoted by the black press in general, not just in her father's *Pittsburgh Courier,* as a role model, and she certainly inspired a generation of black parents to sign their kids up for piano lessons.

But there were pitfalls ahead for the talented youngster. When she was 13, she discovered a scrapbook her mother had kept of her accomplishments, and more and more she began to feel like an exotic flower on display. On tour, especially in the South, she began to experience racial prejudice, something of which she had been mostly unaware during her sheltered upbringing. Bookings began to dry up, except in black-organized concert series. Observers have offered vari-

ous explanations as to why. Schuyler herself and many others pointed to discrimination; the world of classical music has never been a nurturing one for African-American performers, and in the 1940s very few blacks indeed had access to major concert stages. Some felt that Schuyler's playing, although technically flawless, suffered from an emotionless quality brought on by the strictures of her demanding life. And Schuyler faced a problem she had in common with other teenage sensations—the tendency of the spotlight to seek out the next young phenomenon.

Became World Traveler

Schuyler and her mother reacted by once again calling in George Schuyler's connections; he had friends in Latin American countries, and Schuyler began to give concerts there. In 1952 she visited Europe for the first time. Schuyler enjoyed travel, and, like other black performers, found a measure of unprejudiced acceptance among European audiences. Over the next 15 years she would appear in 80 countries and would master four new languages, becoming proficient enough in French, Portuguese, and Italian that she could write for periodicals published in those languages. She traveled to Africa as well as Europe, performing for independence leaders such as Kwame Nkrumah in Ghana and Haile Selassie in Ethiopia—but also passing for white in apartheid-era South Africa. Schuyler began to resist the pressure that still came from her parents, but she remained close to them, writing to her mother almost daily and becoming their chief means of financial support. "Remember, my bitterness requires mobility and relocation," she wrote to her mother shortly before her death in a letter quoted in *Notable Black American Women.*

Her income came not only from music but also from lectures she gave to groups such as the virulently anti-internationalist John Birch Society, for Schuyler had come to share her father's conservative politics. Despite her performances in newly independent African capitals, she came to adopt a positive outlook on European colonialism. A string of romantic relationship all ended badly, and by the early 1960s Schuyler was threatened with financial problems.

Confused and fearful about the future, Schuyler took steps in two new directions. First, since her ethnic identity seemed uncertain to those who had never encountered her, she began in 1962 to bill herself as Felipa Monterro or Felipa Monterro y Schuyler. She even obtained a new passport in that name. Her motivation seems to have been split between a desire to have audiences judge her without knowing of her African-American background, and a broader renunciation of her black identity. The ruse convinced audiences for a time, but the reviews of her concerts were mixed, and she soon abandoned the effort.

Filed Dispatches Amid Unrest

Second, Schuyler began to write. Traveling the globe, she filed stories from political hot spots for United Press International and later for the ultraconservative *Manchester Union Leader* newspaper in New Hampshire. Schuyler found herself in the middle of street violence in the Congo and in Argentina; the demise she met in Vietnam could easily have come earlier. She wrote several books and magazine articles as well, and at her death she left several unpublished novels in various stages of completion. One of them evolved into an autobiography, *Adventures in Black and White,* which was published in 1960.

Schuyler also wrote two books about Africa, one of them, *Who Killed the Congo?,* dealing with the legacy of colonialism and the other, *Jungle Saints,* praising the efforts of Catholic missionaries on the continent. During the last part of her life, she became a devout Catholic herself. In Rome she met two popes. She traveled to Vietnam to do lay missionary work, supporting U.S. military action there and writing a posthumously published book about American soldiers, *Good Men Die.* She founded an organization devoted to the aid of children fathered by U.S. servicemen, and on several occasions she assisted Catholic organizations in evacuating children and convent residents from areas of what was then the nation of South Vietnam as pro-North Vietnamese guerrillas advanced. It was on one of those evacuation missions, on May 9, 1967, that Schuyler's helicopter crashed into Da Nang Bay. She drowned, for she was unable to swim. Shortly before her death, she had written a letter that seemed to suggest a political change of heart, expressing sympathy with black activist leader Stokely Carmichael.

Schuyler's funeral was held at New York's St. Patrick's Cathedral, and in death she was once again in the headlines. Two years after her death, Schuyler's mother hanged herself in her Harlem apartment. A New York City school was named after Schuyler, but her name dropped into temporary obscurity. She became better known with the publication in 1995 of *Composition in Black and White: The Life of Philippa Schuyler,* a biography by Kathryn Talalay. In 2004, star vocalist Alicia Keys was signed to portray Schuyler in a film co-produced by actress Halle Berry. "This story is so much about finding your place in the world," Keys told Japan's *Daily Yomiuri* newspaper. "Where do we really fit in, in a world so full of boxes and categories?"

Selected writings

Adventures in Black and White, foreword by Deems Taylor, Robert Speller, 1960.
Who Killed the Congo?, Devin Adair, 1962.
Jungle Saints: Africa's Heroic Catholic Missionaries, Herder & Herder, 1963.
(With Josephine Schuyler) *Kingdom of Dreams,* Robert Speller, 1963.
Good Men Die, Twin Circle, 1969.

Sources

Books

Notable Black American Women, books 1 and 3, Gale, 1992, 2002.
Talalay, Kathryn, *Composition in Black and White: The Life of Philippa Schuyler,* Oxford, 1995.

Periodicals

Black Book Review, February 28, 1996, p. 23.
Daily Yomiuri (Tokyo), October 14, 2004, p. 14.
Herald Sun (Melbourne, Australia), October 23, 2004, p. 7.
New Pittsburgh Courier, July 20, 1963, p. 14.
New York Times, December 10, 1995, section 7, p. 16.
Sunday Times (London, England), August 4, 1996.
Washington Post, November 24, 1995, p. D3.

—James M. Manheim

Mavis Staples

1939(?)—

Musician

Best known as the lead vocalist of the Staple Singers, a family soul-gospel ensemble that flourished from the 1950s through the 1970s and beyond, Mavis Staples has also released a series of albums as a solo artist. Her voice, not a gospel powerhouse, was instantly compelling with its deep-like-a-river quality of moral conviction. Over her long career, Staples won other musicians, including Bob Dylan and Prince as admirers, and her solo work, which had never quite found its course among the shifting winds of musical fashion, won new recognition with the release of her 2004 album, *Have a Little Faith*. In 2005 Staples was set to accept a Grammy award for lifetime achievement on behalf of the Staple Singers, of whom she was the last surviving original member.

Mavis Staples was born in Chicago, Illinois, on July 10, 1939 (or, according to some sources, 1940). Her father, Roebuck "Pops" Staples, had grown up on Mississippi's Dockery Plantation, a key site in the development of the blues, and had learned to play the guitar from the great early bluesman Charley Patton. After he moved north to Chicago in 1936 he began to

Staples, Mavis, photograph. Carlo Allegri/Getty Images.

organize gospel quartets after finishing work at a meatpacking plant, and it was gospel that Mavis Staples heard at home. "He used to play records by the Dixie Hummingbirds, the Soul Sisters, the Blind Boys of Mississippi as well as the Blind Boys of Alabama, but after I heard [gospel great] Mahalia [Jackson] sing 'Move On Up a Little Higher,' I had to play her music every day," Staples told Greg Quill of the *Toronto Star.*

Sounded Older Than 15 to Listeners

Pops Staples, dissatisfied with the attendance habits of his group the Trumpet Jubilees, recruited his son Pervis and daughters Mavis, Cleo, and Yvonne to form the Staple Singers around 1948. The first song they learned together was the country classic "Will the Circle Be Unbroken," and it would always be among their trademark numbers. The group began performing in Chicago churches and then on a weekly radio program. In 1953 they made a 78 rpm record, "Sit Down Servant," and three years later they scored their first national hit, "Uncloudy Day," after signing with the Chicago blues powerhouse Vee Jay. The Staple Sing-

At a Glance . . .

Born on July 10, 1939(?), in Chicago, IL; daughter of Roebuck "Pops" and Oceala Staples; married (divorced).

Career: Staple Singers (family gospel group), member, 1950–; solo career, 1969–.

Selected awards: "100 Greatest Women of Rock and Roll," VH1 cable network; Rock and Roll Hall of Fame Inductee (with the Staple Singers), 1999; Grammy Award, for lifetime achievement (with the Staple Singers), 2005.

Addresses: *Home*—Chicago, IL. *Agent*—The Rosebud Agency, P.O. Box 170429, San Francisco, CA 94117.

ers stood out not only because of the shimmering electric guitar of Pops Staples, but also because of Mavis's lead vocals. "I was a skinny little knock-kneed girl with a big voice that comes from my mother's side," Staples recalled to *Washington Post* writer Richard Harrington. "Deejays would announce, 'This is little 15-year-old Mavis singing' and people would say it's gotta either be a man or a big lady. People were betting that I was not a little girl."

Staples considered going to nursing school, but finally chose to stay with the family group; she often told a story of how her father, one of 14 children, would put 14 pencils together to show his own children how hard they were to break as compared with breaking each one individually. In the 1960s, some said, the Staple Singers provided the soundtrack to the civil rights revolution. African-American groups found common cause with white folk performers as the Rev. Martin Luther King, Jr., preached the gospel of equal rights across the South.

"I really like this man's message and I think if he can preach it, we can sing it," Pops Staples told his children, as Mavis recalled to Harrington in the *Washington Post.* The Staple Singers performed with the then-acoustic folk musician Bob Dylan and began to record his songs, including the blistering antiwar anthem "Masters of War." Dylan, for his part, had been a Staple Singers fan ever since he heard their recordings on Nashville AM radio powerhouse WLAC as a 12-year-old in Minnesota. A romance sprang up between Dylan and Mavis Staples, although it was not publicly revealed until many years later. Dylan proposed marriage at one point but was turned down even though Pops Staples backed the union. The two remained friends, and Staples later regretted her decision. "It was

really too bad," she told Harrington. "I often wonder when I see Bobby's son Jakob, how would our son have looked and how would he have sounded."

Recorded Secular Music for Stax Labels

Staples made her solo recording debut in 1969 on the Volt imprint of Memphis's Stax label, with the secular *Mavis Staples* album and its 1970 Stax followup *Only for the Lonely.* These albums, with compositional contributions from the Stax songwriting staff, had only moderate success, but the Staple Singers, also recording for Stax by that time, reached the peak of their commercial success in the early 1970s. Staples had a hand in composing several of the group's top hits, including the chart-topping and widely familiar "I'll Take You There" (1972)—a song that seemed to distill into funky gospel cadences the hopeful atmosphere of the civil rights era. In 1974 the group moved to the Chicago-based Curtom label, headed by soul singer Curtis Mayfield, and the following year they scored another number one hit with "Let's Do It Again."

After recording a soundtrack album, *A Piece of the Action,* for Curtom in 1977, Staples made another try at a solo career with the album *Mavis Staples.* Produced by former Motown songwriters Eddie and Brian Holland along with Stax veteran Steve Cropper, and featuring songwriting contributions from Aretha Franklin's younger sister Carolyn, the album spawned only one single that reached the lower levels of the R&B charts. Delayed for several years, the album tanked after its 1984 release on the HDH label, but it remained a personal favorite for Staples.

By the late 1980s, with no recording contract on the horizon, Staples was living in Chicago and facing tax problems and overdue bills. Things turned around when another fan from the pop world, the funk- and rock-influenced Prince, offered her a seven-year contract on his Minneapolis-based Paisley Park label. When asked how it felt to be working with Prince, Staples often directed the questioner to ask Prince how it felt to be working with Mavis Staples. Prince tailored his songwriting to Staples on the two albums she recorded for him, *Time Waits for No One* (1989) and *The Voice* (1993). He avoided the sexual themes of much of his own music, but the albums did not sell well with either youthful urban fans or with the traditional Staple Singers base that was leery of Prince's influence. Still, the two albums earned strongly positive reviews and kept Staples in the public eye, leading to guest slots on 1994's *Rhythm, Country & Blues* collection and other album releases.

Prepared Final Staple Singers Album

In 1996 Staples recorded *Spirituals & Gospel,* a tribute to her idol Mahalia Jackson. She entered the studio in Memphis as producer in 1997 to record a final Pops Staples album. "These were old songs he sang as a boy, and I asked him to record them as simply as possible, just his voice and guitar," Staples told the *Toronto Star*. "I could add other stuff after his work was done." Pops Staples fell ill that year and died in 2000, and Staples also faced the deteriorating health of her sister Cleo, who was diagnosed with Alzheimer's disease. She continued to work periodically on the Pops Staples album, which was slated for release in 2005.

Chicago songwriter Joe Tullio, who lost two friends in the terrorist attacks of September 11, 2001, asked Staples to perform "In Times Like These," a song he had written about the event. The request resonated with Staples' own feelings. "I wanted to sing songs that would be uplifting and healing," she told Keith Spera of the New Orleans *Times-Picayune*. "We're living in troubled times. So many people are living in fear." The result was the album *Have a Little Faith*, financed and mostly co-written by Staples herself. Staples' sister Yvonne was drafted to sing harmony, for Staples said that she still listened for her sister Cleo's voice when she sang. After shopping the project to various companies, Staples reached an agreement with the blues-oriented Chicago label Alligator.

Have a Little Faith appeared in 2004; one of its selections, "I Still Believe in You," became the theme song for the successful World Series drive of baseball's Boston Red Sox that year, and Staples was picked to sing "America the Beautiful" at the 2004 Democratic National Convention. The album also included "Pops Recipe," a tribute to Pops Staples, and a new version of "Will the Circle Be Unbroken." Staples earned a Grammy nomination in 2003 for her duet with Bob Dylan on "Gotta Change My Way of Thinking," and she added three more in 2004 for her contributions to Dr. John's *N'awlinz: Dis Dat or D'uddah* and to *Beautiful Dreamer: The Songs of Stephen Foster*. Perhaps more popular than she had ever been, Staples told *Jet* that "Nobody is going to send me out to pasture. My voice is my gift from God, and I'm going to use it."

Selected discography

Albums

Mavis Staples, Volt, 1969.
Only for the Lonely, Stax, 1970.
A Piece of the Action, Curtom, 1977.
Mavis Staples, HDH, 1984.
Time Waits for No One, Paisley Park, 1987.
The Voice, NPG, 1993.
Spirituals & Gospel, Verve, 1996.
Have a Little Faith, Alligator, 2004.

Sources

Books

Contemporary Musicians, vol. 13, Gale, 1994.

Periodicals

Billboard, September 4, 1993, p. 21.
Jet, November 22, 2004, p. 38.
San Francisco Chronicle, October 6, 2004, p. E1.
Star Tribune (Minneapolis, MN), January 14, 2005, p. E1.
Times-Picayune (New Orleans, LA), September 24, 2004, p. 31.
Toronto Star, December 19, 2004, p. C2.
Washington Post, October 31, 2004, p. N1.

On-line

"Mavis Staples," *All Music Guide,* www.allmusic.com (January 24, 2005).
"Mavis Staples," *Alligator Records,* www.alligator.com/artists/bio.cfm?ArtistID=076 (January 24, 2005).
Mavis Staples, www.mavisstaples.com (February 8, 2005).
"Mavis Staples," *The Rosebud Agency,* www.rosebudus.com/staples (February 8, 2005).
"Staple Singers," *Rock and Roll Hall of Fame,* www.rockhall.com/hof/inductee.asp?id=195 (January 24, 2005).

—James M. Manheim

Michael Stoney

1969—

Fashion designer

Michael Stoney seemed an unlikely candidate to lead a fashion revolution. An orphan, he was reared on a dual diet of poverty and crime. Instead of design school, Stoney attended the police academy, learning how wield guns and shields, not scissors and fabric. When a bullet forced him to retire, he became a man of leisure. That is when he realized he needed clothes for his new lifestyle. "[We] decided to build a fashion line based on my life," Stoney told *Contemporary Black Biography (CBB)*. "I was on pension, I could afford to dress down, be comfortable. We equated being comfortable to success." The result was Dug—Down Under Gear. When it debuted in 1999, both Stoney and men's undergarments came out from under and found fame.

Escaped Streets Through Police Force

Michael Stoney was born in 1969 into a life marred by the ugly statistics of New York's inner-city. His father was unknown to him, his teenaged mother drug-addicted. At birth he was placed in foster care where he stayed until he was five years old. "I was taken from my foster mother who I loved," Stoney told *CBB*. "And after a court case, I was sent back to my mother who still had problems and couldn't take care of me. I finally ended up with my mother's sister who had seven kids already." Stoney spent ten years with his aunt's family in Hollis, Queens, before setting out on his own at 16. He told *CBB* that he "didn't want to have anything to do with anyone. I wanted to do it on my own."

Hollis was home to some of New York's toughest streets. "I saw most of the kids around me get lost," he told *CBB*. "Drugs, prisons, dying on the streets." However, Hollis also gave birth to legendary rappers Run DMC, Murder Inc. Records kingpin Irv Gotti, and Fubu fashion founder Daymond John. These were Stoney's peers, kids from the same bloodied streets who had found a way to channel the bleakness of their surroundings into creativity. Though Stoney got into some trouble—"knucklehead stuff. Riding motorcycles too fast, flipping over cars," he told *CBB*—he also seemed to know instinctively that he did not have to become another inner-city statistic, another boy lost to the streets. He decided to take the police test. "I passed it," Stoney told *CBB*. "That was a big turning point for me."

In 1992 Stoney became a New York City cop. Two years later he was promoted to detective and started working undercover in a Brooklyn narcotics unit. In 1996, during a high-profile case, Stoney was shot. "The bullet went in my left arm and the left side of my chest," he told *CBB*. Stoney lost 60 percent of his blood and nearly died. His injuries forced him to retire from the NYPD in 1997. He received several awards for his police work as well as a lifelong pension. He was just 26 years old. "I still had so much to do in my life," he told *CBB*.

Launched Dug with Only a Logo

Still recovering from the gunshot, Stoney teamed up with a chef to open Blue Goose Café in Queens. The restaurant featured late night jazz dinners and Sunday gospel brunches and was an initial success. It was not

At a Glance . . .

Born in 1969, in New York, NY; married Maria Stoney; children: Michael, Xavier, Halle.

Career: New York Police Department, officer, 1992-94; New York City Police Department, detective, 1994-97; Blue Goose Café, Queens, NY, managing partner, mid-1990s; Dug, New York, NY, CEO, 1999-2004; THElabel, New York, NY, CEO, 2004–.

Selected awards: New York Police Department, Detective Shield, 1995; New York Police Department, Finest of the Month award, 1995; New York Police Department, Medal of Valor, 2003; New York Police Department, Combat Cross, 2003; New York Mayor's Office, Humanitarian Award, 2004.

Addresses: *Office*—178-10 Wexford Terrace, Jamaica Estates, NY, 11432.

the right fit for Stoney, however. "It felt good to have my own place, but it consumed me," he told *CBB*. "I was a slave to the business. I wanted to make money, but also sleep." Stoney next became the personal assistant for an Italian businessman. "It was humbling to go from owner of a nightclub to someone's driver, but I needed to do it," Stoney told *CBB*. "Eventually he took me under his wing and said he would teach me more about business than I could ever learn in college. He said he was doing it because I had a driving personality, a passion for work and people that he couldn't teach to anyone with a business degree," Stoney recalled to *CBB*. Stoney was a quick learner and could have easily pursued partnerships with his boss, but as he told *CBB*, "I wanted to do something more creative, so I started looking for my next move."

Late in 1998 Stoney and childhood friend Jonathan Johnson were sitting around Stoney's kitchen table pitching business ideas when they remembered a pajama party Stoney had attended. Of the party Stoney later told CNNfn's *Business Unusual*, "after exhausting every opportunity to find something that was cool and comfortable and made a statement, a fashion statement, I realized that there was a void that needed to be filled." Stoney and Johnson decided to fill it with Dug, a loungewear line for men. The duo commissioned a logo of a man digging. "We didn't want to come across as being designers," Stoney told the *Daily News Record*. "We wanted a simple and understandable logo. Dug represents a hard-working, masculine, simple man who's digging. Every man, no matter what his color, can relate to him."

With the logo and little else Stoney and Johnson launched Dug. "We bought stuff off the rack and sewed on our label," Stoney confessed to *CBB*. "Then we got people to wear it. I knew people from my club days, some rappers, producers, video directors, and we began chasing after them. We didn't have a line. We had no clothes, no brand, but we built a story around the logo." It worked. "The logo has already been in at least 15 music videos, and it hasn't even hit stores yet," Johnson told the *Daily News Record* in 1999.

Built Star Following for Dug

Stoney directed his electric personality into promoting the Dug lifestyle. "Comfort is the new luxury," he said in an interview on the KriSeLen Web site. He repeated that mantra to anyone and everyone. "We got in front of our peers and were passionate about the story we were selling," Stoney told *CBB*. In 1999 Stoney attended Magic, a mega-trade show for the clothing industry. He and Johnson walked the booths, a few samples in hand, preaching the Dug lifestyle. Eventually they caught the interest of SaraMax, a woman's underwear and sleepwear maker that held licenses for Disney, Harry Potter, and Nascar.

With a $3 million investment SaraMax bought 75 percent of Dug, and Stoney and team launched their first line. It included tank tops and matching boxers, t-shirts, jogging pants and jackets, pajamas, and hooded robes. Fabrics included silk, velour, micro-fiber, and mesh. Colors ranged from basic grays and whites to ice blue, teal, and lemon. Stoney's ambition expanded with the line. "We want to be the male Victoria Secret," he told the *Daily News Record*. "We might be starting in underwear and loungewear, but eventually we want to move into categories such as bath, home, beauty, accessories, razors, condoms, and aromatherapy."

Stoney's flair for publicity propelled Dug into the limelight. At the 2000 Magic show, he rented ten booths, three 50-inch flat screen televisions, and hired a full-time DJ. "We started getting a lot of press," Stoney told *CBB*. "We were featured three times in *DNR* (a men's fashion magazine), also *The Source*, and *Sportswear*. I was on CNNfn.... I just shared my line and my passion and met a lot of people. We spread through word of mouth and ended up with a lot of celebrity fans." Singer R. Kelly wore the label on the cover of an early album. Leonardo DiCaprio was photographed in a Dug tank top. Gwen Stefani, Justin Timberlake, Toni Braxton, Usher, and Ja Rule were all spotted sporting the Dug logo.

Sold Dug to Apparel Giant

Despite the hype, Dug was having trouble getting retail buyers. "We didn't have the corporate power behind us," Stoney told *CBB*. The solution was typical of

Stoney's creativity. "We ended up hiring a couple of white actors, corporate-looking guys and put them up in our offices. We painted a picture of being more corporate than we were," he confessed to *CBB*. It was starting to work. Orders for boutique shops were coming in and business seemed ready to take off. Then 9/11 hit. In the aftermath, Dug lost several deals. Then both SaraMax and Johnson decided to pull out. Though dejected, Stoney refused to be defeated. He hired another childhood friend, Robert Crawford, to take Johnson's place and trudged off to the 2002 Magic show. "We were a featured vendor, but we had nothing left, no money, just our passion," Stoney told *CBB*.

On the plane ride home, Stoney struck up a conversation with the man seated next to him. He related the Dug philosophy and showed off a few samples. "It turns out he is with Kellwood," Stoney told *CBB*. Kellwood, a publicly-traded clothing manufacturer with sales in the billions, was looking to expand into the urban market and Dug seemed just the vehicle. Kellwood bought Dug in March of 2002 and made Stoney CEO of the line.

Kellwood pushed Dug into several major retail outlets including Macy's, Marshall Fields, and Hechts and Robinsons. Ads popped up on billboards and phone kiosks. Stoney told the *Daily News Record*, "Now that Kellwood is behind us, we have the power to make Dug the lifestyle brand we believe it can be." Kellwood agreed. "Dug is the absolute most exciting thing I have seen in this category," a top executive said in the same article.

Infused Spirituality into Clothes and Life

The honeymoon between Dug and Kellwood was short-lived. In 2004 Kellwood acquired Phat Farm fashions from hip-hop mogul Russell Simmons. It quickly became the company's preferred avenue into the urban market. "Dug began to be overlooked," Stoney told *CBB*. "It was phased out of department stores." After two years with Kellwood, Stoney decided not to renew his contract as Dug's CEO. Instead he offered his talents on the open market as a consultant to apparel manufacturers.

One of Stoney's clients was Avirex, a wholesale manufacturer of aviation themed clothing and accessories. In 2004 Avirex asked Stoney to launch a new brand. "It's called THElabel," Stoney told *CBB*. "It is a high-end, high-fashion line for men. It uses exotic leathers, cashmeres, silks. High quality, attention to detail, all done with the same focus and passion I gave to Dug." Expected to launch in January of 2005, THELabel would feature another one of Stoney's innovations—an audio CD hang tag. Stoney hired a composer and spoken word artist to create a series of tracks to go with the line's different items. "The CD will be included with the tags on each piece of clothing. It is about how you get dressed, what your clothes mean to you," he told *CBB*. "I don't want to get too spiritual, but we feel the clothes you wear are a reflection of your inner spirit."

Inner spirit is something Stoney has long understood. It propelled him from inner-city kid to fashion visionary. It is also a trait he has used to reach kids who, like himself, faced despair almost from day one. Because of the fame Dug brought him, Stoney has been invited to speak to at-risk kids at schools and half-way houses. "It can turn out to be a blessing in disguise to have a tough childhood, it makes you stronger," he told *CBB*. He continued, explaining the philosophy he has shared with kids, "You need to get into the core of who you are and understand who you are. I focus on the spiritual aspect of who you are, letting the past go and the present come." If he gets his way, that present is going to be both fashionably and spiritually well-dressed.

Sources

Periodicals

Business Unusual (CNNfn transcripts); December 22, 2000.
Daily News Record August 19, 2002, August 28, 2000.

On-line

"Interview with Michael Stoney," *KriSeLen*, www.kriselen.com/reviews/DUGlife.shtml (December 22, 2004).

Other

Additional information for this profile was obtained through an interview with Michael Stoney on December 28, 2004.

—Candace LaBalle

Cynthia Bramlett Thompson

1949—

National Chair of Girl Scouts USA, business owner, executive

On October 19, 2002, Cynthia Bramlett Thompson was elected chair of the National Board of Directors of Girl Scouts of the USA (GSUSA)—the highest volunteer position in the world's largest female organization, with more than 3.7 million members nationwide. Thompson's business career as a company owner and human resources specialist has been equally successful. In 1993 Thompson and her husband founded Midwest Stamping, Inc. in Maumee, Ohio, near Toledo. By 2003 Midwest Stamping was number 28 on *Black Enterprise*'s list of the 100 largest black-owned industrial/service businesses in the United States.

Born on May 18, 1949, in Highland Park, Michigan, Cynthia Bramlett was the daughter of Carrie Frances Bramlett and Cosby Bramlett, Jr. Her mother was a homemaker and her father was a pharmacist who later worked as a chemist for the federal government. Bramlett grew up in Inkster, Michigan, near Detroit. Her parents had high standards and expectations for their children. Bramlett's public-school experiences were excellent, with inspiring teachers and principals. Her home, school, and the Episcopal Church provided her with a strong community network.

Bramlett entered the five-year pharmacy program at the University of Michigan in Ann Arbor. She attended school year-around, studying literature, science, and the arts (LSA) during the summer when pharmacy courses were not offered. When Bramlett met her future husband, Ronald L. Thompson, her parents insisted that she graduate before marrying. Therefore she took a bachelor of general studies (BGS) degree in LSA in 1970.

Although she planned to return to pharmacy school and eventually go to medical school, Cynthia Thompson followed her husband to Michigan State University (MSU) in East Lansing so that he could pursue his master's and doctoral degrees in agricultural economics. The Thompsons' daughter Sela was born in 1971 and their son Mance in 1973. Meanwhile Cynthia Thompson earned her master's degree in nutrition from MSU.

In 1981 the Thompsons moved to St. Louis, Missouri, where they bought the GR Group—formerly General Railroad—a company that refurbished freight cars. While working in human resources at GR, Thompson decided that she needed a more thorough background in business. She earned her master's in business administration (MBA) from Washington University in St. Louis.

Despite the demands of her family and her full-time career, Thompson was very active in the St. Louis community. She told *Contemporary Black Biography* (*CBB*) that she was particularly proud of her service as a board member of the St. Louis Science Center and the Missouri State Board of Education. Following her tenure on the Board of Education, then-governor John Ashcroft appointed her to the Board of Curators of the University of Missouri System. Thompson also was active in the Links, Inc. and the Alpha Kappa Alpha Sorority.

In 1993 the Thompsons moved to Ohio to establish Midwest Stamping, a manufacturer of automobile parts. Cynthia Thompson became vice president of human resources and her husband became chief execu-

At a Glance . . .

Born Cynthia Bramlett on May 18, 1949, in Highland Park, MI, daughter of Carrie Frances and Cosby Bramlett, Jr.; married Ronald L. Thompson, 1970; children: Sela, Mance. *Education:* University of Michigan, BGS in LSA, 1970; Michigan State University, MS, nutrition, 1973(?); Washington University, St. Louis, MBA, 198(?).

Career: GR Group, St. Louis, co-owner and human resources executive, 1981-93, board member, 1981–; Midwest Stamping, Inc., Maumee, OH, co-founder, major shareholder, vice president of human resources, 1993–.

Selected memberships: St. Louis Science Center, former board member; International Women's Forum, Missouri Chapter, former board member; GSUSA, Girl Scout Council of Greater St. Louis, board member, vice president of corporate planning, program committee chair, 1989-1993, National Board, director, 1996–, second vice president, 1999-2002, chair, 2002-2005, executive, finance, human resources, and fund development committees, Special Committee on Compensation and Benefits, 2002–; University of Missouri System, Board of Curators, 1991-94, vice president, 1993, curator emeritus, 1994–; Girls, Inc., St. Louis, numerous positions and several committee memberships, board member, president of the board, emeritus national board member, 1993–.

Addresses: *Offices*—Midwest Stamping, Inc., 3455 Briarfield Blvd., Suite A, Maumee, OH 43537; Girl Scouts of the USA, 420 Fifth Avenue, New York, NY 10018-2798.

tive officer (CEO). She told *CBB* that she had the "best job in the company" because she was involved in all aspects of the business and interacted with everyone, from the plant floor to engineering, accounting, and finance. The Thompsons built up their company until, by 2003, Midwest Stamping had 580 employees and $130 million in annual sales.

Thompson's involvement with Girl Scouts began while she was in elementary school. Her mother was chair of cookie sales and camped with her daughters' troops.

As a college undergraduate Thompson spent a summer as a counselor at a Girl Scout camp. She loved the experience. While living in Seattle, Washington, in the 1970s, Thompson and her own daughter became active in the Girl Scouts.

After moving to St. Louis Thompson joined the Girl Scout Council of Greater St. Louis. She served as cookie chair, and as a board member, vice president of corporate planning, and chair of the program committee for the Council. Thompson joined the national board of directors of GSUSA in 1996. In 1999 she became second vice president of the board. In June of 2002 Thompson served as a GSUSA delegate to the World Association of Girl Guides and Girl Scouting in Manila, the Philippines. By the time Thompson was elected chair—for a three-year term beginning in the fall 2002—she had been involved with Girl Scouts for more than 35 years. Between 2002 and 2005 Thompson also was a member of the executive, finance, human resources, and fund development committees and served as chair of the Special Committee on Compensation and Benefits.

The stated goal of GSUSA has been to help girls to become the best that they possibly can. In the Spring 2003 issue of *Leader*, a GSUSA publication, Thompson told Ed Levy: "Girl Scouting really does prepare you to interact effectively with others, makes you ready for leadership, and gives you an opportunity to spread your wings…Girl Scouting gives any girl an opportunity to develop leadership skills and character, and to become involved in community service activities that will last throughout her lifetime. The things Girl Scouts do in areas like information technology and the environment are very relevant. The organization has changed because the needs of girls and women have changed. Girl Scouts has kept up with that."

Thompson now headed an organization of almost 980,000 adult members who, along with community leaders and organizations, alumni and other donors, corporations, foundations, and government agencies, worked for the benefit of 2.8 million girls. The influence of New York City-based GSUSA reached across the country and throughout the world, advocating for girls and providing high-quality community and volunteer-based programs. As the chair of GSUSA Thompson tried to visit as many local councils as possible and to improve the dialogue between local volunteers and the national board.

Developing programs for pre-teen and teenage girls, as well as reaching out to Latinas, had become major undertakings for the GSUSA. Although participation in Girl Scout programs was high among elementary-school girls, as they entered their preteens their involvement dropped off dramatically. In her leadership position, Thompson focused on bringing GSUSA into the lives of adolescent girls across the country.

In the Fall 2004 issue of the *Leader*, Thompson announced that she, Kathy Cloninger—CEO of GSUSA—and the National Board were embarking on a business strategy process to redefine the long-range vision of the Girl Scout Movement. They would take into consideration "current and projected social and economic trends, the needs and interests of girls, and the needs of volunteers," while developing a core business strategy.

Although her family was always Thompson's top priority, she remained very career-oriented. She worked full-time while also devoting much time and energy to academic and service organizations. As GSUSA chair, Girl Scouts became her major focus. Thompson decided at the outset of her term that she would serve for three years only.

Selected writings

"Redefining Strategic Leadership for Now and the Future," *Leader*, Fall 2004, p. 4.

Sources

Periodicals

Ebony, March 2003, pp. 46-54.

On-line

"Chair, National Board of Directors, Cynthia Bramlett Thompson," *Executive Bios, Girl Scouts of the USA*, www.girlscouts.org/who_we_are_/executive_bios (January 18, 2005).
"Meet Cynthia Bramlett Thompson Chair, National Board of Directors 2002-2005," *Leader, Girl Scouts of the USA*, www.girlscouts.org/for_adults/leader_magazine/2003_spring/cynthia_thompson.asp (January 18, 2005).

Other

Additional information for this profile was obtained through an interview with Cynthia Bramlett Thompson on January 12, 2005.

—Margaret Alic

Boyd Tinsley

1964—

Musician

Tinsley, Boyd, photograph. Tim Mosenfelder/Getty Images.

A member of the acclaimed Dave Matthews Band, Boyd Tinsley has earned accolades for his innovative work on the violin. Critics have marveled at his ability to move from the traditional to the avant-garde, stretching the limits of an instrument not often associated with contemporary rock music. Tinsley has also recorded a solo album, and has become an impassioned and dedicated advocate for music education in public schools.

Wanted to Learn Guitar

Boyd Calvin Tinsley was born on May 16, 1964, in Charlottesville, Virginia, and grew up in the same neighborhood as saxophonist Leroi Moore and drummer Carter Beauford, who would later be his bandmates with Dave Matthews. Music was a big part of Tinsley's childhood: his father, George Franklin Tinsley, directed the church choir; his uncle played in local jazz bands; and tunes from Motown records filled the Tinsley house.

In sixth grade at Walker Middle School in Charlottesville, Tinsley signed up for a string music class, hoping to learn to play guitar. To his initial dismay, the class was in classical orchestra. Rather than withdraw, he decided to attempt the violin, which he learned relatively quickly. By his teens, Tinsley was an accomplished classical musician. He co-founded the Charlottesville-Albemarle Youth Orchestra and studied under the concertmaster of the Baltimore Symphony Orchestra, Isador Saslav. Indeed, Saslav urged his pupil to apply to the Performing Arts School in Baltimore to further his studies. Tinsley decided against this step, however, and chose to enroll at the University of Virginia in 1982, where he earned a BA in history.

At the university, Tinsley joined the Sigma Nu fraternity. He participated in various activities with the fraternity, including a series of all-night music festivals. He also expanded his musical awareness by listening to innovative violinists such as Stephane Grappeli. "Stephane Grapelli was the first violinist I heard outside of classical or bluegrass or country," he commented in an interview for VH1. "He was a huge influence [on me]. He showed a whole different side of the instrument I didn't even know about…. The more I dug, the more I realized there were a lot of other guys doing unconventional stuff with the violin, like Jean-Luc

At a Glance . . .

Born on May 16, 1964, in Charlottesville, Virginia; son of George Franklin Tinsley and Helen Carter Tinsley; children: two. *Education:* University of Virginia, BA, 1986(?).

Career: Down Boy Down (band), co-founder, 1987-92; Boyd Tinsley Band, cofounder and member, 1988(?)-92; Dave Matthews Band, violinist, 1991–; solo musician and recording artist, 2003–; model.

Awards: (As member of Dave Matthews Band) Chairman's Award, NAACP Image Awards, 2004.

Addresses: *Label*—c/o RCA Records, 1540 Broadway, New York, NY 10036.

Ponty, Jefferson Starship's Papa John Creach, and It's a Beautiful Day's David LaFlamme."

Soon Tinsley began thinking of creating a rock band featuring violin instead of electric guitar. Though it was tricky at first to slough off his classical training and learn to improvise, Tinsley persisted and, in 1987, formed the duo Down Boy Down with guitar player Harry Faulkner. The group later expanded to include drummer Andrew Weaver, and renamed itself the Boyd Tinsley Band.

Impressed Dave Matthews at Frat Party

Tinsley first met Dave Matthews in Charlottesville, where Matthews was working as a bartender and playing in small clubs. "I knew [the Dave Matthews Band] was something special," Tinsley said in an interview for *Defy Magazine*. "This was some of the most powerful music I'd heard in a long time." One night, Matthews attended a fraternity party where Tinsley was playing solo. Matthews was so impressed with the sounds that Tinsley coaxed out of the instrument that he invited the violinist to play with the Dave Matthews Band on the demo of "Tripping Billies," recorded in 1991. Tinsley became a permanent member of the band the following year.

Playing with the Dave Matthews Band has allowed Tinsley to continue his exploration of his instrument. As VH1 interviewer C. Bottomley observed, since joining the band, Tinsley has put rock violin in the spotlight, "mounting wild Hendrix-style solos as often as concocting weepy Appalachian melodies." *Guitar Player* critic Kevin Ransom described Tinsley's playing as "Celtic-cum-country fiddle lines" that contribute to "some wild improvisations" onstage. "It's not really a competition," Tinsley explained in the VH1 interview. The point of playing with the other Dave Matthews Band musicians, he said, is to push each other to achieve something better each time they perform. "The greatest gigs from DMB," he noted, "are gigs when I play stuff I didn't even realize I could play."

In 2003 Tinsley released a solo album, *True Reflections*. The title song had been familiar to Dave Matthews Band fans for several years. Tinsley wrote it around 1989, when he was with the Boyd Tinsley Band; the tune went on to become a staple at Dave Matthews Band concerts. "I planned on doing it again," Tinsley told VH1, "but it took 10 years before I got the opportunity to sit down and spend a lot of time writing."

A writer for *Defy Magazine* described the album as a recording that "walks an unmistakable inner-directed path." The songs, Boyd said in an interview for the magazine, reflect his deep awareness of "what's important in life, what I appreciate about life. So the songs are basically about love and relationships." Among the tracks that critics found especially notable were the title song, on which Dave Matthews contributed vocals, and a slowed-down cover of Neil Young's "Cinnamon Girl."

Promoted Music Education

A firm believer in the importance of music education, Tinsley has supported several initiatives that provide music classes in public schools. In 2003 he became the official spokesperson for the 'Blue for Save the Music Campaign,' a joint endeavor between Blue from American Express and the VH1 Save the Music Foundation. The campaign aimed to raise funds and awareness to support music education. "I joined the Blue for Save the Music campaign because I understand first-hand the powerful impact that music can make on young people's lives," said Tinsley in a press re-lease from the campaign. "As a child, I quickly learned to play the violin through the encouragement of my teachers, and have since turned my passion for music into a career.... I look forward to providing the same hope and opportunity for kids across the country."

Tinsley has also privately supported music education in his hometown of Charlottesville, where he resides with his family. He has provided public schools in the city with scholarship money to pay for private music lessons for low-income students. In its first year, the program provided scholarships to 26 student orchestra members. Additional scholarships are planned for future years.

When not playing music, Tinsley enjoys frequent workouts at the gym. He has also embarked on a side career as a model for such designers as JanSport, Tommy Hilfiger, and Gucci. Modeling, Tinsley explained in a quote on the Dave Matthews Band Web site, offers him a break from the intensity of the concert stage or the recording studio.

Reflecting on his musical success, Tinsley told *Defy Magazine* that he loves taking his playing to ever-new heights. "There are no limits to it," he said of the violin. "I like playing pizzicato, rhythm, playing with a wah-wah pedal. Mostly, it's really cool to see kids playing air violin in the crowd. That's something new. I hope some kids will take what I've done and expand on it."

Selected discography

True Reflections, RCA Records, 2003.

Sources

Periodicals

Guitar Player, February, 1995, p. 19.
New York Times, January 28, 2004; September 25, 2004.

On-line

"Blue From American Express and Infinity Broadcasting to Launch 'Amplify Tomorrow' Tour," *For Release*, www.forrelease.com/D20030610/002/ (January 17, 2005).
"Boyd Tinsley," *Defy Magazine*, www.defymagazine.com/artists/Boyd_Tinsley/ (January 17, 2005).
"Boyd Tinsley Sure Can Pull Some Bow," *VH1*, www.vh1.com/artists/az/tinsley_boyd/artist.jhtml (January 17, 2005).
Dave Matthews Band, www.dmband.com (January 6, 2005).
Charlottesville High School Orchestra, http://avenue.org/chso (January 6, 2005).
"True Reflections: A Profile of Boyd Tinsley," *The Delta of Sigma Nu*, www.sigmanu.com/documents/DeltaW0304.pdf (February 7, 2005).

—E. M. Shostak

Wayman Tisdale

1964—

Professional basketball player, musician

Tisdale, Wayman, photograph. Kent Horner/NBAE via Getty Images.

Bass player Wayman Tisdale played twelve years in the National Basketball Association (NBA) as a power forward before turning his undivided attention to his first love: music. Releasing his first solo album in 1995 while still playing in the NBA, the six-foot, nine-inch tall, 240 pound giant had released his sixth album by 2004. His first four albums reached Billboard's top ten chart and included the number-one hit "Can't Hide Love." He has also contributed to other recordings as a writer and a producer.

The youngest of six children, Wayman Lawrence Tisdale was born on June 8, 1964, in Tulsa, Oklahoma, where his father, the late Rev. Louis Tisdale, served as the pastor of Tulsa's Friendship Baptist Church for over 20 years. When Tisdale was young his father bought each of his three sons a Mickey Mouse guitar, hoping at least one of them would take an interest in music. Tisdale, who loved to watch the bass players at his father's church, was instantly enthralled and began to teach himself to play guitar and bass.

Although music was Tisdale's first love, a rapid growth spurt during his junior high school years—he grew 24 inches and began to tower over his older siblings—drew

him onto the basketball court. Though he did not completely set aside his music, basketball became his first priority. Growing to his full height of six-feet, nine inches, and displaying tremendous athletic ability, Tisdale became a star player at Booker T. Washington High School in Tulsa. By the time he graduated in the spring of 1982, he had his pick from literally hundreds of college scholarship offers.

Choosing to remain close to home, Tisdale attended Oklahoma University. Playing for the Sooners he quickly earned recognition as one of the country's best power forwards. Having watched Tisdale during his high school days, J. V. Haney of the *Tulsa World* recalled his reaction to Tisdale's transition into college basketball: "At 6' 9", he was too much for most high school players to defend against, but I never thought that he displayed the toughness to be a great player. Boy was I wrong. Once he arrived at the University of Oklahoma, the man-child became an honest-to-goodness man."

Tisdale was named first-team All-American in each of his three years of college play, averaging 25.6 points and over 10 rebounds per game. His field goal percent-

At a Glance . . .

Born on June 9, 1964, in Fort Worth, TX; married Regina; four children. *Education:* Attended University of Oklahoma, 1982-85.

Career: Indiana Pacers, professional basketball player, 1985-89; Sacramento Kings, professional basketball player, 1989-94; Phoenix Suns, professional basketball player, 1994-97; recording artist, 1996–.

Memberships: Named to U.S. Olympic basketball team, 1984.

Awards: Olympic gold medal, basketball, 1984; Oklahoma Sports Hall of Fame, 2002; National Smooth Jazz Awards, Bassist of the Year, 2002.

Addresses: *Agent*—Cole Classic Management, P.O. Box 231, Canoga Park, CA 91305. *Record Label*—Rendezvous Entertainment, 2211 Corinth Avenue, Suite 207, Los Angeles, CA 90064.

age was an impressive 57.8 percent. In 1984 he became a member of the then-amateur U.S. Olympic basketball team, which won the gold medal. Tisdale was the first Oklahoma Sooner basketball player to have his jersey number, 23, retired.

In 1985 Tisdale decided to forego his final year of college to enter the NBA draft. He was selected as the second overall pick, after Patrick Ewing, by the Indiana Pacers. During his rookie year Tisdale averaged 14.7 points and 7.2 rebounds per game. By his fourth and final season with the Pacers, Tisdale's numbers had improved to 17.5 points and 7.7 rebounds per game, but the long-suffering Pacers failed to post a winning record during the period. In 1989 Tisdale joined the Sacramento Kings, another losing team, but he had his best season on the floor, scoring a career-high average of 22.3 points per game. The following season he averaged 20 points per game, before falling to just under 17 points per game for the next three seasons. Despite his contribution, the Kings continued to post losing seasons during Tisdale's five-year tenure.

Tisdale signed as a free agent with the Phoenix Suns in 1994. Although his minutes as well as his points per game dropped, he was finally playing on a winning team. The Suns earned first place in the 1995 Pacific Division with a record of 59-23, losing in the Western Conference Semifinals. Over his twelve-year career,

Tisdale scored more than 12,000 points and pulled down over 5,000 rebounds, prompting *Sports Illustrated* Web site writer John Hollinger to add him to the short list of the NBA's best players who were never invited to play in an All-Star game.

As Tisdale's basketball career was winding down, his music career was just getting started. "The guys, especially Charles Barkley, used to tease me on the bus when they'd see me with my bass," Tisdale told *Billboard*. However, before he ever released a solo album, Tisdale was busy writing and producing. He wrote the song "Payday" for The Winans, a cut that featured R. Kelly. He also wrote several songs for SWV's first album, which sold around 3 million copies.

In 1995, after putting together a demo of seven songs, he proved that his interest in music was not just a passing fancy when he scored a recording contract with Motown's MoJazz label. His debut album, aptly titled *Power Forward*, made it to number four on Billboard's contemporary jazz charts. In 1996 Tisdale released his second album, once again taking on a basketball theme with the title *In the Zone*. The unexpected death of his 74-year-old father on March 28, 1997, helped finalize his decision to retire from the NBA following the 1996-97 season to focus solely on his music. It also became the impetus for his third album, *Decisions*, released in 1998, which marked a pivotal moment in his professional and personal life. Although the move to fulltime musician may have surprised those who had followed his NBA career, for Tisdale the transition was natural and smooth. "Music was what I thought I was going to do," he told *Jet*. "I wanted to be an artist even before I started thinking about basketball."

Face to Face, released by Warner Brothers in 2001, hit the number-one spot on Billboard's contemporary jazz charts, confirming that Tisdale's abilities as a bass player rivaled his abilities as a power forward and earning him honors as the Bassist of the Year during the 2002 National Smooth Jazz Awards. The track "Can't Hide Love" was a number one hit. For his fifth album, Tisdale followed an industry trend by forming his own production company, Tisway Records, to produce *21 Days*, which includes contributions from Tisdale's daughter Danielle and his brother Weldon, who followed their father as pastor of Friendship Baptist Church, where Tisdale and his family continue to attend. Tisdale wrote or co-wrote the eleven tracks for this gospel-influenced album, which includes songs such as "We Worship" and "Jesus Is the Answer."

In 2004 Tisdale worked with Rendezvous Entertainment co-founder saxophonist Dave Koz to produce his sixth album, *Hang Time*, featuring Koz's saxophone. The album also includes the re-release of "Glory Glory," which first appeared on *21 Days* and showcases Tisdale's daughter Danielle on vocals. Tisdale spent much of 2004 on the road touring with Koz. He continues to play in a variety of venues as well as work in the studio. He lives in Tulsa with his wife Regina and their four children.

Selected discography

Power Forward, Motown, 1995.
In the Zone, Motown, 1996.
Decisions, Atlantic, 1998.
Face to Face, Warner Brothers, 2001.
21 Days, Tisway Records, 2003.
Hang Time, Rendezvous, 2004.

Sources

Periodicals

Billboard, April 21, 2001, p. 18; November 1, 2003, p. 32.

Jet, August 14, 1995, p. 48; August 23, 2004, p. 35.
Sports Illustrated, July 15, 2002, p. 86.
Tulsa World, August 28, 2002.

On-line

"Interview: Wayman Tisdale," *Manhunt,* www.man hunt.com/features/html/232.html (January 10, 2005).
"The All-Not-Quite-Team," *Sports Illustrated* (January 28, 2003), http://sportsillustrated.cnn. com/statitudes/news/2003/01/27/statitudes_012 8/ (January 10, 2005).
Wayman Tisdale, www.tisway.com (January 10, 2005).
"Wayman Tisdale," *Basketball Reference,* www.bas ketballreference.com/players/playerpage.htm?ilkid =TISDAWA01 (January 10, 2005).

—Kari Bethel

John T. Walker

1925-1989

Episcopalian Bishop

The first African-American bishop of the Episcopal diocese of Washington, D.C., John T. Walker used his ministry to work tirelessly for social justice. He championed the rights of the poor and marginalized, and spoke out forcefully against South Africa's apartheid regime. After his death following heart surgery in 1989, Walker was remembered in *Washington Post* as a "powerful and effective force for change in his church and in this city."

Family Had African Methodist Episcopalian Roots

Born John Thomas Walker in Barnesville, Georgia, in 1925, Walker grew up in Chicago. Religion was important to his extended family, with his grandfather and great-grandfather both serving as ministers in the African Methodist Episcopalian Church. Yet when Walker began attending Wayne State College in the late 1940s, he drifted away from the church, focusing instead on political matters.

At age 23, Walker decided to join the Episcopal Church, to which he had been exposed during his college years. After attending Virginia Seminary Institute, he was assigned to St. Mary's Parish in Detroit. Later, he taught at St. Paul's School, a private high school in Concord, New Hampshire.

When Walker was ordained in the 1950s, the Episcopal Church membership tended to be white, affluent, and mostly of English ancestry. Black priests were relatively few, and the Church—like U.S. society itself—was generally segregated. Walker was among those whose work helped transform the Church's makeup and mission. It now welcomes a diverse population and commits itself to the needs of the poor and the oppressed. Throughout his career, Walker saw the church as a way to provide for the needs of such populations. "You have to give them a faith to live by, help break them from enslavement, be it economic, political, or emotional," he observed in comments quoted in the *New York Times*. "I think being black means I understand enslavement and rejection as well as anybody else."

Took on Apartheid and Women's Rights

One of Walker's most compelling social causes was the fight against apartheid; indeed, he was once arrested during a protest rally at the South African Embassy in Washington, D.C., Rather than focusing on the total removal of U.S. businesses from South Africa, however, Walker urged companies there to concentrate on training blacks for future leadership roles in a post-apartheid society. His position "brought him much reproach" from those who favored more immediate and drastic change at the time, according to his obituary in the *Washington Post*.

Yet Walker did not let such criticism sway his belief in peaceful negotiation as the best way to effect change.

At a Glance . . .

Born John Thomas Walker in 1925 in Barnesville, Georgia; died in 1989 in Washington, DC; married Maria Rosa Flores; children: Thomas, Anna Maria, Charlie. *Education:* Wayne State College, BA, 194(?); Virginia Seminary Institute, divinity degree, 195(?).

Career: St. Mary's Parish, Detroit, MI, parish ministry; St. Paul's School, Concord, NH, teacher; National Cathedral of St. Peter and St. Paul, Washington, DC, ministry, 1967-78; National Cathedral of St. Peter and St. Paul, Washington, DC, dean, 1978-98; Episcopal Diocese of Washington, DC, bishop, 1977-89.

Awards: The Black Student Fund and Africare created annual awards in Bishop John T. Walker's name.

At a time when many activists refused to consider compromise, Walker consistently assumed a mediating rather than confrontational role. Even so, he did not shy away from a stance that might place him in conflict with church authorities. His advocacy in favor of women priests, for example, met with pronounced opposition from his presiding bishop. Nevertheless, Walker continued to support ordination for women and for gays.

Walker also raised funds to fight poverty, and worked to make blacks feel at home in a predominantly white church. After being named the first black bishop of the Episcopalian Diocese of Washington, D.C., in 1967, he committed himself to issues that were important to the capital's inner city residents, including homelessness and crime. Not one to speak only from the pulpit, Walker hosted a local television program, *Overview*, in which he and his guests discussed such topics as joblessness, inflation, and crime.

From 1969 to 1976, Walker chaired the board of trustees of the Black Student Fund, an organization providing funding and support services to Washington's schoolchildren and their families. In recognition of Walker's "exemplary leadership, his moral commitment to an integrated society, and his unselfish devotion to serve all people in the Washington Metropolitan community," the Black Student Fund established the Bishop John T. Walker Awards in 1990.

Walker also served for 15 years as chair of the board of Africare, the oldest and largest African American nonprofit organization devoted to aid for Africa. The organization raises funds for food relief, agricultural development, education, and health projects, including HIV/AIDS initiatives. The organization established the Bishop John T. Walker Memorial Dinner in his honor in 1990. By 2002 the dinner had become the country's largest annual benefit for Africa. Africare also created the annual Bishop John T. Walker Distinguished Humanitarian Service Award in 1992.

Became Dean of National Cathedral

In 1978 Walker was named dean of the National Cathedral of St. Peter and St. Paul in Washington. This appointment marked the first time in more than 50 years that the Episcopal bishop of Washington also held the office of dean. Walker used the position to connect the cathedral's work more closely with the needs of city residents. He also promoted the work of lay ministers in the church, whose role, he claimed, was central to the work of caring for the destitute and the abandoned. "Priest and bishops are the teachers," he remarked in comments quoted in the *New York Times*. But it is "through the ordinary person who sits in the pew that the church's mission is done."

In 1985 Walker was one of four candidates for the position of presiding bishop of the Episcopal Church. Though he was ahead in early voting, another candidate, Bishop Edmond Lee Browning, was elected to this position.

Walker remained an influential figure in Washington until his death in 1989 at age 64. He was survived by his wife, Maria Rosa, whom he had met while teaching at a summer program in Costa Rica, and their three children. Many dignitaries attended his funeral, including President George Bush, South African Archbishop Desmond Tutu, civil rights leader Jesse Jackson, and Washington mayor Marion Barry.

In the House of Representatives, Hon. Ronald V. Dellums eulogized Walker as "truly a man for all seasons" who "daily lived out the gospel mandate that, here on Earth, God's work must truly be our own." In the Senate, Walker was eulogized by Senator John Danforth, who hailed him as a "man of principle, a man of determination, a man of gentleness, and a man of justice." Noting that Walker "was determined to show that racism has no place in the church or in society," Danforth concluded that "We must honor the life of this remarkable man by taking up his banner [to] become ambassadors of reconciliation."

Sources

Books

Hein, David, and Shattuck, Gardiner H., Jr., *The Episcopalians*, Praeger, 2004.

Periodicals

Boston Globe, September 11, 1985, p. 1; October 6, 1989, p. 69.

Congressional Record, October 4, 1989; October 5, 1989.

New York Times, January 16, 1978, p. A16.

Washington Post, October 2, 1989, p. A14.

On-line

"Bishop John T. Walker Awards," *Black Student Fund,* www.blackstudentfund.org/programs/bishop walkerawards.htm (January 3, 2005).

—E. M. Shostak

Rebecca Walker

1969—

Writer

Rebecca Walker, daughter of novelist Alice Walker, has forged her own successful career and identity as a writer, activist, and leading American advocate for women's issues. Author of the best-selling *Black, White, and Jewish: Autobiography of a Shifting Self,* Walker has written extensively on race, gender politics, and the changing face of contemporary American feminism.

Born in 1969 in Jackson, Mississippi, Walker came into the world as a symbol of the civil-rights era and harbinger of a new age. Her Georgia-born

Walker, Rebecca, photograph. AP/Wide World Photos. reproduced by permission.

mother, a published poet by then, had become active in the civil rights movement and met a white attorney, Mel Leventhal, while working on a voter-registration drive in Mississippi. When they married, they became Mississippi's first legally married biracial couple. By 1974, they had settled with their daughter in the New York City area, but divorced when Rebecca was eight. Hoping to share child-rearing duties equally, her parents decided that Walker would spent two-year intervals with each of them. Thus she attended schools in Westchester County, an affluent suburban area of New York City, as well as in the more free-spirited community of San Francisco, to which her mother had moved.

Walker attended Yale University, where she won a prize for academic excellence. By the time she graduated in 1992, Walker was already a contributing editor to *Ms.* magazine. Keenly interested in women's issues, she realized that while the generation of feminists to which her mother belonged had worked to achieve many important gains for young women, a new direction was necessary to set the tone for the 1990s and beyond. Thus Walker co-founded a national, non-profit organization called Third Wave Direct Action Corporation, which worked to promote new leadership ideas and activist strategies for women. Their massive voter registration drive, which targeted women in urban areas in time for the 1992 presidential elections, earned Walker several kudos, including the Feminist of the Year award from the Fund for the Feminist Majority.

Walker's first book was *To Be Real: Telling the Truth and Changing the Face of Feminism,* a 1995 tome for which she served as editor and author of the introduction. Contributors included Naomi Wolf, bell hooks, and Veronica Webb. The book-tour events shaped the form of her next project, as she told writer

At a Glance . . .

Born Rebecca Leventhal Walker on November 11, 1969, in Jackson, MS; daughter of Alice Walker (a writer) and Mel Leventhal (an attorney); partner of Me'shell N'degeocello (a singer), beginning 1996; children: one son. *Education:* Yale University, BA (cum laude), 1992.

Career: *Ms.* magazine, New York, NY, contributing editor, 1989–; Third Wave Direct Action Corporation, New York, NY, co-founder, 1992; Kokobar, Brooklyn, NY, co-owner, 1996-97. *Essence, Mademoiselle, Black Scholar, Ms., New York Daily News, Spin, Harper's,* and *Sassy,* contributor, 1980s–.

Awards: Fund for the Feminist Majority, Feminist of the Year award, 1992; Paz y Justicia award, Vanguard Foundation.

Addresses: *Home*—Berkeley, CA. *Office*—Riverhead Books, Author Mail, 375 Hudson St., New York, NY 10014.

Erin Raber of *Curve* magazine. "I would meet these young mixed-blood people, and I'd always look at them and feel like we knew each other," she said of those who came to the readings. "We recognized something similar, but yet there was no story underneath, no way to really access it."

Six years later, Walker's result of that exploration, *Black, White, and Jewish: Autobiography of a Shifting Self,* was published by Riverhead Books. In it, she recounts the lingering effects of her parents' split, which came during the mid-1970s when race relations had changed dramatically over the preceding decade. "With the rise of Black Power, my parents' interracial defiance, so in tune with the radicalism of Dr. King and civil rights, is suddenly suspect," she writes. "Black-on-black love is the new recipe for revolution…. The only problem, of course, is me. My little copper-colored body that held so much promise and broke so many rules…. I am a remnant, a throwaway, a painful reminder of a happier and more optimistic but ultimately unsustainable time."

Walker delved extensively into her childhood and adolescent experiences as a mixed-race American in her memoir. The necessity of changing residences every two years, between her father's and mother's homes, seemed to add an element of additional instability for

her in forming an identity with which she felt comfortable. Added to that was the fact that her parents lived in vastly different cultural and social milieus. "I had that sense," she explained to *Kansas City Star* reporter John Mark Eberhart, "of no matter where I was, no matter which community, there was a part of me that always liked something that community didn't approve of…. When I was listening to Prince with my friends, I couldn't say, 'Oh, did you hear that Led Zeppelin song?'" Some barbs came from within her own family, she also noted. She had an uncle on her mother's side whom she adored, but who sometimes teased her about mannerisms he termed "cracker," a pejorative term for a white Southerner. "A part of me feels pushed away when they say this," she wrote in her book, "like I have something inside of me I know they hate."

Black, White, and Jewish touched upon other issues, including Walker's Jewish heritage and her bisexuality. Reviewers of it praised her candor. "Walker has written, in blunt, stunning and intelligent language, a vital story about what it meant to come of age in two worlds that existed, largely, in diametric opposition," declared novelist Asha Bandele in a *Black Issues Book Review* critique.

After a long post-collegiate stint in New York City, where she owned a Brooklyn cyber café, Walker eventually settled in Berkeley, California, with her partner, recording artist Me'shell N'degeocello. The two have a son, and her own experiences as a parent partly inspired her next work, the anthology *What Makes a Man: 22 Writers Imagine the Future,* published in 2004. "For the last 50 years, women have been intensely re-envisioning femininity and what it means to be a woman," she explained to Deborah Solomon in a *New York Times Magazine* article. "I think that same scrutiny should be applied to men….. The feminist movement came into being because women were fundamentally in pain and unable to develop to their full potential. And men are similarly hampered by this masculine ideal, in which they are expected to repress their emotions."

Walker admitted to Solomon that she tried to write a novel a few years back, but found it difficult to find her voice in such a medium. In most interviews, she avoids discussion of the relationship of her career to that of her mother, who won the 1983 Pulitzer Prize for *The Color Purple,* but it seems evident that she has inherited not just her mother's literary gifts but the sense of confidence so crucial to the women's movement and all its achievements. "I'm very secretive," Walker told Raber in the *Curve* interview. "I'm not like, 'Here, come read my stuff, tell me what you think.' I'm more like, I'm doing this, when I know it's totally done, then I can share it to people. I mean, she read it before I published it, but I didn't give it to her like, 'Tell me what you think.' I gave it to her like, 'Here's my book.'"

Selected writings

Books

(Editor and author of introduction) *To Be Real: Telling the Truth and Changing the Face of Feminism,* Anchor, 1995.
Black, White, and Jewish: Autobiography of a Shifting Self, Riverhead Books, 2001.
What Makes a Man: 22 Writers Imagine the Future, Riverhead Books, 2004.

Sources

Books

Feminist Writers, St. James Press, 1996.

Periodicals

Advocate, February 27, 2001, p. 65.
American Prospect, September 10, 2001, p. 42.
Black Issues Book Review, January 2001, p. 49.
Curve, June 2001, p. 43.
Essence, May 1995, p. 173; January 1996, p. 123; June 2002, p. 111.
Kansas City Star, January 22, 2002.
Lambda Book Report, May 2002, p. 30.
Library Journal, March 15, 2004, p. 96.
New York Times Magazine, June 13, 2004, p. 19.
Publishers Weekly, November 6, 2000, p. 78.

On-line

Contemporary Authors Online, www.galenet.com/servlet/BioRC (January 21, 2005).

—Carol Brennan

James Melvin Washington

1948-1997

Historian, educator, minister

The church is recognized as an institution of paramount importance in African-American life, and its character and development have been traced in detail by historians and popular writers. The lives of individual African-American religious believers, however, received less attention until the Rev. Dr. James Melvin Washington published *Conversations with God: Two Centuries of Prayers by African Americans* in 1994. That book became a bestseller and, according to the Rev. James A. Forbes Jr. of the Riverside (New York) Church, speaking to the *New York Times,* was "a source of inspiration to many" that "reflected the dignity and power of the African-American religious heritage." *Conversations with God* was the last of several influential books by Washington, who was a professor at New York's Union Theological Seminary.

Born on April 24, 1948, Washington was a native of Knoxville, Tennessee. His family was poor, and his mother, unable to make a rent payment, once dreamed of a lottery number, played it, and won, crediting the narrow escape to divine intervention. Washington's path to the ministry began with the religious faith of his mother and her disabled friend, Helen Grady, who would sometimes turn to Washington (as he told Knight-Ridder Newspapers) and say, "Honey, let's talk to the Lord." The two women, Washington said, "taught me that it is a privilege to call on God. It is not simply for the privileged. No, it is the most radical form of democracy conceivable."

After having preached to congregations for several years as a teenager, Washington was ordained as a

Baptist minister in Nashville at the age of 19. He grew up when the South was still segregated, and he remembers riding in the back of Knoxville city buses and seeing Western films at a theater with blacks-only entrances. By the time he began his preaching career, however, Southern universities were beginning to open up slowly to African-American students, and Washington enrolled at the University of Tennessee. After earning a bachelor's degree in 1970, he moved on to the prestigious Harvard Divinity School, finishing a master's in theology in 1972.

With the help of fellowships from the Rockefeller Foundation and other funders, Washington completed two advanced degrees at the Yale Divinity School, receiving his Ph.D. in 1979. He began his teaching career at Yale in 1974, and in 1976 he was hired as an associate professor at the Union Theological Seminary. He spent the rest of his life there, rising to the rank of Professor of Modern and American Church History in 1987. Washington was also much in demand as a visiting professor, teaching along the way at Columbia University and Haverford College in 1984, Oberlin College in 1985 and 1986, and Princeton University in 1982, 1989, and 1990.

Washington's career was notable for his involvement in public spheres in addition to these academic posts. He remained active in his ministry as a board member of the American Baptist Church denomination and, from 1985 to 1987, of the National Council of Churches, where he served on the executive committee of the Faith and Order Commission. Beginning in 1989,

At a Glance . . .

Born on April 24, 1948, in Knoxville, TN; died May 3, 1997, of hypertensive stroke, in New York, NY; son of James William (a laborer) and Annie Beatrice (a homemaker; maiden name Moore) Washington; married Patricia Anne Alexander (an executive assistant), December 19, 1970; one daughter, Ayanna Nicole. *Education:* University of Tennessee, BA, 1970; Harvard University, MTS, 1972; Yale University, MPhil, 1975, PhD, 1979. *Religion:* Baptist.

Career: Union Theological Seminary, New York, assistant professor, 1976-83, associate professor, 1983-86, professor of modern and American church history, 1986-97; visiting lectureships at Princeton and Columbia universities, Haverford and Oberlin colleges; associate editor, *American National Biography,* 1989.

Selected memberships: National Council of Churches; American Historical Association; American Society of Church History; American Baptist Historical Society; American Academy of Religion.

Selected awards: Rockefeller Fund for Theological Education doctoral fellowship, 1972-74; National Endowment for the Humanities grant, 1981; Christopher Award, 1987, for *A Testament of Hope;* Black Caucus of the American Library Association honor award, 1995, for *Conversations with God.*

Washington was an associate editor of the American National Biography encyclopedia series.

His publications, too, addressed both academic and public audiences. His first book, based on his Yale doctoral dissertation, was *Frustrated Fellowship: The Black Baptist Quest for Social Power,* published in 1986. That book examined the development of the African-American Baptist church in the years after the civil war, focusing on the trend toward separatism as blacks' dreams of social equality were violently dashed. As he looked back on the years around 1900, Washington told Knight-Ridder Newspapers, he thought that despite his belief in the power of prayer, "there was too much patience.... Between 1889 and 1920 there were 3,900 black people lynched and burned in this country. That's almost one a week. That's terrorism."

That book, primarily intended for academic audiences, was reissued after Washington's death with a new

afterword by scholar Cornel West. Washington also edited a collection of articles, *Afro-American Protestant Spirituality,* published in 1986. That same year Washington edited *A Testament of Hope: The Essential Writings of Martin Luther King, Jr.,* a popular one-volume compendium of the great civil rights leader's words. The book won the Christopher Award in 1987 and was later issued as *I Have a Dream: Writings and Speeches That Changed the World.*

In the early 1990s, Washington set to work on *Conversations with God* without any idea that it would become a publishing blockbuster. In fact, he had mixed feelings about entering an arena that he saw as dominated by stereotypes. "As a historian of African American religion," he wrote in the book's introduction, "I was quite aware of the cynicism that has often made the spiritual life of my people part of a cultural menagerie. This indecency callously subjects genuine spiritual struggles to ridicule, dismissing them as superstitions and escapist, or reducing them to various doctrinaire theories of group frustration."

The book was published in 1994 by HarperCollins, however, and rose onto bestseller lists. It reproduced prayers offered by 190 African Americans, from all walks of life and throughout America's violent history. Some were famous preachers; some key figures in the antislavery and civil rights struggle such as Frederick Douglass; some were literary figures who included the prayers of characters in their books; and some were ordinary people whose prayers had moved observers to write them down. "Here are verse and prose, folk English and high oratory, and a growing awakening that if God is good, slavery must be wrong and must fall," noted the *Christian Science Monitor* in one of many positive reviews the book received.

In his book, Washington quoted a poem by Paul Lawrence Dunbar: "When storms arise // And dark'ning skies // About me threat'ning lower, // To thee, O Lord, I raise mine eyes, // To Thee my tortured spirit flies // For solace in that hour." But Washington deplored trends in contemporary African-American life that, he believed, sapped the strength prayer had historically given the community through times of trouble. One, he told the *Seattle Times,* was "a kind of pseudo-intellectual approach to Scripture" that could not succeed in addressing "questions relating to the tragedy of life, which cannot be answered through a rational means...." More disturbing still were people "walking around and spreading death" because of the prevalence of violence and drug abuse.

Washington reached a new level of prominence after *Conversations with God* was published. But as he turned his attention to new projects, he was felled by a stroke on May 3, 1997. He had suffered from high blood pressure. Washington was survived by his wife, the former Patricia Anne Alexander, by five of his six siblings, by one daughter, Ayanna Nicole Washington, and by his mother Annie, to whom *Conversations with God* was dedicated.

Selected writings

(Editor) *A Testament of Hope: The Essential Writings of Martin Luther King, Jr.,* 1986 (reissued as *I Have a Dream: Writings and Speeches That Changed the World,* Harper, 1992).

Frustrated Fellowship: The Black Baptist Quest for Social Power, Mercer University Press, 1986.

(Editor) *Afro-American Protestant Spirituality,* Paulist Press, 1986.

Conversations with God: Two Centuries of Prayers by African Americans, Harper, 1994.

Sources

Periodicals

Christian Science Monitor, February 21, 1996, p. 14.
Knight Ridder/Tribune News Service, January 25, 1995.
New York Times, May 8, 1997, pp. D26, D46.
Seattle Times, January 7, 1995, p. A12.
Washington Post, December 17, 1994, p. D7.

On-line

"James Melvin Washington," *Biography Resource Center,* www.galenet.com/servlet/BioRC (February 7, 2005).

—James M. Manheim

Kenny Washington

1918-1971

Football player

While the pathbreaking accomplishments of his college teammate Jackie Robinson are known even to casual sports fans, Kenny Washington is not a familiar name even though he was the first African American to play in the modern-day National Football League (NFL). The difference in recognition may be due to the fact that baseball was the undisputed king of sports in the late 1940s, while professional football was just beginning its climb to popularity. But the historical injustice done to Washington was significant: he was one of the top college football players in the United States in the late 1930s, but by the time he broke into the pros he was injury-ridden and past his prime years as a player.

Kenneth S. Washington was born in Los Angeles on August 31, 1918. He inherited his athletic prowess from his father, Edgar "Blue" Washington. The elder Washington played with the Kansas City Monarchs and Chicago American Giants of baseball's Negro Leagues, and also worked as an actor; his small parts included one in *Gone with the Wind*. These activities kept him away from home much of the time, and Washington was raised by his father's brother, Rocky, whom Washington considered his real father. Rocky Washington was the highest-ranking black officer in the Los Angeles Police Department.

Completed Bomb as High Schooler

Playing football at Lincoln High School in Los Angeles, Washington demonstrated his abilities early on by throwing a 60-yard touchdown pass in 1935. He graduated in 1936 and was admitted to the University of California at Los Angeles (UCLA). At the time, black football players outside the orbit of historically black colleges numbered only in the dozens, but Washington won a place on the squad. Over three years at UCLA he consistently improved. Washington was a left halfback, a position that in the era of the single-wing offense cast the player in the role of both runner and passer.

In 1939, with Jackie Robinson (a transfer from Pasadena City College) as his new receiver, Washington raised his career passing total to 1,300 yards and rushed in that single season for 1,915 yards, both long-time UCLA records. He led college football in total offense, and he completed one pass that traveled 72 yards in the air. His career total offense of 3,206 yards and his six pass interceptions in 1939 were also UCLA records.

Another impressive feat, of which Washington himself was especially proud, was that he played all but 20 minutes of the 1939 season; he took the field on defense as well as offense, as a safety. "Records are made to be broken," Washington was quoted as saying by *USA Today,* "but when somebody breaks my endurance record, let me hear about it." On top of all these gridiron accomplishments Washington also played baseball, notching batting averages of .454 in 1937 and .350 in 1938. "Next to me, Jackie [Robinson] was the best competitor I ever saw," Washington was quoted as saying in the *Los Angeles Sentinel.*

At a Glance . . .

Born Kenneth S. Washington on August 31, 1918, in Los Angeles, CA; died June 24, 1971 in Los Angeles, of circulatory failure; son of Edgar "Blue" Washington, a baseball player and actor; raised by uncle Rocky Washington, a Los Angeles police officer; children: Kenny Jr. *Education:* University of California at Los Angeles, BA, 1940.

Career: Hollywood Bears, Pacific Coast League, professional football player, 1940-43; San Francisco Clippers, American Football League, professional football player, 1944; Los Angeles Rams, National Football League, professional football player, 1946-48; worked as liquor public relations executive and baseball scout later in life.

Awards: Douglas Fairbanks Trophy, given to top U.S. collegiate player, 1939; inducted into National Football Foundation Hall of Fame, 1956.

"But when he became a baseball star it kind of shook me. I outhit him by at least two hundred points at UCLA."

Snubbed in All-American Balloting

Soon, overt discrimination marred Washington's career. Although he was certainly one of the top college players in the United States in 1939, he was named only to the second team in the annual official All-American selection. A *Liberty* magazine poll then asked college players themselves to select an All-American team; out of 664 nominees, Washington was the only one to receive the votes of every player who had taken the field against him. He won the Douglas Fairbanks Trophy, awarded to America's top collegiate player. The six-foot-one-inch, 200-pound Washington was dubbed "the Kingfish."

In the early days of professional football, with small competing leagues scattered across the country, a few African Americans had played for various small teams. In 1933, however, National Football League owners imposed a ban on black players. In August of 1940, Washington played on a team of college all-stars in an annual exhibition game at Chicago's Soldier Field against the NFL champion, that year the Green Bay Packers. Although the Packers won the game, Washington scored a touchdown and played well, inspiring

speculation that an NFL owner might try to break the apartheid rule. Speculation intensified when Chicago Bears owner George Halas asked Washington to stay on for a week in Chicago, and NBC radio sports anchor Sam Balter supported his cause. But Halas did not succeed in persuading his fellow NFL owners to lift the ban.

So Washington headed for the Hollywood Bears of the Pacific Coast League, where he was so popular that tickets for the team's games billed them as "The Hollywood Bears with Kenny Washington." Washington's teammate, Woody Strode, told football historian Charles Kenyatta Rose. Washington was paid on a par with NFL players of the day, but part of his salary was diverted to his uncle Rocky to disguise the fact that he was taking home more than his fellow players. He also worked as a Los Angeles police officer on the side. Two serious knee operations slowed Washington down and kept him out of World War II. He played for the San Francisco Clippers of the American Football League in 1944.

Anti-Discrimination Ordinance Led to Signing

After the war, which led to gains for the idea of integration in many areas of American life, Cleveland Rams owner Dan Reeves announced plans to move his team to the rapidly growing city of Los Angeles. A city anti-discrimination ordinance, however, threatened to block the team from using the publicly owned Los Angeles Coliseum. Largely as a result, Washington was signed by the Rams on March 21, 1946. As he prepared to undergo a third knee operation, his uncle Rocky negotiated a no-cut clause for his contract. There was still resistance from other NFL owners—"all hell broke loose," Rams backfield coach Bob Snyder was quoted as saying in *USA Today*—but Strode was also signed to the Rams, and two other black players, Marion Motley and Bill Willis, joined the new Cleveland Browns. By the time baseball's Brooklyn Dodgers signed Jackie Robinson in 1947, pro football was on the road to integration.

With Washington's knees ailing, white NFL players made things worse with physical attacks. "When he first began to play, they'd tee off on him," Snyder was quoted as saying in the *Chicago Sun-Times.* "They'd drop knees on him." But Washington performed well over three seasons in the NFL, averaging over six yards per carry and leading the league with a 7.4 yard-per-carry average in 1947. He gained 859 yards for the Rams before retiring in 1948, including one thrilling 92-yard run that still holds the Rams record for longest run from scrimmage. In 1950, he still had enough raw athletic ability that he was given a tryout by baseball's New York Giants.

Later in life, Washington worked as a scout for the Los Angeles Dodgers and did public relations work for a Scotch whisky distillery. He also became a skillful golfer. He had one son, Kenny Jr., who played professional baseball. Inducted into the National Football Foundation Hall of Fame in 1956 but not, at this writing, into the Pro Football Hall of Fame, Washington suffered from circulatory problems in later years. Over a thousand of the many fans he retained in the Los Angeles area turned out for a celebration of his career at the Hollywood Palladium in 1970. On June 24, 1971, he died at UCLA Medical Center. "I'm sure he had a deep hurt over the fact he never had become a national figure in professional sports," Jackie Robinson wrote in a *Gridiron* magazine essay quoted in *USA Today*.

Sources

Books

Levy, Alan H., *Tackling Jim Crow: Racial Segregation in Professional Football,* McFarland, 2003.

Rose, Charles Kenyatta, *Outside the Lines: African Americans and the Integration of the National Football League,* New York University Press, 1999.

Periodicals

Chicago Sun-Times, June 24, 1996, p. 25.
Los Angeles Sentinel, September 22, 1999, p. B3.
Los Angeles Times, January 8, 1956, p. B7.
Sporting News, March 19, 2001, p. 7.
USA Today, September 20, 1995, p. C1.
Washington Post, June 26, 1971, p. B3.

—James M. Manheim

Carlos Watson

1970—

Political analyst, television commentator

A political analyst and commentator who joined CNN's political team in 2003, Carlos Watson has been described as a rising star at the network, representing a new generation of political journalists and interested as much in personalities as he is in policies and political goals. A graduate of Harvard University and Stanford Law School, Watson previously worked for several major law firms, acted as campaign manager for Florida Republican Daryl Jones, and wrote for the *Miami Herald* and the *Detroit Free Press*. Before moving to CNN Watson hosted CNBC's one-hour interview series "The Edge," where he interviewed high-profile guests such as Florida Governor Jeb Bush, brother of president George W. Bush. In October 2004 he hosted the first of an occasional series of one-off specials for CNN. Titled "Off Topic with Carlos Watson," the prime-time show allowed him to discuss unusual and wide-ranging subjects with celebrities and politicians. "Off Topic" suits Watson's knockabout style, which has earned him a reputation as a fresh voice in political journalism. Critics argue that Watson's departure from the solemn approach of old-style commentating reduces it to a form of entertainment, but he sees himself as setting new standards. His dramatic rise to the elite in the American media gives him the chance to do just that.

Watson was born in 1970 in Miami, Florida. His parents were Jamaican immigrants, and he attended a local kindergarten followed by a campus school at the University of Miami, West Lab Elementary. Watson had a difficult early schooling; by the age of six he had been thrown out of kindergarten for disruptive behavior, had seen a child psychologist to be assessed for a learning disability, and was attending his second elementary school. Watson attributes his bad start to boredom: he told *Essence* magazine that he had already learned a lot of what he was being taught from his older sister. He also cites the experience as one of his motivations for founding Achieva in 1996, a company providing materials to help high school students get into college. After high school Watson attended Harvard University, where he studied government and journalism, graduating cum laude in 1992. He then went on to study law at Stanford University Law School and graduated in 1995.

Was a Student Journalist

Watson's media career began while he was still in college, when he wrote for newspapers such as the *Miami Herald* and the *Detroit Free Press*. He also began to develop an interest in politics, working for Miami Mayor Xavier Suarez, Senator Bob Graham, and the Democratic National Committee Chair, Ron Brown. After graduating from Harvard he became chief of staff and campaign manager for Florida Republican Daryl Jones. Watson's interest in journalism continued after he moved to California to attend law school. There he served as editor of the Stanford Law Review as well as working as an intern for the White House Office of the Legal Counsel.

At a Glance . . .

Born in 1970 in Miami. *Education:* Harvard University, BA, 1992; Stanford University Law School, JD, 1995.

Career: McKinsey and Company, management consultant, 1995-97; Achieva College Prep Services, co-founder, 1996-2002; CNBC, political interviewer, 2002-03; CNN, political analyst and talk-show host, 2003–.

Memberships: California Bar; College Track, board member.

Awards: *People Weekly* "Hot Bachelor" 2004.

Addresses: *Office*—c/o CNN, One CNN Center, Atlanta, GA 30303.

After graduating from Stanford he joined the management consultancy firm McKinsey and Company, where he worked as an adviser in strategy and operations. In 1996, along with his younger sister Carolyn and his best friend Jeff Livingstone, he co-founded Achieva, a company that provides software, books, workshops, and other materials to help schools prepare students for college. Watson told *Essence* magazine that "I realized how critical a second (or even third) chance could be in a young person's life. The indelible memory of being counted out, then helped back in, inspired me to help others." Helping others was also good business: Watson left McKinsey in 1997 to work full-time as CEO of Achieva, developing it into a multi-million dollar company by the time he sold it in 2002. He continues to pursue his interest in education and assisting disadvantaged students through his work as a director of College Track, an organization that provides help for high school students as they work towards college.

Phoned by Producer

Not long after selling Achieva, Watson was trying to work out what his next move would be when he returned home to find a message on his answering machine from a TV producer asking if he had considered a career in television. Watson told *Mountain View Voice* that he thought the message was a joke and ignored it, but the producer called again. Within a few months Watson was hosting CNBC's interview series "The Edge." His brand of quick-fire interview and his ability to persuade celebrities to open up on a wide range of topics soon came to the attention of CNN. He was hired in 2003 to help with CNN's coverage in the build-up to the 2004 presidential election; by the time the election came around he was appearing on the network eight or nine times a week, more often at busy times.

By the autumn of 2004 Watson had become an important figure in CNN's news line-up. During the election he provided analysis and commentary across the network, including a regular column on the CNN Web site, called "The Inside Edge, with Carlos Watson," where he is able to discuss in depth his observations on the political scene. Like many commentators Watson observed that the 2004 election was one of the most important in U.S. history, not least because of its effect on the Democratic Party in the aftermath of a win for President Bush. As far back as March 2004 he noted, for example, that the Republicans were making a huge effort to register voters in areas where the GOP was likely to pick up votes; Bush's win has since been attributed in part to this aggressive registration drive in key states such as Ohio. One of Watson's strengths is his willingness to do extensive research before interviewing or talking on camera, and the depth of his knowledge is often greater than his easy style might suggest. Off-camera Watson has a reputation for being an exacting and at times difficult colleague.

Despite his relative youthfulness and inexperience, Watson proved himself an able anchor, commentator, and interviewer over the course of 2004 and in the autumn he was rewarded with his own show, "Off Topic with Carlos Watson," which first aired on October 15. The show's format involves celebrities, politicians, and business leaders talking "off topic" on subjects other than those for which they are best known. Within a matter of months "Off Topic," which airs only a few times each year, had become an important show for public figures wanting to raise their media profile. Early guests included Heidi Klum, and Barak Obama, while in January 2005 Watson talked to the biggest guest of the series up to that point, California Governor Arnold Schwarzenegger.

Multiple Careers

Watson's multi-faceted career includes law, journalism, media, education, and politics; he stands out from older commentators whose media image depends on their reputations as journalists of long standing. But Watson revels in being unconventional and seems relentlessly modern in his attitude to traditional ways of doing things. One example is his refusal to move to the east coast from his home in California, despite his career in the media which would traditionally have centered on New York City and Washington, D.C. In the past decade or so technological advances have made geography less important, but Watson's sense of belonging to a new media generation goes further than simply being able to do his job wherever he chooses. He told the *Mountain View Voice* in 2004: "I don't want to be IBM, I want to be Google."

Watson is not without his critics, who attack him for simplifying politics, for displaying bias, and for favoring celebrity over substance. But his achievement is to have begun a process of change in the American news media towards a more irreverent, direct approach. Despite his youthful style and "new media" image, Watson's fan base is surprisingly diverse. He says proudly that his most loyal fans are grandmothers, but his role as one of CNN's key analysts and interviewers suggests that the network sees his appeal as being much wider than that. Besides his high-profile television work Watson is a member of the California bar, sits on several boards, and regularly gives talks and presentations in schools, colleges, and for other organizations.

Sources

Periodicals

Black Enterprise, September 2001.
Contra Costa Times, October 1, 2004.
Essence, November 2004, p.148.
Mountain View Voice (California), September 3, 2004.
People Weekly, June 28, 2004, p. 126.

On-line

"Board of Directors," *College Track*, www.college-track.org/organization/board.html (January 21, 2005).
"Carlos Watson," *CNN*, http://cnnstudentnews.cnn.com/CNN/anchors_reporters/watson.carlos.html (February 8, 2005).
"Transcript: Carlos Watson," *Tavis Smiley Archive*, www.pbs.org/kcet/tavissmiley/archive/200411/20041118_transcript.html#1 (January 25, 2005).

—Chris Routledge

Edward T. Welburn

1950—

Automotive executive

Edward T. Welburn became chief designer of General Motors Corporation, the world's largest automaker, in 2003. The appointment made him the first African American to rise to what is considered one of the most prestigious jobs in the automotive industry. Welburn's mission for the dozens of GM models he oversees is to lead their styling and concept teams into an exciting and visually distinctive brand identity for the twenty-first century. "I feel very fortunate," he said in an *Automotive News* interview not long after taking the job. "I am coming in at a time when the corporation has a real understanding of the value of design and its importance to the future of the company."

Welburn, Edward T., photograph. AP/Wide World Photos. Reproduced by permission.

father had done of 1930s Dusenbergs and similar classics. Welburn grew intensely involved in the hobby as he grew older, and even wrote to General Motors when he was eleven asking about a future with the company as a car designer. The company replied with a helpful letter that recommended what he might study in school to prepare for such a career, and provided information about its internship program. This bid for a job, coming as it did in the early 1960s, seemed all the more remarkable given the fact that the profession was an elite one and minorities were nonexistent in such corners of the automotive world during the era.

Fascinated by Vintage Autos

Welburn was born in December of 1950 and grew up in the Philadelphia area. His father was a co-owner of a body shop with his brothers and instilled in a very young Welburn an appreciation for automotive design. The two would spend hours drawing cars of vintage design, with Welburn tracing over the sketches his

Welburn followed the suggestions of that response, and studied fine arts and sculpture at Howard University in Washington, D.C. He won a slot in the GM internship program while still in school, and worked tirelessly from his first day forward, churning out sketches and posting them for all to see. "It was the first time somebody black was putting sketches up on the board," he recalled in an interview with *Newsweek*'s Keith Naughton. "I quickly realized I was representing more people than just myself."

At a Glance . . .

Born Edward Thomas Welburn, Jr., in December 14, 1950, in Philadelphia, PA; son of Edward Sr. (an auto-body repair shop owner) and Evelyn Welburn. *Education:* Howard University, BA, fine arts, 1972.

Career: General Motors Corporation, design studio intern, early 1970s; General Motors Corporation, Buick division employee, 1972; GM Oldsmobile division employee, 1975; GM, various management positions 1980s-90s; GM Corporate Brand Character Center, director, 1998; GM executive director of body-on-frame architecture, 2002-03; GM chief designer, 2003.

Addresses: *Office*—General Motors Corporation, 300 Renaissance Center, Detroit, MI 48265-3000.

Welburn was hired full-time after graduation, and spent his three years with the company in the design studio of GM's Buick division. As a newcomer, fresh out of college, he joined the ranks at the right time, for a major shift was taking place in the design studios of the Big Three domestic automakers, with veterans suddenly forced to come up with smaller vehicles as the gas-guzzling automotive-behemoth era ended. In 1975, Welburn moved over to the Oldsmobile studio, and would spent the next two decades of his GM career there. He had a hand in the design of a top-seller during the early 1980s, the Cutlass Supreme, but also worked on a car that was a one-shot project, not for the consumer market: the Oldsmobile Aerotech. Knowing that GM was eager to make a new high-performance race car to compete with a 1,000-horsepower Mercedes model, he sketched out what became the teardrop-shaped Aerotech one day on a napkin and gave it to his boss. His design chief looked at it and said, "'This is it,'" Welburn recalled in the *Newsweek* article, but Welburn told him, "I have other ideas." His stunned boss replied, "'What are you talking about? This is it.'"

Met A.J. Foyt

Welburn's Aerotech was built by a special GM team, and in August of 1987 was taken out to a track in Fort Stockton, Texas, with racing legend A. J. Foyt behind the wheel. It set a new world land-speed record for a closed course at 259 miles per hour that day. Foyt had long been one of Welburn's idol, he told *Automotive Industries* writer Gary Witzenburg. "Nothing made me happier than the day when...Foyt first drove that vehicle," he asserted, and recalled that the Indy 500 champion "teased me about my 'Detroit shoes.' After setting the record, he went to his transporter and came

back with a pair of Tony Lama ostrich skin boots. He said, 'Here, I don't want to see you ever wearing those Detroit shoes again.' I still have those boots, and I love them."

Welburn worked for GM's Saturn division for a time, and spent a year overseas at the company's Opel facilities in Russelsheim, Germany. By the mid-1990s, he had been elevated to chief designer at Oldsmobile. There, the Oldsmobile Antares concept car he oversaw, a hit on the auto-show circuit, morphed into a production vehicle that debuted in the 1998 model year, the Oldsmobile Intrigue. It was another top seller for GM and sealed Welburn's reputation as a designer with a sharp eye for consumer preferences. That same year, he was made director of GM's Corporate Brand Character Center (BCC), a relatively new design-management concept where all of the stylistic elements for the fleet of cars among GM's various divisions were closely monitored so that a strong brand identity could be forged. Detractors named the BCC the "brand police" and deemed Welburn the "brand cop," but he defended the strategy in an *Automotive Industries* profile by Lindsay Brooke. "The various chief designers are all building their brands, and they want to keep them separate," Welburn explained. "To have a location where they can congregate and see where the opportunities—and potential overlaps between brands—exist is important to all of us."

Welburn was said to enjoy good rapport with GM chief executive officer Rick Wagoner as well as the company's design chief, Wayne Cherry. After 2001, Welburn oversaw the trio of studios that brought out trucks and sport-utility vehicles like the Cadillac Escalade, Hummer H2, a retro hot-rod Chevy pick-up called SSR, and the top-selling Chevrolet Avalanche. Nearly all of the models in which he had a hand at the design stage were excellent sellers for the company, but GM did take a hit for the overly plastic-cladded Pontiac Aztek. "It's controversial," he conceded, in the interview with Brooke in *Automotive Industries,* "and yes, it's absolutely right for the Pontiac brand. I say that with total confidence. We saw an opportunity and we went after it. Aztek's a vehicle that will take a bit of time with some people. Others may never embrace it. That's OK. We have other products for them."

Welburn's job also entailed the supervision of the concept cars, which debut at events like Detroit's North American International Auto Show and serve as a harbinger of future design trends industry-wide. But his track record on the sport-utility vehicles and trucks that are the profit center for GM was unparalleled, as Phil Patton asserted in the *New York Times;* eschewing "brand cues like fake exhaust ports on the sides of Buicks and flaring nostril grilles on Pontiacs, Mr. Welburn was taking a more thoughtful view of Chevrolet's tradition and character. The resulting concepts helped shape the Cheyenne pickup, a powerful but restrained design study displayed at auto shows this year and a likely precursor of Chevy's next-generation pickups."

Rose to Chief Design Post

On September 26, 2003, GM announced that Welburn would succeed Cherry as GM's chief designer, making him only the sixth person to hold the job in company history, but also the first African American among any of the Big Three domestic automakers to be promoted to such an influential post. His duties included overseeing the work of some 600 designers for GM, spread out across eleven studios. There were, however, an entirely new set of challenges for anyone who came to the job, and Welburn's first responsibility was to work to strengthen brand identities among the GM lineup. "GM design is at a crossroads," noted Naughton in the *Newsweek* profile. "Over the three decades that Welburn has toiled in GM's studios, a burgeoning bureaucracy has sapped stylists of the almighty power they had back in the days of tailfins and gleaming chrome. Engineers and focus groups have dictated design. The result: blandmobiles that GM marketed on price rather than style."

Welburn is a low-key executive who seems to lack the press-courting ego of many of the predecessors in the GM chief-designer job. Those he succeeded were legendary figures in the automotive industry, such as Harley Earl and Bill Mitchell, under whom Welburn worked when he first started at GM. As Patton wrote in the *New York Times*, Welburn had "a daunting job, as implied by Buick television commercials that feature a Harley Earl character whose impersonation of the original is a somewhat loose reading of reality. The advertisements suggest how deeply G.M. is both haunted by the achievements of its past and intimidated by the challenge of matching them."

Inside the design studios, he remains "Ed," not "Mr. Welburn," among designers working on the company's next highly anticipated new model, the Buick Velite convertible. Welburn's own car is a classic, a hot rod 1969 Chevrolet Camaro. Though he has participated in a media campaign aimed at African American buyers, Welburn downplays his role as the first black to steer GM's design process into the next few decades. "It's interesting because it's something I don't celebrate," he reflected in an interview with *Ward's Auto World* writer Drew Winter, "because to celebrate it means there are so many years it didn't occur. . . . But I know it is very important. It can't be ignored. I know it isn't ignored, and I know there are a lot of people in the African-American community that really, really consider this something very significant, so I don't take it lightly. If it has an effect on young people, then I think that's great."

Sources

Periodicals

Automotive Industries, December 2000, p. 31; December 2003, p. 14..
Automotive News, January 5, 2004, p. 28.
Newsweek, May 31, 2004, p. 54.
New York Times, October 13, 2003, p. D13.
Ward's Auto World, February 1, 2004.

—Carol Brennan

Kelvin R. Westbrook

1955—

Corporate executive

President, CEO, and co-founder of Millennium Digital Media LLC, Kelvin R. Westbrook is one of the most sought-after executives and among the most influential black business leaders of the early twenty-first century. He sits on the boards of numerous high-profile companies, including the National Cable Satellite Corporation, better known as C-SPAN. In his early career Westbrook was a partner in the national law firm, Paul, Hastings, Janofsky, and Walker, and he remains a member of the American Bar Association. Founded in 1997, Millennium Digital Media is one of the 30 largest cable providers in the United States in 2005, providing broadband services to over 150,000 customers in Maryland, Michigan, Missouri, Washington, and Oregon. A private company, in 2002 it posted sales of about $125 million.

Born in 1955, Westbrook was educated at the University of Washington, where he was awarded a degree in business administration in 1977, and at Harvard Law School, where he received his Juris Doctorate in 1982. He went on to work at the New York City-based national law firm of Paul, Hastings, Janofsky, and Walker, where he became a partner specializing in corporate mergers, acquisitions, and finance. He was co-chair of the firm's Telecommunications Practice Group, as well as being vice-chair of its recruiting committee and a member of its policy committee. He is married to Valerie Bell, a former senior counsel for the New York State Urban Development Corporation. They moved with their three children to St. Louis in 1997 when Millennium Digital Media was setting up its headquarters there. Since then Bell, a public policy

expert, has become a full-time civic volunteer, applying her legal skills to community projects such as schools and healthcare facilities.

In 1993 Westbrook founded LEB Communications, Inc., his first commercial venture into the business of telecommunications. LEB negotiated deals with Charter Communications to manage cable television systems around the country. It was his experience with LEB and Charter that prompted Westbrook to branch out into the wider area of broadband communications. In 1997, along with John Brooks, Jeffrey Sanders, and Charles Payer, Jr., he founded Millennium Digital Media, a cable company providing broadband services such as high-speed internet access, cable television, and telephony. They began buying up cable companies around the country, starting with Baltimore-based North Arundel Cable, for a purchase price of around $108 million. Within seven years the company was one of the top 30 cable providers in the United States, with over 150,000 customers in four states. Operating out of three regional centers in Maryland, Michigan, and Washington, privately-owned Millennium Digital Media is headquartered in St. Louis.

The rapid growth of Millennium Digital Media has made Westbrook into a high-profile figure in American business. He has been an outspoken critic of the control wielded by program makers over cable operators and was one of few supporters prepared to speak out for Time Warner Cable in their contract dispute with ABC-TV in 2000. He has accepted offers of directorships from companies as diverse as Angelica

At a Glance . . .

Born in 1955; married Valerie Bell; three children. *Education:* University of Washington, BA, Business Administration, 1977; Harvard Law School, JD, 1982. *Religion:* Christian.

Career: Paul, Hastings, Janofsky, and Walker, New York City, partner; LEB Communications, Inc., founder, president, and chairman, 1993-97; Millennium Digital Media, Clayton, MO, founder and CEO, 1997–.

Selected memberships: American Bar Association; Business Program Advisory Council of Harris Stowe State College; Federal Communications Commission Advisory Committee for the Diversity of Communications in the Digital Age, 2004–; board member: Millennium Digital Media; Archer Daniels Midland Company; Angelica Corporation; National Cable and Telecommunications Association; National Cable Satellite Corporation (C-SPAN); BJC HealthCare; Christian Hospital Northeast-Northwest; St. Louis Internship Program; and Chesterfield Day School.

Addresses: *Office*—Millennium Digital Media, 120 S. Central Ave., Suite 150, Clayton, MO 63105.

Corporation, which offers textile rental and laundry services to the healthcare industry, and the Archer Daniels Midland Company, a global cereals processor and exporter. With his diverse interests and obvious talent for understanding businesses of different kinds, Westbrook is among the most successful black business leaders of his generation. His company Millennium

Digital Media takes in over $125 million in sales each year and is expanding into new high-tech services, such as Voice over Internet Protocol (VoIP), through deals with other companies. Un 2005 Millennium Digital Media looked set to become a major Web portal service provider as well as a cable company.

Each year since 2001 Westbrook has been featured by *Black Enterprise* magazine as the CEO of one the nation's 100 largest businesses owned by African Americans. Although he has been hugely successful in business, he has also devoted energy to community projects and charity work in his home town of St. Louis. Along with his wife Valerie Bell, Westbrook has campaigned for schemes to help improve wealth-creation opportunities for African Americans, as well as sitting on the boards of several schools and hospital groups in the St. Louis area. He is also a community volunteer on several other projects.

Sources

Periodicals

Baltimore Business Journal, May 8, 1998.
Black Enterprise Magazine, June 2001, June 2002, June 2003, June 2004.
Forbes, June 12, 2000.
St Louis Business Journal, June 12, 2000 v20 i40 p2; January 31, 2003.

On-line

"Top of the List," *St Louis Business Journal*, www. bizjournals.com/stlouis/stories/2003/02/03/tid bits.html (January 5, 2005).
"The Next New Thing," *NCTA The National Show 2004*, http://cable2004.com/ncta2004/attendee/ speakers.asp?Task=ShowDetails&SpeakerID=125 (January 5, 2005).

—Chris Routledge

Reggie White

1961-2004

Football player, minister, philanthropist

For a decade and a half, Reggie White dominated the National Football League as one of its most ferocious defensive players. White habitually struck terror into opposing offenses with his great strength, but he also possessed speed, stamina, and the ability to size up situations for maximum impact. Former Philadelphia Eagles head coach Buddy Ryan once called White the "perfect defensive lineman…probably the most gifted defensive athlete I've ever been around." After eight seasons with the Eagles, in 1993 White signed a four-year, $17-million contract with the Green Bay Packers; it was an unprecedented amount for a defensive player. Upon his retirement from the NFL in 2001, White was credited with a record 198 career sacks; he had been named to the Pro Bowl an impressive 13 times in succession (although he failed to play in 1994 due to injury). In 1999, the Green Bay Packers retired White's jersey number (92) after his retirement from that team.

Loved His Tennessee Home

Reginald Howard White was born and raised in Tennessee. He went to college there—at the University of Tennessee—and he called that state home his entire life. As a child he lived in Chattanooga, where he was raised by his mother and his grandparents. The family was deeply religious. They attended the local Baptist church regularly, and as a youngster White was inspired by the ministers and teachers he met there. He did not undergo a single, charismatic experience of faith, but rather found his ties to Christianity growing stronger over the entire period of his youth. His mother, Thelma Collier, told *Sports Illustrated* that when he was 12 years old he announced that he wanted to be two things: a football player and a minister.

Football was a welcome outlet for a young Christian who was teased and goaded by bullies. "When I was a child, I was always bigger than the other kids," White told *Sports Illustrated*. "Kids used to call me Bigfoot or Land of the Giant. They'd tease me and run away. Around seventh grade, I found something I was good at. I could play football, and I could use my size and achieve success by playing within the rules. I remember telling my mother that someday I would be a professional football player and I'd take care of her for the rest of her life."

White's strength and size indeed seemed to be God-given. He never lifted weights or conditioned himself rigorously, but he was always in shape. At Howard High School in Chattanooga, he played both football and basketball, earning All-America honors in football and all-state honors in basketball. Numerous colleges recruited him, but he chose to stay near home and enrolled at the University of Tennessee, whose team, the Volunteers, were glad to have him. He was a talented and determined athlete who spent his Sundays preaching sermons in churches all over the state. As a senior in 1983, he was a consensus All-American and one of four finalists for the Lombardi Award given annually to the outstanding college lineman. (He did not win.) During his years with the Volunteers, White

At a Glance . . .

Born Reginald Howard White on December 19, 1961, in Chattanooga, TN; died December 26, 2005, near Knoxville, TN; son of Charles White and Thelma Dodds Collier; married Sara Copeland, January 5, 1985; children: Jeremy, Jecolia. *Education*: University of Tennessee, BA, 1983. *Religion*: Baptist.

Career: Memphis Showboats (USFL), professional football player, 1984-85; Philadelphia Eagles (NFL), professional football player, 1985-93; Green Bay Packers (NFL), professional football player, 1993-98; Carolina Panthers (NFL), professional football player, 1999-2000. Alpha & Omega Ministry, founder (with wife, Sara) and president, 1988-2004; Hope Place, founder and president, 1991. Served as a spokesperson for Nike; active in fund-raising and blood drives for Children's Hospital of Chattanooga and Eagles Fly for Leukemia.

Memberships: Fellowship of Christian Athletes.

Awards: Named Southeast Conference Player of the Year, 1984; named NFC rookie of the year, 1986; named NFL defensive player of the year by Associated Press 1986 and 1998; named to 1980s All-Decade Team *Pro Football Weekly*, 1991; named defensive player of the year by *Pro Football Weekly*, 1991; named to NFL Pro Bowl, 1986-98; Pro Bowl MVP, 1987; White's Jersey Number (92) retired by the Green Bay Packer's, 1999; named to NFL's All-time Team, 2000.

earned the nickname "minister of defense." The named followed him into his professional career, which began in 1984.

For a while it appeared that Reggie White might never leave Tennessee. After graduating from college he signed a five-year, $4 million contract with the Memphis Showboats, one of the teams in the fledgling United States Football League (USFL). The USFL began as an alternative league for cities starved for professional football action. From the outset it was dwarfed by the better-known, better-staffed National Football League, and soon the upstart teams foundered financially. White viewed this financial instability with concern. He also wanted to prove himself against the best players in the game. He began the 1985 season with the USFL but defected to the Philadelphia Eagles.

With his wife, Sara—whom he had met in church—he ventured north to join the NFL.

Jumped from USFL to NFL

White took a salary cut in Philadelphia. The Eagles signed him to a four-year, $1.85 million deal after buying out the remaining three years on his Memphis contract. At the time White was still an unproven entity, but his anonymity did not last long. He joined the Eagles after the 1985 season had begun, missing the first few games. When he finally did start, he made ten tackles and two-and-a-half sacks in his very first game. By season's end he had turned in 13 sacks in as many games, and he was named NFC defensive rookie of the year.

Curiously enough, White's singular gift for mayhem began and ended on the gridiron during his 15-year career with the NFL. The rest of his time was always been spent in pursuing humanitarian work inspired by his deep Christian faith. The citizens of Philadelphia soon discovered that they had won the services of more than just a star athlete. "I believe that I've been blessed with physical ability in order to gain a platform to preach the gospel," White told *Sports Illustrated*. "A lot of people look at athletes as role models, and to be successful as an athlete, I've got to do what I do, hard but fair.... I try to live a certain way, and maybe that'll have some kind of effect. I think God has allowed me to have an impact on a few people's lives." White spent hours and hours of his spare time preaching on street corners in Philadelphia's troubled inner-city neighborhoods. He gave money to dozens of Christian outreach organizations and spoke as a member of the Fellowship of Christian Athletes. And he led by example. In the rough-and-tumble world of professional football, none of his opponents or teammates could ever recall hearing him curse or seeing him fight.

White blossomed in 1986 with the arrival of Buddy Ryan as the Eagles' head coach. Ryan had made a name for himself as a defensive coordinator and had worked with some great lines, including the Chicago Bears and the Minnesota Vikings. Quickly Ryan assessed White's potential and built the defense around him. Opponents tried to double- and triple-team White, but still he achieved more than 11 quarterback sacks each season. In his first season under Ryan, he made 18 sacks in 16 games. He was also named Most Valuable Player at the annual Pro Bowl after sacking the opposing quarterback four times in that game. In 1987 he led the league with an NFC-record 21 sacks, and most certainly would have broken the all-time record had the season not been shortened by a players' strike.

Emerged as Team Leader

That players' strike—a particularly bitter one—saw

White emerge as a team leader. As one of the team-voted union representatives, White worked hard to keep his fellow Eagles united in the face of "replacement" teams and fan apathy. Didinger wrote in the *Philadelphia Daily News*: "One of the more memorable images of that 1987 season was White wearing a picket sign and blocking a bus loaded with replacement players as it attempted to pull into a South Jersey hotel…. [White] spoke loudly and passionately about the need for the veterans to stick together. Other teams broke ranks: the Eagles never did."

The hard feelings between White and the Eagles' front office probably began to develop during this strike season, intensifying as the years passed, but White's continued dominance on the field allayed any talk of trade or release. In 1988 he led the NFL in sacks for the second straight year. Between 1989 and 1991 he was joined on the defensive line by several equally ferocious teammates, including Clyde Simmons, Seth Joyner, and Jerome Brown. This potent defense—with White still as anchor—was widely considered the best in pro football by 1991.

Observers marveled at the way White roared into every play of every game without ever seeming tired or distracted. White told *Sports Illustrated*: "In high school and college you're taught to hit the ground on a double team. Here you're expected to take it on. I get double-teamed on every play, so I expect it. Sacks are great, and they get you elected to the Pro Bowl. But I've always felt that a great defensive lineman has to play the run and the pass equally well…. The so-called men of the game pride themselves on being complete players."

In 1989 White signed a four-year, $6.1 million contract that made him the highest-paid defensive player in the NFL at the time. The deal came at the tail end of considerable acrimony between White and the Eagles' ownership and management. Didinger described the relationship between White and the Eagles' brass, headed by owner Norman Braman: "They split on so many issues—the 1987 players' strike, the 1990 firing of head coach Buddy Ryan, the 1992 loss of free agent Keith Jackson—that in the end they had nothing to build on. There was no trust, no goodwill to serve as the foundation for constructive talks." Although he continued to play at the top of his game under new Eagles coach Rich Kotite, White became privately convinced that owner Braman was not pursuing a championship with any great vigor.

As the end of his 1989 contract approached, White grew more and more critical of Braman and his decisions. In the press White suggested that the Eagles' training facilities were inadequate. White spoke of the growing chasm between Braman and the Eagles players, using his own chilly relations with the owner as an example. Not surprisingly, White became one of the plaintiffs in a 1992 lawsuit against the NFL ownership to enlarge the powers of free agency.

Joined the Packers

Unrestricted free agency descended upon the NFL officially on March 1, 1993. Reggie White quickly became the most visible—and sought-after—unrestricted free agent after the 1992-93 football season. His contract with the Eagles had expired, and although he claimed that he would not mind staying in Philadelphia, he was not tendered another offer there. As it happened, Green Bay was one of a half dozen teams that bid quite openly for White's services at that time. He flew to Atlanta, Cleveland, Detroit, Green Bay, New York City, and Washington, D.C., as an all-out war erupted to sign the powerful defensive end. Everywhere he went he was courted not only by team owners, management, and player personnel, but also by ordinary citizens who had heard about his community work and his Christian ethics. In the end, White signed with Wisconsin's Green Bay Packers. The Packers' offer was the most generous financially, with guaranteed earnings of $17 million over four years. Under the contract White became the most highly paid defender in the NFL and a pioneer in the heady new world of unrestricted free agent contracts.

Joining the Packers for the 1993 season, White left behind good will in Philadelphia, where he played for the Eagles through eight seasons. *Philadelphia Daily News* correspondent Ray Didinger called White "a man who made a giant impact…a symbol of hope, for the Eagles and for the city in general." Didinger added: "White is more than just a superb football player. He is an ordained Baptist minister whose tireless work in the community touched thousands of lives. He is a man who always wore his heart on his extra-long sleeve."

During his years with the Eagles, White had was named annually to play in the Pro Bowl beginning in 1986; he continued the tradition during his years with Green Bay through 1998, to realize the longest consecutive run of Pro Bowl participation on record. When the Packers won the world championship at the Super Bowl in 1997, White set a Super Bowl game record with three quarterback sacks. The Associated Press named White the defensive player of the year for the second time in his career after the 1998 season, and he announced his retirement soon afterward in 1999. Green Bay honored White's retirement by retiring his jersey number, which was 92, and he spent one year out of football and involved in his ministry.

White returned for one final season in the NFL, lured from retirement for the 2000 season by the Carolina Panthers who paid him one million dollars for the effort. He retired for the second time at the end of that season, leaving behind an NFL record of 198 career sacks after 15 seasons of play. White was voted by the NFL Hall of Fame to the NFL All-time Team in 2000.

Retired to Ministry

White's other career—carrying the gospel of Christ to those in need—will last his entire life. He and his wife built Hope Place, a shelter for unwed mothers, on property near their home in rural Tennessee; they also founded the Alpha & Omega Ministry to sponsor a community development bank in Knoxville. "I'm trying to build up black people's morale, self-confidence and self-reliance to show them that the Jesus I'm talking about is real," White explained in *Ebony*.

One of the most trying moments in White's career in the ministry came in 1996, when his church was burnt to the ground, one of dozens of black churches torched throughout the South in a string of hate crimes. Throughout the off-season that year, White badgered investigators to discover the arsonist, lobbied lawmakers—including then vice president Al Gore of Tennessee—to speak out against racial violence, and raised money to help his and other black churches throughout the nation. In addition to this work, White pursued missionary work among teenaged gang members, abused children, and young women seeking an alternative to abortion. He also tithed a good portion of his NFL income to several Baptist churches. Reflecting on his work in the *Philadelphia Daily News*, the "minister of defense" concluded: "The Bible says, 'Faith without works is dead.' That is just another way of saying: 'Put your money where your mouth is.'"

White's life work came to an untimely end on December 26, 2004, when he was rushed to the hospital for what was termed a respiratory illness and soon pronounced dead. According to *Jet*, family spokesman Keith Johnson stated that White's death "was not only unexpected, but it was also a complete surprise. Reggie wasn't a sick man…he was vibrant. He had lots and lots of energy, lots of passion." In his local church and across the NFL, friends, former players, and fans of White spoke of their sadness at his passing. NFL commissioner Paul Tagliabue issued a statement which read in part: "Reggie White was a gentle warrior who will be remembered as one of the greatest defensive players in NFL history. Equally as impressive as his achievements on the field was the positive impact he made off the field and the way he served as a positive influence on so many young people."

Selected writings

(With Terry Hill) *Reggie White: Minister of Defense,* Wolgemuth & Hyatt, 1991.
(With Jim Denney) *Reggie White in the Trenches: The Autobiography,* T. Nelson, 1996.
(With Steve Hubbard) *God's Playbook: The Bible's Game Plan for Life,* T. Nelson, 1998.
Broken Promises, Blinded Dreams: Take Charge of Your Destiny, Treasure House, 2003.

Sources

Periodicals

Atlanta Journal and Constitution, August 29, 1993, p. TS-5.
Ebony, December 1993, pp. 47-48.
Jet, September 15, 1986; April 26, 1993; January 29, 1996; November 1, 1999; August 21, 2000; March 19, 2001; January 17, 2005.
Los Angeles Times, October 21, 1989, p. C-1.
New York Times, April 7, 1993, p. B-11.
Philadelphia Daily News, June 7, 1991; April 7, 1993; April 8, 1993.
Sporting News, July 12, 1993, p. 30; September 13, 1993, p. 30; July 8, 1996; January 14, 2005, p. 41.
Sports Illustrated, September 3, 1986; November 27, 1989, p. 64; March 15, 1993, p. 20; May 3, 1993; September 2, 1996; January 10, 2005, p. 30.
USA Today, February 11, 1991, p. C-6; August 4, 1993, p. C-8.
Wall Street Journal, August 20, 1993, p. A-9.
Washington Post, March 14, 1993, p. D-4; March 18, 1993, p. C-1.

—Mark Kram and Tom Pendergast

David Rudyard Williams

1954—

Research scientist, professor of sociology and public health

Born into working-class poverty in a colonized society, David Williams observed the effects of racial and economic oppression from an early age. With the support of his family and his deeply held religious beliefs, he not only grew to believe in his ideas and abilities, but he also determined to live a life of service to others. Travelling far away from the tiny island that had been his home, Williams worked hard to gain an advanced education and employment at prestigious universities. More importantly, he stayed true to his youthful goal of service and has devoted his life to improving the health of society's most vulnerable members. In the process, he has become one of the foremost experts on the health issues of racial minorities and the poor.

David Rudyard Williams was born on June 12, 1954, on the westernmost Caribbean island of Aruba. His father, William R. Williams, had come to Aruba from his home on another Caribbean island, St. Lucia, as a member of a British army regiment during World War II. He had stayed to work in the island's oil refineries. While working on Aruba he met and married his wife, Zenobia, and together they began a family. David was the fourth of their five children. While he was still a child, the family moved back to St. Lucia, and David grew to consider that island his home.

Raised in Working-Class Family

Twenty-seven miles long and fourteen miles wide, St. Lucia is a small tropical island in the eastern Caribbean chain of islands called the Lesser Antilles. Once colo-

nized by both the Dutch and the French, it was a British possession when the Williams family moved there during the late 1950s. Life in the beautiful tropics was not easy for a working-class black family. William and Zenobia were resourceful, however, and both worked at many different jobs as the need arose. William had various jobs, as a book salesman, a factory supervisor, a construction foreman, and an office clerk, before starting his own business as a customs agent, helping importers and exporters fill out papers and pay fees on their products. Zenobia took care of the children and the small family farm which helped feed them. She also worked periodically, both as an elementary school teacher and as a maid for the island's wealthy white families.

The children, too, contributed to the family by doing the constant chores that arise on a rural homestead. Williams milked cows and delivered milk to the neighbors who bought it. He also took care of the sheep, turkeys, and chickens that contributed to the family income or its dinner table. As he got older, he joined his brothers and sisters working at his father's customs business. There was not much extra cash, but the Williams children earned spending money by collecting coconuts from the trees on their property and selling them for five cents apiece.

When not occupied with chores or playing with his sisters and brothers, Williams developed a love of reading. Since television did not come to the island until almost 1970, he relied on the radio and books for entertainment and news of the outside world. During

At a Glance . . .

Born David Rudyard Williams on June 12, 1954, in Aruba; married Opal Reid on June 7, 1981; children: Delia, Alysia. *Education:* Caribbean Union College, BTh, theology, 1976; Andrews University, MDiv, 1979; Loma Linda University, MPH, 1981; University of Michigan, MA, sociology, 1984, PhD, sociology, 1986. *Religion:* Seventh-Day Adventist.

Career: Yale University, Department of Sociology, director of undergraduate studies, 1989-90; Yale University, assistant professor of sociology and public health, 1986-91; Yale University, associate professor of sociology, 1991-92; Yale School of Medicine, associate professor of public health, 1991-1992; U of M, associate professor of sociology and associate research scientist,1992-98; U of M, African American Mental Health Research Center, faculty associate, 1992–; U of M, Center for Afro-American and African Studies, faculty associate1992–; U of M, professor of sociology and senior research scientist, 1998–; U of M, Survey Research Center, Research Center on Religion, Race, and Health, co-director, 1999–; U of M, Harold W. Cruse collegiate professor of sociology, 2002–; U of M, Institute for Social Research, professor, 2004–; U of M, Center for Afroamerican and African Studies, South Africa Initiative Office, director, 2004–; U of M, professor of epidemiology, 2004–.

Selected memberships: American Sociological Association; American Public Health Association; Association of Black Sociologists; Caribbean Studies Association;

Selected awards: Robert Wood Johnson Foundation, Investigator Award in Health Policy Research, 1995-96; U of M, Harold R. Johnson Diversity Award, 1998; National Academy of Sciences, Institute of Medicine, elected member, 2001; Decade of Behavior Research Award, 2004.

Addresses: *Office*—University of Michigan, Institute for Social Research, 426 Thompson Street, Room 2230, Ann Arbor, MI 48106-1248.

the 1960s and early 1970s, he closely followed the exciting developments of the civil rights and black power movements in the nearby United States. Some of the major figures in these movements were closely tied to the Caribbean, such as Stokely Carmichael, who had been born in Trinidad, and Malcolm X, whose mother had been a West Indian immigrant. At the same time, the people of St. Lucia were beginning to demand independence from Britain. To a boy living in an island nation that was fighting its way out of colonialism, the ideas and passion of the U.S. civil rights movement were fascinating and inspiring. The ideas of social justice he absorbed during his youth would be important to him throughout his life and career.

Williams graduated from St. Lucia Adventist Academy in 1971. Neither of his parents had finished high school, but they encouraged their children to seek higher education. Though he never felt pressured to achieve, Williams expected that he would follow his older siblings to college, and he entered Caribbean Union College in Trinidad. He majored in theology, the study of religion. Religion and spirituality had long been important to Williams, who had been raised in the Seventh-day Adventist faith, an international Protestant denomination which has almost thirteen million members throughout the world.

Founded during the mid-1800s in New England, Adventists are Christians who hold the belief that Jesus Christ will return to earth, not on some distant, unforeseeable day, but in the near future. Adventists celebrate their sabbath or holy day of rest on Saturday, rather than Sunday as most other Christian denominations do. They place great value on independent thinking, personal freedom, and healthy living habits, such as a wholesome diet. Caffeine, alcohol, meat, and tobacco are all prohibited by Adventism, and many studies have shown that Adventists tend to be healthier because of the lifestyle their religion demands. Though Adventists look to a joyous future in heaven, they also have a strong belief in serving humankind while on Earth, much as they believe Jesus did. Growing up in the Adventist church, Williams learned to value personal health and community service, and his education reinforced those values.

Continued Education in the United States

After his graduation from Caribbean Union in 1976, Williams decided to take a big risk to further his education. He had heard stories from other Caribbean students that by working in a sales job in Canada, one could make enough money to enter college in the United States. In the summer of 1976, he went to Toronto, carrying only a few personal possessions and $50 that his father had given him for graduation. He did earn enough money working there to enter graduate school at Andrews University, an Adventist college in Berrien Springs, Michigan, to further his religious studies and pursue his masters degree in divinity.

It was while studying divinity that Williams began to feel that to be of real use to the world, his service had to be both practical and meaningful. The Adventist focus on health led him to the conviction that through helping people become healthier, he could truly make the world a better place. He felt that by working in the field of public health, he could help the most vulnerable members of society, the poor and people of color who were often overlooked by the health care system. He continued his education at Loma Linda University in Southern California, where he earned another masters degree, this time in public health.

While working on his degree at Loma Linda, he was required to do a semester of supervised work in the field of public health. He went back to Michigan in 1980 to do his fieldwork at the Battle Creek Adventist Hospital. The Adventist Hospital in Battle Creek had once been under the supervision of the famous John Harvey Kellogg, an Adventist doctor who had worked to improve the community's health during the nineteenth century. Kellogg is probably best remembered for inventing such healthy breakfast alternatives as granola and corn flakes.

Began Work in Public Health

At the hospital, Williams got his first practical experience in involving the black community in its own health care. Though the hospital's Battle Creek neighborhood had become largely African American, the staff and patients at the hospital had remained predominantly white. Williams' goal became to make sure that African-American people were included in hospital health programs. He soon realized that simply offering classes and clinics at the hospital would not be enough to accomplish this. When few blacks showed up at a hypertension, or high blood pressure, clinic at the hospital, Williams and his co-workers took the clinic to the local African-American church, where they were able to educate many more blacks about the dangers of high blood pressure in their community.

As Williams worked with the black community in Battle Creek, he began to understand that simply providing health information was not enough; many factors contributed to an individual's ability to make use of public health programs, such as family and community support and access to money and leisure time. He began to feel that the stresses of living with racism and poverty had a direct effect on the health of people in poor and minority communities. He wanted to research these effects further, and this research would take him into the field of sociology.

Studied Minority Health Issues

Williams continued to work in Battle Creek until the fall of 1982, when he entered the University of Michigan to seek his Ph.D. in sociology. In 1986, after earning another masters and his doctorate, he received a job offer to teach sociology at Yale University, a prestigious college in Connecticut. He taught at Yale for six years, then returned to the University of Michigan to teach both sociology and public health.

Though he has continued to teach, becoming a full professor in both of his fields, Williams has also continued to research the various social influences on health, especially the effects of poverty and racism on the health of the poor. He has become a tireless spokesperson for the most vulnerable members of American society, pointing out over and over in articles and speeches that in the world's wealthiest nation, the poor are still becoming increasingly less healthy than the rich, and exploring the reasons behind this fact. As a diligent research scientist, he has supported his ideas with many thorough research studies on the health issues of poor people of color. Through this work, Williams has become a highly regarded member of the scientific community. He has written over a hundred papers and is a member of the board of five scientific journals, as well as dozens of other boards, task forces, and professional organizations. He continues to see his work as part of his service to society and his pursuit of social justice.

Selected writings

"Health Issues in the Black Community," *Contemporary Sociology,* Vol. 22, No. 5, September 1993, pp. 746-48.
(With M.S.Spencer and J.S.Jackson) "Race, Stress and Physical Health: The Role of Group Identity," *Self and Identity: Fundamental Issues,* edited by R. J. Contrada and R. D. Ashmore, Oxford University Press, 1999, pp. 71-100.
(With Toni D. Rucker) "Understanding and Addressing Racial Disparities in Health Care," *Health Care Financing Review,* Vol. 21, No. 4, Summer 2000, pp. 75-95.
"Discrimination and Health," in *Encyclopedia of Health and Behavior, Vol. 1,* edited by N.B. Anderson, Sage Publications, 2004, pp. 254-59.
"Racism and Health," in *Closing the Gap: Improving the Health of Minority Elders in the New Millennium,* edited by Keith E.Whitfield, Gerontological Society of America, 2004, pp. 69-80.

Sources

Periodicals

Detroit Free Press, July 23, 2004.

On-line

"David R. Williams on the Influence of Socioeconomic Status, Race and Geography on Health," *Inequality.*

org, www.inequality.org/williamstranscript.pdf (December 14, 2004).

"David Williams," *John D. and Catherine T. Mac-Arthur Research Network on Socioeconomic Status and Health,* www.macses.ucsf.edu/Network/david.htm (December 14, 2004).

"Seventh-Day Adventists: The Heritage Continues," *Seventh-Day Adventist,* www.adventist.org/world_church/facts_and_figures/history/index.html.en (December 14, 2004).

Other

Information for this profile was obtained through an interview with David R.Williams on December 14, 2004.

—Tina Gianoulis

Cumulative Nationality Index

Volume numbers appear in **bold**

American

Aaliyah **30**
Aaron, Hank **5**
Abbott, Robert Sengstacke **27**
Abdul-Jabbar, Kareem **8**
Abdur-Rahim, Shareef **28**
Abernathy, Ralph David **1**
Abu-Jamal, Mumia **15**
Ace, Johnny **36**
Adams Earley, Charity **13, 34**
Adams, Eula L. **39**
Adams, Floyd, Jr. **12**
Adams, Johnny **39**
Adams, Leslie **39**
Adams, Oleta **18**
Adams, Osceola Macarthy **31**
Adams, Sheila J. **25**
Adams, Yolanda **17**
Adams-Ender, Clara **40**
Adderley, Julian "Cannonball" **30**
Adderley, Nat **29**
Adkins, Rod **41**
Adkins, Rutherford H. **21**
Agyeman, Jaramogi Abebe **10**
Ailey, Alvin **8**
Al-Amin, Jamil Abdullah **6**
Albright, Gerald **23**
Alert, Kool DJ Red **33**
Alexander, Archie Alphonso **14**
Alexander, Clifford **26**
Alexander, Joyce London **18**
Alexander, Khandi **43**
Alexander, Margaret Walker **22**
Alexander, Sadie Tanner Mossell
  22
Ali, Laila **27**
Ali, Muhammad **2, 16**
Allain, Stephanie **49**
Allen, Byron **3, 24**
Allen, Debbie **13, 42**
Allen, Ethel D. **13**
Allen, Marcus **20**
Allen, Robert L. **38**
Allen, Samuel W. **38**
Allen, Tina **22**
Alston, Charles **33**
Ames, Wilmer **27**
Amos, John **8**
Amos, Wally **9**
Anderson, Carl **48**
Anderson, Charles Edward **37**
Anderson, Eddie "Rochester" **30**
Anderson, Elmer **25**
Anderson, Jamal **22**

Anderson, Marian **2, 33**
Anderson, Michael P. **40**
Anderson, Norman B. **45**
Andrews, Benny **22**
Andrews, Bert **13**
Andrews, Raymond **4**
Angelou, Maya **1, 15**
Ansa, Tina McElroy **14**
Anthony, Carmelo **46**
Anthony, Wendell **25**
Archer, Dennis **7, 36**
Archie-Hudson, Marguerite **44**
Arkadie, Kevin **17**
Armstrong, Louis **2**
Armstrong, Robb **15**
Armstrong, Vanessa Bell **24**
Arnwine, Barbara **28**
Arrington, Richard **24**
Arroyo, Martina **30**
Asante, Molefi Kete **3**
Ashanti **37**
Ashe, Arthur **1, 18**
Ashford, Emmett **22**
Ashford, Nickolas **21**
Ashley-Ward, Amelia **23**
Atkins, Cholly **40**
Atkins, Erica **34**
Atkins, Juan **50**
Atkins, Russell **45**
Atkins, Tina **34**
Aubert, Alvin **41**
Auguste, Donna **29**
Austin, Junius C. **44**
Austin, Lovie **40**
Austin, Patti **24**
Avant, Clarence **19**
Ayers, Roy **16**
Babatunde, Obba **35**
Bacon-Bercey, June **38**
Badu, Erykah **22**
Bailey, Buster **38**
Bailey, Clyde **45**
Bailey, DeFord **33**
Bailey, Radcliffe **19**
Bailey, Xenobia **11**
Baines, Harold **32**
Baiocchi, Regina Harris **41**
Baisden, Michael **25**
Baker, Anita **21, 48**
Baker, Augusta **38**
Baker, Dusty **8, 43**
Baker, Ella **5**
Baker, Gwendolyn Calvert **9**
Baker, Houston A., Jr. **6**

Baker, Josephine **3**
Baker, LaVern **26**
Baker, Maxine B. **28**
Baker, Thurbert **22**
Baldwin, James **1**
Ballance, Frank W. **41**
Ballard, Allen Butler, Jr. **40**
Ballard, Hank **41**
Bambaataa, Afrika **34**
Bambara, Toni Cade **10**
Bandele, Asha **36**
Banks, Ernie **33**
Banks, Jeffrey **17**
Banks, Tyra **11, 50**
Banks, William **11**
Baraka, Amiri **1, 38**
Barber, Ronde **41**
Barboza, Anthony **10**
Barclay, Paris **37**
Barden, Don H. **9, 20**
Barker, Danny **32**
Barkley, Charles **5**
Barlow, Roosevelt **49**
Barnes, Roosevelt "Booba" **33**
Barnett, Amy Du Bois **46**
Barnett, Marguerite **46**
Barney, Lem **26**
Barnhill, David **30**
Barrax, Gerald William **45**
Barrett, Andrew C. **12**
Barrett, Jacquelyn **28**
Barry, Marion S(hepilov, Jr.) **7, 44**
Barthe, Richmond **15**
Basie, Count **23**
Basquiat, Jean-Michel **5**
Bass, Charlotta Spears **40**
Bassett, Angela **6, 23**
Bates, Daisy **13**
Bates, Karen Grigsby **40**
Bates, Peg Leg **14**
Bath, Patricia E. **37**
Baugh, David **23**
Baylor, Don **6**
Baylor, Helen **36**
Beach, Michael **26**
Beal, Bernard B. **46**
Beals, Jennifer **12**
Beals, Melba Patillo **15**
Bearden, Romare **2, 50**
Beasley, Jamar **29**
Beasley, Phoebe **34**
Beatty, Talley **35**
Bechet, Sidney **18**
Beckford, Tyson **11**

Beckham, Barry **41**
Belafonte, Harry **4**
Bell, Derrick **6**
Bell, James "Cool Papa" **36**
Bell, James A. **50**
Bell, James Madison **40**
Bell, Michael **40**
Bell, Robert Mack **22**
Bellamy, Bill **12**
Belle, Albert **10**
Belle, Regina **1**
Belton, Sharon Sayles **9, 16**
Benét, Eric **28**
Ben-Israel, Ben Ami **11**
Benjamin, Andre **45**
Benjamin, Regina **20**
Bennett, George Harold "Hal" **45**
Bennett, Lerone, Jr. **5**
Benson, Angela **34**
Berry, Bertice **8**
Berry, Chuck **29**
Berry, Fred "Rerun" **48**
Berry, Halle **4, 19**
Berry, Mary Frances **7**
Berry, Theodore **31**
Berrysmith, Don Reginald **49**
Bethune, Mary McLeod **4**
Betsch, MaVynee **28**
Beverly, Frankie **25**
Bibb, Eric **49**
Bickerstaff, Bernie **21**
Biggers, John **20, 33**
Bing, Dave **3**
Bishop, Sanford D. Jr. **24**
Black, Barry C. **47**
Black, Keith Lanier **18**
Blackburn, Robert **28**
Blackwell, Unita **17**
Blair, Jayson **50**
Blair, Paul **36**
Blake, Asha **26**
Blake, Eubie **29**
Blake, James **43**
Blakey, Art **37**
Blanchard, Terence **43**
Bland, Bobby "Blue" **36**
Bland, Eleanor Taylor **39**
Blanks, Billy **22**
Blanton, Dain **29**
Blassingame, John Wesley **40**
Blige, Mary J. **20, 34**
Blockson, Charles L. **42**
Blow, Kurtis **31**
Bluford, Guy **2, 35**

Cumulative Occupation Index

Volume numbers appear in **bold**

Art and design

Adjaye, David **38**
Allen, Tina **22**
Alston, Charles **33**
Andrews, Benny **22**
Andrews, Bert **13**
Armstrong, Robb **15**
Bailey, Radcliffe **19**
Bailey, Xenobia **11**
Barboza, Anthony **10**
Barnes, Ernie **16**
Barthe, Richmond **15**
Basquiat, Jean-Michel **5**
Bearden, Romare **2, 50**
Beasley, Phoebe **34**
Biggers, John **20, 33**
Blacknurn, Robert **28**
Brandon, Barbara **3**
Brown, Donald **19**
Burke, Selma **16**
Burroughs, Margaret Taylor **9**
Camp, Kimberly **19**
Campbell, E. Simms **13**
Campbell, Mary Schmidt **43**
Catlett, Elizabeth **2**
Chase-Riboud, Barbara **20, 46**
Cortor, Eldzier **42**
Cowans, Adger W. **20**
Crite, Alan Rohan **29**
De Veaux, Alexis **44**
DeCarava, Roy **42**
Delaney, Beauford **19**
Delaney, Joseph **30**
Delsarte, Louis **34**
Donaldson, Jeff **46**
Douglas, Aaron **7**
Driskell, David C. **7**
Edwards, Melvin **22**
El Wilson, Barbara **35**
Ewing, Patrick A. **17**
Fax, Elton **48**
Feelings, Tom **11, 47**
Freeman, Leonard **27**
Fuller, Meta Vaux Warrick **27**
Gantt, Harvey **1**
Gilliam, Sam **16**
Golden, Thelma **10**
Goodnight, Paul **32**
Guyton, Tyree **9**
Harkless, Necia Desiree **19**
Harrington, Oliver W. **9**
Hathaway, Isaac Scott **33**
Hayden, Palmer **13**

Hayes, Cecil N. **46**
Hope, John **8**
Hudson, Cheryl **15**
Hudson, Wade **15**
Hunt, Richard **6**
Hunter, Clementine **45**
Hutson, Jean Blackwell **16**
Jackson, Earl **31**
Jackson, Vera **40**
John, Daymond **23**
Johnson, Jeh Vincent **44**
Johnson, William Henry **3**
Jones, Lois Mailou **13**
Kitt, Sandra **23**
Knox, Simmie **49**
Lawrence, Jacob **4, 28**
Lee, Annie Francis **22**
Lee-Smith, Hughie **5, 22**
Lewis, Edmonia **10**
Lewis, Norman **39**
Lewis, Samella **25**
Loving, Alvin **35**
Manley, Edna **26**
Mayhew, Richard **39**
McGee, Charles **10**
McGruder, Aaron **28**
Mitchell, Corinne **8**
Moody, Ronald **30**
Morrison, Keith **13**
Motley, Archibald Jr. **30**
Moutoussamy-Ashe, Jeanne **7**
Mutu, Wangechi **44**
N'Namdi, George R. **17**
Nugent, Richard Bruce **39**
Olden, Georg(e) **44**
Ouattara **43**
Perkins, Marion **38**
Pierre, Andre **17**
Pinderhughes, John **47**
Pinkney, Jerry **15**
Pippin, Horace **9**
Porter, James A. **11**
Prophet, Nancy Elizabeth **42**
Puryear, Martin **42**
Ringgold, Faith **4**
Ruley, Ellis **38**
Saar, Alison **16**
Saint James, Synthia **12**
Sallee, Charles **38**
Sanders, Joseph R., Jr. **11**
Savage, Augusta **12**
Sebree, Charles **40**
Serrano, Andres **3**
Shabazz, Attallah **6**

Simpson, Lorna **4, 36**
Sims, Lowery Stokes **27**
Sklarek, Norma Merrick **25**
Sleet, Moneta, Jr. **5**
Smith, Marvin **46**
Smith, Morgan **46**
Smith, Vincent D. **48**
Tanksley, Ann **37**
Tanner, Henry Ossawa **1**
Thomas, Alma **14**
Thrash, Dox **35**
Tolliver, William **9**
VanDerZee, James **6**
Wainwright, Joscelyn **46**
Walker, A'lelia **14**
Walker, Kara **16**
Washington, Alonzo **29**
Washington, James, Jr. **38**
Wells, James Lesesne **10**
White, Charles **39**
White, Dondi **34**
White, John H. **27**
Williams, Billy Dee **8**
Williams, O. S. **13**
Williams, Paul R. **9**
Williams, William T. **11**
Wilson, Ellis **39**
Woodruff, Hale **9**

Business

Abbot, Robert Sengstacke **27**
Abdul-Jabbar, Kareem **8**
Adams, Eula L. **39**
Adkins, Rod **41**
Ailey, Alvin **8**
Al-Amin, Jamil Abdullah **6**
Alexander, Archie Alphonso **14**
Allen, Byron **24**
Ames, Wilmer **27**
Amos, Wally **9**
Auguste, Donna **29**
Avant, Clarence **19**
Beal, Bernard B. **46**
Beamon, Bob **30**
Baker, Dusty **8, 43**
Baker, Ella **5**
Baker, Gwendolyn Calvert **9**
Baker, Maxine **28**
Banks, Jeffrey **17**
Banks, William **11**
Barden, Don H. **9, 20**
Barrett, Andrew C. **12**
Beasley, Phoebe **34**
Bell, James A. **50**

Bennett, Lerone, Jr. **5**
Bing, Dave **3**
Bolden, Frank E. **44**
Borders, James **9**
Boston, Kelvin E. **25**
Boston, Lloyd **24**
Boyd, Gwendolyn **49**
Boyd, John W., Jr. **20**
Boyd, T. B., III **6**
Bradley, Jennette B. **40**
Bridges, Shelia **36**
Bridgforth, Glinda **36**
Brimmer, Andrew F. **2, 48**
Bronner, Nathaniel H., Sr. **32**
Brown, Eddie C. **35**
Brown, Les **5**
Brown, Marie Dutton **12**
Brunson, Dorothy **1**
Bryant, John **26**
Burrell, Thomas J. **21**
Burroughs, Margaret Taylor **9**
Burrus, William Henry "Bill" **45**
Busby, Jheryl **3**
Cain, Herman **15**
CasSelle, Malcolm **11**
Chamberlain, Wilt **18, 47**
Chapman, Nathan A. Jr. **21**
Chappell, Emma **18**
Chase, Debra Martin **49**
Chenault, Kenneth I. **4, 36**
Cherry, Deron **40**
Chisholm, Samuel J. **32**
Clark, Celeste **15**
Clark, Patrick **14**
Clay, William Lacy **8**
Clayton, Xernona **3, 45**
Cobbs, Price M. **9**
Colbert, Virgis William **17**
Coleman, Donald A. **24**
Combs, Sean "Puffy" **17, 43**
Connerly, Ward **14**
Conyers, Nathan G. **24**
Cooper, Barry **33**
Cooper, Evern **40**
Corbi, Lana **42**
Cornelius, Don **4**
Cosby, Bill **7, 26**
Cottrell, Comer **11**
Creagh, Milton **27**
Cullers, Vincent T. **49**
Daniels-Carter, Valerie **23**
Darden, Calvin **38**
Dash, Darien **29**
Davis, Ed **24**

Zollar, Alfred **40**

Dance
Ailey, Alvin **8**
Alexander, Khandi **43**
Allen, Debbie **13, 42**
Atkins, Cholly **40**
Babatunde, Obba **35**
Baker, Josephine **3**
Bates, Peg Leg **14**
Beals, Jennifer **12**
Beatty, Talley **35**
Byrd, Donald **10**
Clarke, Hope **14**
Collins, Janet **33**
Davis, Chuck **33**
Davis, Sammy Jr. **18**
Dove, Ulysses **5**
Dunham, Katherine **4**
Ellington, Mercedes **34**
Fagan, Garth **18**
Falana, Lola **42**
Glover, Savion **14**
Guy, Jasmine **2**
Hall, Arthur **39**
Hammer, M. C. **20**
Henson, Darrin **33**
Hines, Gregory **1, 42**
Horne, Lena **5**
Jackson, Michael **19**
Jamison, Judith **7**
Johnson, Virginia **9**
Jones, Bill T. **1, 46**
King, Alonzo **38**
McQueen, Butterfly **6**
Miller, Bebe **3**
Mills, Florence **22**
Mitchell, Arthur **2, 47**
Moten, Etta **18**
Muse, Clarence Edouard **21**
Nicholas, Fayard **20**
Nicholas, Harold **20**
Nichols, Nichelle **11**
Powell, Maxine **8**
Premice, Josephine **41**
Primus, Pearl **6**
Ray, Gene Anthony **47**
Rhoden, Dwight **40**
Ribeiro, Alfonso, **17**
Richardson, Desmond **39**
Robinson, Bill "Bojangles" **11**
Robinson, Cleo Parker **38**
Robinson, Fatima **34**
Rodgers, Rod **36**
Rolle, Esther **13, 21**
Sims, Howard "Sandman" **48**
Tyson, Andre **40**
Vereen, Ben **4**
Walker, Cedric "Ricky" **19**
Washington, Fredi **10**
Williams, Vanessa L. **4, 17**
Zollar, Jawole Willa Jo **28**

Education
Achebe, Chinua **6**
Adams, Leslie **39**
Adams-Ender, Clara **40**
Adkins, Rutherford H. **21**
Aidoo, Ama Ata **38**
Ake, Claude **30**
Alexander, Margaret Walker **22**
Allen, Robert L. **38**
Allen, Samuel W. **38**

Alston, Charles **33**
Amadi, Elechi **40**
Anderson, Charles Edward **37**
Archer, Dennis **7**
Archie-Hudson, Marguerite **44**
Aristide, Jean-Bertrand **6, 45**
Asante, Molefi Kete **3**
Aubert, Alvin **41**
Awoonor, Kofi **37**
Bacon-Bercey, June **38**
Baiocchi, Regina Harris **41**
Baker, Augusta **38**
Baker, Gwendolyn Calvert **9**
Baker, Houston A., Jr. **6**
Ballard, Allen Butler, Jr. **40**
Bambara, Toni Cade **10**
Baraka, Amiri **1, 38**
Barboza, Anthony **10**
Barnett, Marguerite **46**
Bath, Patricia E. **37**
Beckham, Barry **41**
Bell, Derrick **6**
Berry, Bertice **8**
Berry, Mary Frances **7**
Bethune, Mary McLeod **4**
Biggers, John **20, 33**
Black, Keith Lanier **18**
Blassingame, John Wesley **40**
Blockson, Charles L. **42**
Bluitt, Juliann S. **14**
Bogle, Donald **34**
Bolden, Tonya **32**
Bosley, Freeman, Jr. **7**
Boyd, T. B., III **6**
Bradley, David Henry, Jr. **39**
Branch, William Blackwell **39**
Brathwaite, Kamau **36**
Braun, Carol Moseley **4, 42**
Briscoe, Marlin **37**
Brooks, Avery **9**
Brown, Claude **38**
Brown, Joyce F. **25**
Brown, Sterling **10**
Brown, Uzee **42**
Brown, Wesley **23**
Brown, Willa **40**
Bruce, Blanche Kelso **33**
Brutus, Dennis **38**
Bryan, Ashley F. **41**
Burke, Selma **16**
Burke, Yvonne Braithwaite **42**
Burks, Mary Fair **40**
Burnim, Mickey L. **48**
Burroughs, Margaret Taylor **9**
Burton, LeVar **8**
Butler, Paul D. **17**
Callender, Clive O. **3**
Campbell, Bebe Moore **6, 24**
Campbell, Mary Schmidt **43**
Cannon, Katie **10**
Carby, Hazel **27**
Cardozo, Francis L. **33**
Carnegie, Herbert **25**
Carruthers, George R. **40**
Carter, Joye Maureen **41**
Carter, Warrick L. **27**
Cartey, Wilfred **47**
Carver, George Washington **4**
Cary, Lorene **3**
Cary, Mary Ann Shadd **30**
Catlett, Elizabeth **2**
Cayton, Horace **26**
Cheney-Coker, Syl **43**

Clark, Joe **1**
Clark, Kenneth B. **5**
Clark, Septima **7**
Clarke, Cheryl **32**
Clarke, George **32**
Clarke, John Henrik **20**
Clayton, Constance **1**
Cleaver, Kathleen Neal **29**
Clements, George **2**
Clemmons, Reginal G. **41**
Clifton, Lucille **14**
Cobb, Jewel Plummer **42**
Cobb, W. Montague **39**
Cobbs, Price M. **9**
Cohen, Anthony **15**
Cole, Johnnetta B. **5, 43**
Collins, Janet **33**
Collins, Marva **3**
Comer, James P. **6**
Cone, James H. **3**
Coney, PonJola **48**
Cook, Mercer **40**
Cook, Samuel DuBois **14**
Cook, Toni **23**
Cooper Cafritz, Peggy **43**
Cooper, Anna Julia **20**
Cooper, Edward S. **6**
Copeland, Michael **47**
Cortez, Jayne **43**
Cosby, Bill **7, 26**
Cotter, Joseph Seamon, Sr. **40**
Cottrell, Comer **11**
Creagh, Milton **27**
Crew, Rudolph F. **16**
Cross, Dolores E. **23**
Crouch, Stanley **11**
Cullen, Countee **8**
Daly, Marie Maynard **37**
Davis, Allison **12**
Davis, Angela **5**
Davis, Arthur P. **41**
Davis, Charles T. **48**
Davis, George **36**
Dawson, William Levi **39**
Days, Drew S., III **10**
Delany, Sadie **12**
Delany, Samuel R., Jr. **9**
Delco, Wilhemina R. **33**
Delsarte, Louis **34**
Dennard, Brazeal **37**
DePriest, James **37**
Dickens, Helen Octavia **14**
Diop, Cheikh Anta **4**
Dixon, Margaret **14**
Dodson, Howard, Jr. **7**
Dodson, Owen Vincent **38**
Donaldson, Jeff **46**
Douglas, Aaron **7**
Dove, Rita **6**
Dove, Ulysses **5**
Draper, Sharon Mills **16, 43**
Driskell, David C. **7**
Drummond, William J. **40**
Du Bois, David Graham **45**
Dumas, Henry **41**
Dunbar-Nelson, Alice Ruth Moore **44**
Dunnigan, Alice Allison **41**
Dunston, Georgia Mae **48**
Dymally, Mervyn **42**
Dyson, Michael Eric **11, 40**
Early, Gerald **15**
Edelin, Ramona Hoage **19**

Edelman, Marian Wright **5, 42**
Edley, Christopher **2, 48**
Edley, Christopher F., Jr. **48**
Edwards, Harry **2**
Elders, Joycelyn **6**
Elliot, Lorris **37**
Ellis, Clarence A. **38**
Ellison, Ralph **7**
Epps, Archie C., III **45**
Evans, Mari **26**
Fauset, Jessie **7**
Favors, Steve **23**
Feelings, Muriel **44**
Figueroa, John J. **40**
Fleming, Raymond **48**
Fletcher, Bill, Jr. **41**
Floyd, Elson S. **41**
Ford, Jack **39**
Foster, Ezola **28**
Foster, Henry W., Jr. **26**
Franklin, John Hope **5**
Franklin, Robert M. **13**
Frazier, E. Franklin **10**
Freeman, Al, Jr. **11**
Fuller, A. Oveta **43**
Fuller, Arthur **27**
Fuller, Howard L. **37**
Fuller, Solomon Carter, Jr. **15**
Futrell, Mary Hatwood **33**
Gaines, Ernest J. **7**
Gates, Henry Louis, Jr. **3, 38**
Gates, Sylvester James, Jr. **15**
Gayle, Addison, Jr. **41**
George, Zelma Watson **42**
Gerima, Haile **38**
Gibson, Donald Bernard **40**
Giddings, Paula **11**
Giovanni, Nikki **9, 39**
Golden, Marita **19**
Gomes, Peter J. **15**
Gomez, Jewelle **30**
Granville, Evelyn Boyd **36**
Greenfield, Eloise **9**
Guinier, Lani **7, 30**
Guy-Sheftall, Beverly **13**
Hageman, Hans and Ivan **36**
Halliburton, Warren J. **49**
Hale, Lorraine **8**
Handy, W. C. **8**
Hansberry, William Leo **11**
Harkless, Necia Desiree **19**
Harper, Michael S. **34**
Harris, Alice **7**
Harris, Jay T. **19**
Harris, Patricia Roberts **2**
Harsh, Vivian Gordon **14**
Harvey, William R. **42**
Haskins, James **36**
Hathaway, Isaac Scott **33**
Hayden, Carla D. **47**
Hayden, Robert **12**
Haynes, George Edmund **8**
Henderson, Stephen E. **45**
Henries, A. Doris Banks **44**
Herenton, Willie W. **24**
Hill, Anita **5**
Hill, Bonnie Guiton **20**
Hill, Errol **40**
Hill, Leslie Pinckney **44**
Hine, Darlene Clark **24**
Hinton, William Augustus **8**
Hoagland, Everett H. **45**
Hogan, Beverly Wade **50**

Cumulative Subject Index

Volume numbers appear in **bold**

Gumbel, Greg **8**
Hansberry, Lorraine **6**
Hare, Nathan **44**
Harrington, Oliver W. **9**
Harris, Claire **34**
Harris, Jay **19**
Haynes, Trudy **44**
Henriques, Julian **37**
Hickman, Fred **11**
Hunter-Gault, Charlayne **6, 31**
Ifill, Gwen **28**
Jarret, Vernon D. **42**
Jasper, Kenji **39**
Joachim, Paulin **34**
Johnson, Georgia Douglas **41**
Johnson, James Weldon **5**
Khanga, Yelena **6**
Knight, Etheridge **37**
LaGuma, Alex **30**
Lacy, Sam **30, 46**
Lampkin, Daisy **19**
Leavell, Dorothy R. **17**
Lewis, Edward T. **21**
Mabrey, Vicki **26**
Mabuza-Suttle, Felicia **43**
Madison, Paula **37**
Martin, Louis E. **16**
Martin, Roland S. **49**
Mason, Felicia **31**
Maynard, Robert C. **7**
McBride, James **35**
McCall, Nathan **8**
McGruder, Robert **22, 35**
McKay, Claude **6**
Mickelbury, Penny **28**
Mitchell, Russ **21**
Mkapa, Benjamin **16**
Mossell, Gertrude Bustill **40**
Murphy, John H. **42**
Murray, Pauli **38**
Nelson, Jill **6**
Nkosi, Lewis **46**
Page, Clarence **4**
Palmer, Everard **37**
Parks, Gordon **1, 35**
Payne, Ethel L. **28**
Perez, Anna **1**
Perkins, Tony **24**
Pinkston, W. Randall **24**
Pressley, Condace L. **41**
Price, Hugh B. **9**
Quarles, Norma **25**
Raspberry, William **2**
Reed, Ishmael **8**
Reeves, Rachel J. **23**
Riley, Rochelle **50**
Roberts, Robin **16**
Robinson, Max **3**
Rodgers, Johnathan **6**
Rowan, Carl T. **1, 30**
Salih, Al-Tayyib **37**
Schuyler, George Samuel **40**
Schuyler, Philippa **50**
Senior, Olive **37**
Shaw, Bernard **2, 28**
Shipp, E. R. **15**
Simpson, Carole **6, 30**
Smith, Clarence O. **21**
Smith, Danyel **40**
Sowell, Thomas **2**
Staples, Brent **8**
Stewart, Alison **13**
Stokes, Carl B. **10**

Stone, Chuck **9**
Tate, Eleanora E. **20**
Taylor, Kristin Clark **8**
Taylor, Susan L. **10**
Thurman, Wallace **16**
Tolson, Melvin B. **37**
Trotter, Monroe **9**
Tucker, Cynthia **15**
Wallace, Michele Faith **13**
Watson, Carlos **50**
Watts, Rolonda **9**
Webb, Veronica **10**
Wells-Barnett, Ida B. **8**
Wesley, Valerie Wilson **18**
Whitaker, Mark **21, 47**
Wiley, Ralph **8**
Wilkins, Roger **2**
Williams, Armstrong **29**
Williams, Juan **35**
Williams, Patricia J. **11**

Journal of Negro History
Woodson, Carter G. **2**

Juanita Bynum Ministries
Bynum, Juanita **31**

Juju music
Ade, King Sunny **41**

Just Us Books
Hudson, Cheryl **15**
Hudson, Wade **15**

Kansas City Athletics baseball team
Paige, Satchel **7**

Kansas City Chiefs football team
Allen, Marcus **20**
Cherry, Deron **40**
Dungy, Tony **17, 42**
Thomas, Derrick **25**

Kansas City government
Cleaver, Emanuel **4, 45**

Kansas City Monarchs baseball team
Bell, James "Cool Papa" **36**
Brown, Willard **36**

KANU
See Kenya African National Union

Kappa Alpha Psi
Hamilton, Samuel C. **47**

Karl Kani Infinity
Kani, Karl **10**

KAU
See Kenya African Union

KCA
See Kikuyu Central Association

Kentucky Derby
Winkfield, Jimmy **42**

Kentucky state government
Kidd, Mae Street **39**

Kentucky Negro Educational Association
Cotter, Joseph Seamon, Sr. **40**

Kenya African National Union (KANU)
Kenyatta, Jomo **5**
Moi, Daniel arap **1, 35**

Kenya African Union (KAU)
Kenyatta, Jomo **5**

Kenya National Council of Churchs (NCCK)
Kobia, Rev. Dr. Samuel **43**

Keyan government
Maathai, Wangari **43**

Kikuyu Central Association (KCA)
Kenyatta, Jomo **5**

King Center
See Martin Luther King Jr. Center for Nonviolent Social Change

King Oliver's Creole Band
Armstrong, (Daniel) Louis **2**
Hardin Armstrong, Lil **39**
Oliver, Joe "King" **42**

King's Troop of the Royal Horse Artillery
Scantlebury, Janna **47**

King Sunny Ade Foundation
Ade, King Sunny **41**

Kitchen Table: Women of Color Press
Smith, Barbara **28**

Koko Taylor's Celebrity
Taylor, Koko **40**

Kraft General Foods
Fudge, Ann **11**
Sneed, Paula A. **18**

Kwanzaa
Karenga, Maulana **10**

Kwazulu Territorial Authority
Buthelezi, Mangosuthu Gatsha **9**

Labour Party
Amos, Valerie **41**

Ladies Professional Golfers' Association (LPGA)
Gibson, Althea **8, 43**
Powell, Renee **34**

LaFace Records
Benjamin, Andre **45**
Edmonds, Kenneth "Babyface" **10, 31**
Patton, Antwan **45**
Reid, Antonio "L.A." **28**
OutKast **35**

Lamb of God Ministry
Falana, Lola **42**

Langston (OK) city government
Tolson, Melvin B. **37**

LAPD
See Los Angeles Police Department

Latin American folk music
Nascimento, Milton **2**

Latin baseball leagues
Kaiser, Cecil **42**

Law enforcement
Alexander, Joyce London **18**
Barrett, Jacquelyn **28**
Bolton, Terrell D. **25**
Bradley, Thomas **2, 20**
Brown, Lee P. **1, 24**
Freeman, Charles **19**
Gibson, Johnnie Mae **23**
Glover, Nathaniel, Jr. **12**
Gomez-Preston, Cheryl **9**
Harvard, Beverly **11**
Hillard, Terry **25**
Holton, Hugh, Jr. **39**
Hurtt, Harold **46**
Johnson, Norma L. Holloway **17**
Johnson, Robert T. **17**
Keith, Damon J. **16**
McKinnon, Isaiah **9**
Moose, Charles **40**
Napoleon, Benny N. **23**
Noble, Ronald **46**
Oliver, Jerry **37**
Parks, Bernard C. **17**
Ramsey, Charles H. **21**
Schmoke, Kurt **1, 48**
Thomas, Franklin A. **5, 49**
Wainwright, Joscelyn **46**
Williams, Willie L. **4**
Wilson, Jimmy **45**

Lawrence Steele Design
Steele, Lawrence **28**

Lawyers' Committee for Civil Rights Under Law
Arnwine, Barbara **28**
Hubbard, Arnette **38**
McDougall, Gay J. **11, 43**

LDF
See NAACP Legal Defense and Educational Fund

Leadership Conference on Civil Rights (LCCR)
Henderson, Wade J. **14**

League of Nations
Haile Selassie **7**

League of Women Voters
Meek, Carrie **36**

Leary Group Inc.
Leary, Kathryn D. **10**

"Leave No Child Behind"
Edelman, Marian Wright **5, 42**

Lee Elder Scholarship Fund
Elder, Lee **6**

Legal Defense Fund
See NAACP Legal Defense and Educational Fund

Les Brown Unlimited, Inc.
Brown, Les **5**

Lexicography
Major, Clarence **9**

Cumulative Name Index

Volume numbers appear in **bold**